Alone with th

Or, 3,800 miles on

Yezo and a cruise to the Kurile Islands.

Arnold Henry Savage Landor

Alpha Editions

This edition published in 2024

ISBN : 9789366383743

Design and Setting By
Alpha Editions
www.alphaedis.com
Email - info@alphaedis.com

PREFACE.

This book is not meant as a literary work, for I am not and do not pretend to be a literary man. It is but a record—an amplified log-book, as it were—of what befell me during my solitary peregrinations in Hokkaido, and a collection of notes and observations which I hope will prove interesting to anthropologists and ethnologists as well as to the general public.

Without any claim to infallibility I have tried to take an open-minded and sensible view of everything I have attempted to describe; in most cases, however, I have given facts without passing an opinion at all, and all I have said I have tried to express as simply and plainly as possible, so as not to give rise to misunderstandings.

There are a few points which I want to make quite clear.

First, that I went to Hokkaido entirely on my own account and for my own satisfaction. Next, that I accomplished the whole journey (some 4200 miles, out of which 3800 were ridden on horseback and on a rough pack-saddle) perfectly alone. By alone I mean that I had with me no friends, no servants, and no guides. My baggage consisted of next to nothing, so far as articles for my own convenience or comfort were concerned. I carried no provisions and no tent.

I am endowed with a very sensitive nature, and I pride myself in possessing the gift of adaptability to an extreme degree, and this may partly explain why and how I could live so long with and like the Ainu, whose habits and customs, as my readers will see, are somewhat different to ours.

When I go to a country I do my best to be like one of the natives themselves, and, whether they are savage or not, I endeavour to show respect for them and their ideas, and to conform to their customs for the time being. I make up my mind that what is good for them must be good enough for me, and though I have occasionally had to swear at myself for "doing in Ainuland as the Ainu does," especially as regards the food, I was not much the worse for it in the end. I never use force when I can win with kindness, and in my small experience in Hokkaido and other countries I have always found that real savages in their simplicity are most "gentleman-like" people. With few exceptions they are good-natured, dignified, and sensible, and the chances are that if you are fair to them they will be fair to you. Civilised savages and barbarians I always found untrustworthy and dangerous.

The Island of Yezo, with the smaller islands near its coast, and the Kurile group, taken together, are called "the Hokkaido." The Hokkaido extends roughly from 41° to 51° latitude north, and between 139° and 157° longitude east of Greenwich.

My view of the origin of the word Ainu is this: *Ainu* is but a corruption or abbreviation of *Ai-num*, "they with hair," or "hairy men," or else of *Hain-num*, "come with hair," or "descended hairy." Considering that the Ainu pride themselves above all things on their hairiness, it does not seem improbable to me that this may be the correct origin of the word, and that they called themselves after the distinguishing characteristic of their race.

The word Ainu is a generic term, and is used both in the singular and plural; but when specifying, the words *Kuru* (people, men), *utaragesh* (woman), etc., are generally added to it: viz., *Ainu kuru*, Ainu people, Ainu men; *Ainu utaragesh*, an Ainu woman; *Ainu utaragesh utara*, several Ainu women.

The Ainu population of Yezo is roughly reckoned by the Japanese at about 15,000 or 17,000 souls, but at least half this number are half-castes, and in my opinion (and I have visited nearly every Ainu village in Yezo) the number of thoroughbred Ainu does not exceed 8000 souls.

The illustrations in this book are my own, and are the reproductions from sketches which I took on the spot. They may not show much artistic merit, but they seem to me to be characteristic of the country and the people, and I hope that my readers will be impressed with them in the same way.

A. HENRY SAVAGE LANDOR.

CHAPTER I.

From Hakodate to Mororran—Volcano Bay—The first Ainu—A strange Institution among them.

I have often asked myself *why* I went to Yezo; and, when there, what possessed me to undertake the laborious task of going round the island, up its largest rivers, travelling through jungles and round lakes, climbing its highest peaks, and then proceeding to the Kuriles. There are certain things in one's life that cannot be accounted for, and the journey which I am going to relate is one of them.

Pleasure and rest were the two principal objects which had primarily induced me to steer northwards; but it was my fate not to get either the one or the other.

I was on the Japanese ship the *Satsuma Maru*. Rapidly nearing the Hakodate Head, which we soon passed, we entered the well-protected bay and the town of Hakodate at the foot of the Peak came into view. It looked extremely pretty, with its paper-walled houses and its tiled roofs, set against the background of brown rock with its fringe of green at the foot. As we cast anchor, hundreds of coolies, carrying on their backs loads of dried fish and seaweed, were running along the *bund* or wharf. A few *musemes* (girls), in their pretty *kimonos* (gowns) and with oil-paper umbrellas, were toddling along on their wooden clogs, and a crowd of loafers stood gazing at the ship as she came to anchor. The Peak, more than 1000 feet high, was towering on our south side, forming a peninsula, joined to the mainland by a sandy isthmus, and the large bay swept round us, forming nearly a circle. The place has a striking resemblance to Gibraltar.

I landed, and put up at a tea-house, where I was in hopes of learning something regarding the island from the Japanese settlers, but no one knew anything. The reports that there were no roads extending beyond a few miles; that there was but very poor and scarce accommodation along the coast; that the Ainu, who lived further north, were dirty people; and that the country was full of bears, were certainly not encouraging to an intending traveller.

I must confess that my first day in Yezo was a dull one; but the second day I had the pleasure of meeting a Mr. H., a resident, who kindly offered me his hospitality, and the next two were pleasantly spent at his house. In conversation with a friend of his, I heard the remark that no man alone could possibly complete the circuit of the island of Yezo, owing to the difficulties of travel; and my readers can imagine the astonishment of my interlocutors when I meekly said, that if no one had ever done it, I was going to do it; and, indeed, that I intended to set out alone the next morning.

"Impossible!" said one, "you are too young and too delicate."

"Absurd!" said my kind host, "it would take a very strong man to do it—a man who could stand any amount of hardships and roughing." At the same time he gave me a pitiful look, which undoubtedly meant, "You are a mere bag of skin and bones."

However, the bag of skin and bones kept his word, notwithstanding the poor opinion that his new friends had formed of him.

The preparations for my journey were simple. In two large Japanese baskets I packed three hundred small wooden panels for oil-painting, a large supply of oil colours and brushes, a dozen small sketch-books, my diary, three pairs of boots, three shirts, an equal number of pairs of woollen stockings, a revolver, and a hundred cartridges. The remainder of my luggage was left in charge of Mr. H. till my return. I did not burden myself with either provisions or a tent.

I rose early the following morning and bade good-bye to my kind host. "Good-bye," said he, "I expect we shall see you back to-night to dinner." The word "dinner" was the last English word I heard from the mouth of an Englishman, and it was five long months before I heard another.

The first thirty miles of my journey were ridden in a *basha*, a covered cart built on four wheels that ought to have been round, but were not. There were no springs for the comfort of the traveller, and no cushions on the seats. The conveyance was public, and was drawn by two sturdy ponies. The driver, a Japanese, carried a brass trumpet, on which he continually played.

I might have begun my story by the usual "One fine day," if, unfortunately, the day on which I started the rain had not poured in torrents. A Japanese policeman and a girl were my only fellow-passengers. Travelling at full gallop, on a rough road, in a trap with unsymmetrical wheels and with no springs, during a heavy storm, is scarcely what one would call a pleasant mode of progression; but after some hours of "being knocked about," we went zig-zag fashion, first up a steep hill, then down on the other side, giving the horses a rest at a roadside tea-house by the famous lakes of Zenzai. The larger of these two lakes—the Ko-numa—is extremely picturesque, with its numerous little islands wooded with deciduous trees. In shape it is very irregular, and many points, which project into the lake, add to the loveliness of the scene, while the high ridge over which I had come, on the one side, and the rugged volcano of Komagatake on the other, form a beautiful background to the limpid sheet of water. The outlet of this lake empties itself into Volcano Bay, S.E. of the Komagatake Volcano. The other lake, though smaller, is quite as striking, and possesses the same characteristics of its larger brother. It goes by the name of Ono-numa. A peculiarity of these lakes is that they abound in a smallish fish—the *funa*—which is greatly appreciated by the Japanese.

I sat down in the tea-house on the soft mats, and my *bento*—Japanese lunch— was served to me on a tiny table. There was water soup; there was sea-weed; there was a bowl of rice, and raw fish. The fish—a small *funa*—was in a diminutive dish and its back was covered by a leaf; the head projected over the side of the plate. On the leaf were placed several neatly-cut pieces of the raw flesh, which had apparently been removed from the back of the underlying animal. As I had been long accustomed to Japanese food of this kind I ate to my heart's content, when, to my great horror, the *funa*, which had been staring at me with its round eyes, relieved of the weight that had passed from its back into my digestive organs, leaped up, leaf and all, from the dish and fell on the mat. All the vital parts had carefully been left in the fish, and the wretched creature was still alive!

"Horrible!" I cried, violently pushing away the table and walking out disgusted, to the great surprise of the people present, who expected me to revel in the deliciousness of the dish.

For days and days after I could see in my mind the staring eyes of the *funa*, watching each movement of my chopsticks, and its own back being eaten piecemeal! Wherever I went this big eye stood before me, and increased or diminished in size according to my being more or less lonely, more or less hungry. I had often eaten raw fish before, but never had I eaten live fish!

The journey in the *basha* was resumed that afternoon, and, more dead than alive, I alighted in the evening at Mori, a small Japanese village at the foot of the Komagatake Volcano. The peak of this mountain is 4000 feet above the level of the sea, but its basin-like crater is at a somewhat lower altitude. Up to a certain height it is thickly wooded with deciduous trees and firs, thence its slopes are bare of vegetation, rugged in form, and very rich in colour. It makes part of a volcanic mass which extends from the Esan Volcano, further south, to the limit of the Shiribeshi province, crossing straight through the province of Oshima as far as the Yurapdake Mountain. Komagatake is one of the most majestic and picturesque mountains I have ever seen, as it possesses lovely lines on nearly every side. Its isolation and sudden sharp elevation, rising as it does directly from the sea, gives, of course, a grand appearance to its weird and sterile slopes, which are covered with warmly-tinted cinders, pumice, and lava.

I went over to Mororran, across Volcano Bay, and the following morning I risked my life on a small craft, which took me over to Mombets. From this place I rode on to Uso and Aputa, two Ainu villages at a short distance from each other.

Coming from Japan the first thing that strikes a traveller in the Ainu country is the odour of dried fish, which one can smell everywhere; the next is the great number of crows—the scavengers of the country; lastly, the volcanic nature of the island. On visiting an Ainu village what impressed me most were the miserable and filthy huts, compared with the neat and clean Japanese houses; the poverty and almost appalling dirt of the people and their gentle, submissive nature.

I shall not dwell at length on these Volcano Bay Ainu, as this part of the country is comparatively civilised, and has been travelled over by many people previous to my going there. Besides, most of them have intermarried with Japanese, and have consequently adopted many Japanese customs and manners.

The Ainu of the coast build their huts generally on a single line, near the shore, and each family has its "dug out" canoe drawn up on the beach, ready to hand when wanted. The huts are small and miserable-looking, and they have no furniture or bedding to speak of. The roof and walls are thatched with *arundinaria*, but so imperfectly that wind and rain find easy access through their reedy covering. Curiosity is the only good quality which I ever possessed, and in obedience to it I poked my nose into several of the huts along the beach. This was a mistake on my part, for in the Ainu country the nose is the last thing one ought to poke in anywhere. I was more than astonished to see how human beings could live in such filth! The natives kindly asked me to enter, and I of course did so, stooping low through the small door and raising the mat which protects the aperture. When I was in I could smell a great deal more than I could see, for the east window—the size of a small handkerchief, and the only one in the hut—did not give light enough to illuminate the premises. However, I soon got accustomed to the dimness, and then I could make out my surroundings clearly enough. There was an old man, perfectly naked, with a fine head, long white hair and beard, sitting on the ground among a mass of seaweeds, which he was disentangling and packing. Two young women and two young men, with bright, intelligent eyes and high cheek-bones, were helping him in his work. In their quiet, gentle way they all brought their hands forward, each rubbed the palms together, and, lifting the arms, slowly stroked their hair, and the men their beard with the backs of their hands, while the women rubbed the first finger under the nose from the left to the right. This is their salutation, and it is most graceful. They seemed pleased to see me, and asked me to sit down. As there were neither chairs nor sofas, stools nor cushions, I squatted on the ground.

AINU WOMAN SALUTING.

Most Ainu of Volcano Bay understand Japanese, and they also speak it, interpolating Ainu words when necessary, so I began a conversation. My presence did not seem to disturb them or arouse their curiosity, and, beyond gazing at the mother-of-pearl buttons on my white coat, they did not appear to be struck by me. Evidently the buttons were much more interesting to them than the person who wore them. Now and then they uttered a few words, but whenever one spoke some of the company seemed to be angry, as at an impertinence or a breach of etiquette. Men and women wore large ear-rings or pieces of red or black cloth, which added a great deal to their picturesqueness; but the women were disfigured by a long moustache tattooed across the face from ear to ear. Rough drawings adorn the arms and hands of the women, and some of the younger females would undoubtedly be fine-looking if not disfigured by the tattoos, for they carry themselves well when walking, and possess comely features. Judging from appearances, I should think them very passionate.

Coming out of the hut I saw a scene which I shall never forget. Two naked boys, covered with horrible skin eruptions, had got hold of a large fish-bone, out of which they were endeavouring to make a meal. Round them were gathered about thirty dogs, wild with hunger, barking furiously at the frightened children, and attacking and fighting them for that miserable repast.

I walked along the beach, and endeavoured to make friends with some of the Ainu who were less shy than the others. One little girl was especially picturesque. She was only about ten, and her large eyes, tanned complexion, white teeth, the tiny bluish-black tattoo on her upper lip, her uncombed long black hair flying around her, and her red cloth ear-rings, made her indeed one of the quaintest studies of colour that I have seen in my life. I got her to sit for me; and while I was painting her, an old man, the chief of the village, dressed up in a gaudy costume, with a crown of willow shavings on his head, came to me and made his "salaams." He bore the name of Angotsuro, and before all his salaams were over he found himself "caught in the action" in my sketch-book. Many of the villagers had collected round, and one of them, a half-caste, expressed the wish that I should paint the chief in colours, like the picture of the girl. I asked for nothing better, and started an oil-sketch of him. The excitement of the natives who were witnessing the operation grew greater and greater as each new ornament in the chief's dress was put in the picture. Some seemed to approve of it, others were grumpy, and apparently objected to the picture being taken at all. The *séance* was indeed a stormy one; and though the chief had his regal crown knocked off his head two or three times by the anti-artistic party, he sat well for his likeness, especially as I promised him in Japanese, that when the picture was completed he should be given a few coins and two buttons off my coat.

It was while portraying him that I noticed what extraordinary effects colours produce on those whose eyes are unaccustomed to them. A man in the crowd would get excited, and open his eyes wide and show his teeth every time I happened to touch with my brush the cobalt blue on my palette. Other colours had not the same effect on him. His eyes were continually fixed on the blue, anxiously waiting for the brush to dip in it, and this would then send him into fits of merriment. I squeezed some blue paint from a tube on to the palm of his hand, and he nearly went off his head with delight. He sprang and jumped and yelled, and then ran some way off, where he squatted on the sand, still in admiration of the blue dab on his hand, still grinning at intervals with irrepressible enjoyment. Where the point of the joke was no one but himself ever knew.

When the picture was finished I had no little trouble to keep the many fingers of my audience off the wet painting. Moreover, some person endowed with kindly feelings threw a handful of sand in my face, which nearly blinded me for the moment and partly ruined the two pictures I had painted. The money and the buttons were duly paid to Angotsuro and I moved on.

That same evening I went out for a walk. It was a very dark night, and I love dark nights. When for some years you have done nothing but see strange things and new places there is indeed a great fascination in going about in complete darkness; it rests both your eyes and your brain. I walked for some time along the beach, stumbling against the canoes drawn on shore and against anything that was in my way. Hut after hut was passed, but everything was silent; there was not a sound to be heard, not a light to be seen. The Ainu are early people; they retire with the sun. I walked on yet farther and farther afield, till through the thatched wall of one of the huts I discerned a faint light. I stood and listened. The sad voice of a man was singing a weird, weird song, the weirdest song I have ever heard. Then came a pause, and another voice, even more plaintive than the first, continued the same air.

What with the strange melody in the hut, the soothing noise of the waves gently breaking on the shingle, and the distant howling of dogs or wolves, the mystic effect was such that I could not resist the temptation, and I crept into the hut. A fire was burning in the centre, but it had almost gone out, leaving a lot of smoke. Three old men were sitting on the ground. They decidedly looked as if they did not expect me, but, after their first astonishment was over, they asked me to squat down in a corner, and there I was left to amuse myself, while they resumed their singing and drinking. Of the latter they seemed to have had enough already; but, all the same, several wooden bowls, about five inches in diameter and two deep, were passed round and emptied in no time. The more they drank, the wilder and more melancholy the song became. Only one at a time sang, and he would begin in a very low tone of voice and go up in a *crescendo*, gradually getting awfully excited; then all at once he would stop, as if the effort had been too great for him. His head drooped, and he seemed to sleep. Then, suddenly waking up, coming back to his full senses in a startling manner, he drained one of the bowls, which meantime had been refilled, and resumed the song. The three men were facing each other, and so absorbed were they in their music that, though I was not more than four feet away from them, they seemed to have forgotten me altogether.

I was so impressed with the strangeness of the song that I pulled out my pencil and paper to write down the air. As there was no light but the flicker of the fire, I turned the white leaf of my sketch-book toward it to see what I was writing. This caught the eye of one of the men. He woke up, startled from his musical dream, jumped to his feet, and made a dash for me, yelling some words which I did not understand, and holding over my head something that I could not distinguish at the moment owing to the dimness of the light. Standing thus he paused, evidently waiting for an answer to something he had said. It came from one of the other fellows, who pushed him so violently as to send him sprawling on the floor, while, what he held in his hand—a big, heavy, pointed knife—fell and stuck deep in the ground about an inch from my toes. A dispute arose among themselves, but among the Ainu everything ends up in a drink. The large wooden bowls were again refilled; grand bows were made to me, and they all stroked their hair and beard several times—a sign of great respect. I was then handed one of the bowls and made to swallow the contents. But, heavens! never have I felt any liquid work its way down so far. Had I swallowed fire it could not have been as bad; and, indeed, it was neither more nor less than liquid fire.

As the night was wearing fast, and the old fellows had got on well with their drink, the sing-song became rather too languid and monotonous; and I crept out of the hut as quietly as I had entered it, not without first giving the inmates something for their trouble. I had some difficulty in finding my way back to my less musical quarters; and passing too close to some of the other huts, the dogs—which infest all Ainu villages—barked furiously and roused the whole place.

I learned afterwards that it is an Ainu fashion to try a man's courage. This is done in the way in which my musical friends tried mine, namely, by making a sudden rush with a knife as if death and destruction were imminent, which to a perfect stranger, unconscious of the strain of "bluff" in the action, is not very reassuring. If the person to be tested is aware of this fashion he has to submit to an unlimited number of whacks, administered to him on his bare back, with a heavy war-club. These tests of a man's courage and endurance are called the *Ukorra*.

In the first instance it is done, in a certain sense, good-naturedly, and not meaning to hurt one. Should, however, the person apparently so dangerously threatened show fright or signs of cowardice, he loses the respect of the Ainu, unless he has the happy thought of giving them a sufficient quantity of some intoxicating liquor to make them all drunk—which is a sure means of turning the most inimical Ainu you may meet into your fast friend, even if you have had a deadly feud with him.

The second way—with the war-club—of course is a painful process, and the Ainu have recourse to it when it is necessary to determine the relative amount of courage possessed by certain members of a community. The one that can stand the greater number of blows is naturally entitled to the respect and admiration of his neighbours, and he is elected leader in bear-hunts or similar expeditions. At the election of a new chief—when the chief's line of descendants dies out—this process, I was told, is often practised; for bravery is the first quality which an Ainu chief must possess.

At Aputa, through some of the half-castes, I was able to pick up a great number of Ainu words, which were most useful to me afterwards; and from that, gradually increasing my stock of words, I soon knew enough to understand a little and also to make myself understood.

One day I went along the coast to the next village of Repun, and then retraced my steps to Aputa, as there was nothing of interest at the former place.

An excursion which I enjoyed more was to the Toya Lake, with its three pretty islands in the centre and the magnificent Uso Volcano on its southern shores. The walk there and back was hardly fifteen miles, over a mountain track and through forests of pine-trees and oaks. The lake is about 250 feet above the level of the sea, and is about five miles in diameter. Its shores are surrounded with thickly-wooded hills, which have grassy terraces at a certain altitude, extending especially towards the north-western shores of the lake.

The barren Uso Volcano, with its sterile slopes, is a great contrast to the beautiful green of the comparatively luxuriant vegetation of the lower altitudes. The lake finds an outlet into the Osaru River by means of a high waterfall.

The following day I rode back to Mombets, and the next on to Shin-Mororran (the *new* Mororran, distinguished by this affix from Kiu-Mororran, the *old* settlement on the northern shore).

Mororran has a well-protected harbour, and it would be the best future port in Hokkaido if the anchorage were of a larger capacity. In more speculative hands than the Japanese this port would be a great rival to Hakodate. It consists of a thickly-wooded peninsula, which forms a well-sheltered bay, at the entrance of which the picturesque island of Daikuku stands high above the sea-level. In the harbour itself, smaller islets and huge rocks contribute to its beauty.

The village of Mororran is a mere streak of fourth-rate tea-houses along the road by the side of the cliffs. Apart from the natural loveliness of the harbour, it has, indeed, no claims to consideration at present. In former days it was called by the Ainu, Tokri-moi, "the home of the seals," for these valuable amphibious animals were said to be then plentiful in the bay.

TOYA LAKE, NEAR APUTA.

FISHERMAN'S HUT.

CHAPTER II.
From Mororran to the Saru River.

Thirteen more miles in a *basha*—for I was still in civilised regions—took me to Horobets—a village half Ainu and half Japanese.

The Ainu often name their villages after rivers, and this word Horobets, which in English means "large river," is an instance of this custom. In Southern Japan, previous to my visiting Yezo, I was told that nearly all the Ainu of Horobets had become "good Christians." If such were the case, which I do not wish my readers to doubt, the small experience which I had here, led me to believe that "good Christians" often make "very bad heathens."

I left all my baggage in a tea-house at the entrance of the village, and, taking my paint-box with me, I went for a walk along the beach. I saw a crowd of Ainu in the distance, and I hurried up to them. They were busy skinning a large Ushi-sakana (cow-fish), cutting it into pieces with their long knives. They did not pay much attention to me, and this disregard of what would be to others a cause of curiosity and interruption I afterwards found to be a characteristic of the Ainu. They are seldom distracted from any particular idea that occupies their mind at a certain moment. In fact, they are so little accustomed to reflect at all, that it seems almost impossible for them to think of two things at the same time. Of all the existing races of mankind they may be said to be the most purely one-idea'd.

Stark naked, with their long hair streaming in the wind, they formed a picturesque group. What a chance for a sketch! I sat down on the sand, opened my paint-box, and dashed off a picture, when a young lad, who had taken his share of the fish, came over to see what I was doing. "What is it?" he asked me in broken Japanese, to which question I answered that I was painting the group of them. The news seemed to give him a shock. He rejoined the others, excitedly muttered some words, and apparently told them that I had painted the whole group, fish and all. Had anyone among them been struck by lightning, they could certainly not have looked more dismayed. I never knew until then that painting could have such an overpowering effect on people, except, perhaps, when one has sat to an amateur artist for one's own likeness, the result of which is often one of dumb and blank amazement. Anger and disgust naturally followed. The fish was thrown aside, but not the knives, armed with which they all rushed at my back. The sudden change of ideas had evidently made them exceedingly angry. The grumbling became very loud, and louder still when they saw me complacently giving the finishing touches to the fish, which was now left alone, and not as before shifted about every second. They grew wilder and wilder, until one of the crowd shouted in my ears some words which sounded remarkably like swearing. Nevertheless it takes more than that to stop me from sketching; but ... "By Jove!" I exclaimed, when, all of a sudden, a rush was made on me. My paint-box, picture, palette and brushes were snatched out of my hands and smashed or flung away, and I found myself stretched on the sand, my late involuntary sitters holding me down fast by the legs and arms. A big knife was kept well over my head, so that I should not attempt to move, while the painting, on a heavy wooden panel, was being mercilessly destroyed by others. "If these are Christians, well I am ..." were, I must confess, the first words that rose to my lips.

It is, indeed, difficult to describe how and what one feels when, to all appearance, one is going to be murdered—for painting a fish! My first thought, of course, went to my parents. My next was, what a nuisance it was to be murdered with the sun shining in my eyes, so that I could not even see who would give me the "finishing touch." All the events of my life, the bad ones first, flashed across my mind in those few seconds, and then I almost began to feel as if I had made my first steps into the other world, and I could see angels and devils disputing for my company—the devils, of course, having by far the largest claims. The bitterness of death had in some sense passed, when, to my great astonishment, and with a few, but very sound, kicks I was made to understand that I could get up and go.

The sensation of being brought back to life, when one has made up one's mind to be dead, notwithstanding the abrupt manner in which it was produced, was indeed pleasant one. I did get up, and pretty quick, I can tell you; but only to see my poor wooden paint-box floating half-smashed in the sea, my brushes stuck here and there in the sand, and the sketch utterly destroyed.

My assailants were about fifteen or twenty, and I was alone. Stupidly enough, and relying on the Christianity of the people, I had not burdened myself with the extra weight of my revolver; I had left it with my heavy luggage in the small Japanese tea-house where I had put up, nearly a mile away. The Japanese police-station was at Washibets, another village some miles off. Nothing was left for me but to pick up the few unbroken brushes which were within easy reach and retire; but I was neither frightened nor conquered, and I swore to myself that I would have my revenge. I hurried to the tea-house, took my revolver, and filled my pocket with cartridges, then I ran back to the spot where I had sketched and been assaulted. There they all were as I had left them, one of them mimicking me with the broken palette, which he had fished out of the sea. I had kept well behind some thick brushwood, so that they should not see me, and for some time watched them unobserved. The imitation was perfect. The impromptu Raphael's hair was long enough to give him the look of an artist, and he was sufficiently brave to carry on his imitation sketching under a shower of missiles and sand thrown at him by his friends and companions. As he turned his head I recognised in my brother-artist the man who had been holding the knife over my head about an hour before, and also the very person who had given me the soundest kick. Just like a brother-artist! If my sketching had not lasted long, his parody was even shorter. I sprang out from the brushwood screen and caught him by the throat, pointing my revolver at his head, and telling him in Japanese to follow me to the police-station. Another man, attacking me from behind, stabbed me in my left arm, but not very severely, as I saw him just in time to avoid his blow. The sight of my revolver had a salutary effect on my hairy friends, and they were done out of their fun when, keeping them at bay, I told them that if they did not follow me they would all be dead men before they knew where they were. They had seen guns of the Japanese, and they knew the effects of them, so the saucy gentlemen stroked their hair and beard and made signs of submission and obedience. However, I was not to be easily appeased, as it was necessary to give them a lesson to prevent the same thing happening to future travellers; so I made them march in front of me, not caring to have them at my back, and thus took them all to the Japanese police-station, where they were duly arrested. The Japanese are very severe with recalcitrant Ainu, and my assailants would have been unmercifully dealt with had it not been for their wives and children, who came to me begging me to forgive their husbands and fathers for what they had done. I willingly did so, on condition that they should all come and prostrate themselves at my feet, imploring pardon and forgiveness and offering submission, as well as confessing their sorrow. This penitential function was reluctantly fixed by the Japanese policeman—the only one in the place—at a late hour in the afternoon. During the interval, as I fortunately had a large supply of painting materials, I managed to repaint from memory the scene represented in the sketch destroyed. The evening came, and the little Japanese policeman brought the resigned and humbled Ainu to the inn. Their wives and relatives followed, and they all looked supremely mournful and sad. I sat, Japanese fashion, on the small verandah on the ground-floor, and the policeman placed the Ainu on a line in front of me, and then came to sit by my side. He then addressed them, partly in the Ainu language, partly in Japanese, and bestowed on them names which went well to the point. He scolded them harshly, and asked them why they had assaulted me.

One of them, as grave as a judge, with his eyes cast down, and in a half-broken voice, came forward and said, that if once you have your likeness taken you have to give up your life to it, and it brings illness to yourself, to your children, your parents, and your neighbours. Not only that, but as I had *taken* many people together, famine was sure to fall on the country. "Then," he added—and he seemed positive of what he was talking about—"then there was a fish the stranger *made*"—the Ainu have no word for painting—

"and had we not destroyed his *makings* all the fish would have disappeared from the sea, and all the Ainu would have died of starvation"—which was a terrible contingency, as the Ainu live mainly by fishing. "We have not hurt the stranger," continued this hairy representative of Master Eustache de St. Pierre, "and now that all the Ainu and the fish he made are destroyed we are safe."

"You are mistaken," said I, when, by the aid of the policeman, I understood the meaning of this long harangue, and I produced the large sketch of the scene which I had repainted from memory. This certainly beat them. They could hardly believe their own eyes, and looked at each other as if some great calamity were approaching. I have no doubt that they considered me an evil spirit, and, as such, too powerful to be contended with. Discretion was their best part of valour, as they proved. One by one they approached the verandah, sat cross-legged in front of me, rubbed their hands together, stroked their hair and beard three times, and three times each put his head down to my feet, begging my pardon. The Ainu women and children who had assembled in the back yard, where the function took place, were crying and moaning piteously. The most trying part for me was, of course, to keep serious during this long tragi-comic performance, and I was indeed glad when it was all over; when my supremacy was acknowledged, and my immunity from further insult secured; when submission had been made, and such whips and stings of outrageous fortune as might come from the painting of a fish had been humbly accepted.

The Ainu are gentle and mild by nature, but, like all ignorant people, they are extremely superstitious, and superstition is a powerful excitant. Nevertheless, they are good people in their own way, and it must not be inferred from this small experience of mine that they are bullies, for they are not. The superstition regarding the reproduction of images is common all through the East, with the exception of the Japanese, and in many parts of Europe itself strange ideas are connected with portrait-painting. In Spain or Italy many a girl of the lower classes would think herself dishonoured if she happened to be sketched unawares, or if her picture were shown without the consent of her parents, brothers, relatives, and the parish priest.

However, these Horobets Ainu are said, since civilisation has set in in that part of Yezo, of late years to have become untrustworthy and violent. They are more given to drunkenness than their neighbours, as they can procure from the Japanese stronger beverages than their own. *Sake* (Japanese wine) of inferior quality is sold and exchanged in large quantities, and has the same fatal effects on them as rum—our fire-water—had on the American Indians.

I was not sorry to leave a village which had displayed so little appreciation of my art. I took two ponies and two pack-saddles, to one of which was lashed my baggage, while I sat on the other. Riding is a delightful pastime when you have a good horse and a good saddle; but not when you have to look after two vicious animals, and are yourself perched on a rough wooden pack-saddle. Moreover, Ainu pack-saddles are perhaps the most uncomfortable of their kind. The illustration shows one of them. It is made with a rough, solid wooden frame, of which the front and back parts are semicircular. One large hole is perforated in each of these to allow ropes to be passed through. Under this frame are two mat cushions or pads, which are somehow supposed to fit the pony's back; and by means of three ropes, one of which is passed under the pony's body and fastened on each side of the saddle, while the others hang loose across its chest and under its tail respectively, the pack-saddle is made to remain in position either going uphill, downhill, or on level ground. Stirrups, of course, there are none; and mounting involves some difficulties at first. One has to face one's pony and place the left foot on the breast-piece, lift oneself up and swing right round, describing three-quarters of a circle before attaining one's seat in the saddle. If distances are miscalculated in this gymnastic feat, it is a common occurrence to find oneself seated on the pony's neck, or else landed heavily on either of the two hard wooden arches of the saddle, instead of gracefully falling between them. Keeping your equilibrium when you are on is also a trying exercise to anybody not born and bred a circus rider, and balancing your baggage perfectly on each side of the saddle is somewhat more difficult than it sounds.

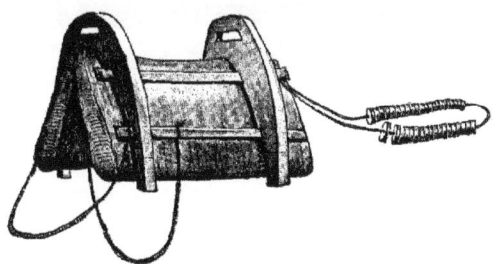

PACK-SADDLE.

Nine miles from Horobets one comes across the Nobori-bets[1] hot-springs. There was, formerly, a *geiser* here, but it is seldom active now. These hot-springs are situated two-and-a-half miles from the sea-coast, and a miserable building, which is a mere shanty, is built in the vicinity of them, where people who wish to be cured of different complaints put up and take the waters.

I rode on to the Noboribets village, consisting of a few houses only; and, though I reached it late in the evening, I had to ride fourteen miles further to Shiraoi, "a place of horse-flies."[2]

At sunrise I was up again and on my way to Tomakomai,[3] the largest Japanese fishing village between Mororran and Cape Erimo.

NOBORIBETS VOLCANO.

Sardine fishing is the principal and, indeed, the only industry of the place. It is carried on in a practical way. When the long nets are ready, and one end of them is fastened to the shore, they launch the boat, which is rowed rapidly by twenty or thirty strong men, while the net is dropped as the boat goes along. Having thus described a semicircle, the boat is beached. All on board jump out, and the net is pulled on shore amid the shrieks and yells of the excited fishermen. Myriads of sardines are caught each time the net is hauled in; and it is a fantastic scene to see the naked crowd which, in clearing the nets from the beheaded fish, get covered with silver scales, which stick to their arms, legs, and body, and give them a strange appearance.

Look-out towers are built on four high posts, where a watchman is posted to signal the arrival and approach of the shoals. The sea is so dense with them that it changes its colour, and these moving banks of sardines are distinguishable four or five miles from the coast. This method is the same as that adopted in Cornwall when the pilchards are expected, and the same discoloration of the sea takes place.

From Tomakomai a road branches to the north leading to Sappro, the capital of Hokkaido, and it is the last place on the southern coast which is visited by that rare specimen of the globe-trotter who ventures to Yezo. He hastily makes his way from here to Sappro and Otaru on the northern coast, and waits for a ship to be conveyed back to Hakodate. He then, of course, tells his friends that he has been round and about and through Yezo, while in fact he has seen absolutely nothing of Yezo or its inhabitants. About half-a-dozen Europeans, however, have been further on—as far as the Saru River; and each one has written a book on the Ainu, for the most part copying what the previous author had written.

As far as Tomakomai there is a road—a sure sign of civilisation—but nothing but a horse-track is to be found all along the southern coast after this place has been passed.

Changing my ponies at Yuhuts,[4] nine miles east, and again at Mukawa and Saru-buto, I was able to reach Saru Mombets that same night. Many Ainu and Japanese fishermen's huts are scattered between Horohuts[5] and Yuhuts, on the sandy track along the sea.

The traveller then leaves the sea on the right, and by a very uneven track, and after fording several rivers of little importance comes to Mukawa, a dirty little village fourteen miles from Yuhuts. My lunch that day consisted of a large piece of raw salmon, which was easily digested in riding nine more miles to Saru-buto. Sharu in Ainu, corrupted into Saru, means a grassy plain; and *buto* is a Japanese corruption of the Ainu word *huts*, the mouth of a river. My ponies must have known of this "grassy plain," for they went remarkably well, and I reached the latter village some time before dark, so that I was able to push on to Saru Mombets, a larger village nearly four miles further. Saru Mombets translated means "a tranquil river in a grassy plain," a name thoroughly appropriate to the locality.

There is nothing to interest the traveller along the coast, unless he be a geologist. Almost the whole of the western part of the Iburi district is of volcanic formation. The eastern part is abundant in sandstones, breccias, and shales. In the neighbourhood of Yuhuts, and all along the coast as far west as Horobets, pumice forms the surface soil, showing that in former days frequent eruptions must have taken place. Vegetable mould alternates with pumice. Sand, clay, tufa, with beds of peat and gravel, are the components of the soil which is found filling up the declivities of mountains, covering lowlands and sea-beaches in this part of the island. Specimens of the palæozoic group are found in the pebbles of the Mukawa River and valley, like amphibolite, limestone, phyllite, sandstone, and clay-slate, besides variegated quartzite of greenish and red layers. Primary rocks are common all through Iburi and Hidaka.

The terraces surrounding the Saru valley are mostly wooded with oak, and the swampy region between the Mukawa and Sarubuto has many patches of green grass, and a thick growth of high swamp reeds.

HOROBETS.

STOREHOUSES AT PIRATORI.

CHAPTER III.
Up the Saru River—Piratori and its chief.

A large number of Ainu have taken up their abode on the banks of the River Saru, or Sharu, as it is called by them, and Piratori, nearly fifteen miles from the coast, is the largest village of the whole series.

The scenery from the coast to this village is not grand, but pretty, through a thickly-wooded country and along grassy plains. The Ainu give to the plain itself the name of Sharu-Ru, which corresponds in English to a "track in a grassy plain." Along this water-way, or not far from it, one meets with numerous small Ainu villages and scattered huts until Piratori is reached.

Piratori is a string or succession of many villages on undulating ground, the last of them being situated on a high cliff overlooking the river. In the Ainu language *Pira* means "a cliff," and *Tori* "a residence." As in all Ainu villages, the huts are in one line, some few yards one from the other. Each has a separate structure—a small storehouse built on piles—generally at the west end of the hut.

On my arrival at Piratori, I was welcomed by Benry, the *Ottena* (chief) of the village, who invited me to his hut and *salaamed* me in the most solemn manner, not forgetting to mention incidentally that "his throat was very dry," and that *sake* (Japanese wine) could be obtained from a Japanese who lives opposite to his hut.

"He is a bad man," said Benry confidentially; "but he sells very good *sake*."

The *sake* was procured, and Benry, beaming with joy, poured it with his shaky, drunken hands into a large bowl. He then produced a wooden stick, shaped like a paper-knife, about five inches in length, and waved it in the air five or six times with his right hand, dipping the point of it each time into the fluid. "*Nishpa*"—sir, master—said he. Then, leaning forwards and lifting up his heavy moustache with the small stick, he swallowed the contents of the bowl at a draught. The same performance took place each time that some fresh *sake* was poured into his bowl, and then Benry, with an inimitable cunning, and a comically self-sacrificing expression on his face, meekly enquired whether I would care to see "how much an Ainu could drink."

"Yes," said I, "we will go down to the river, and you shall show me there if you can drink it dry."

"Yie, yie, yie"—no, no, no—hurriedly replied in Japanese the Ainu chief; "water is too heavy, and I meant wine." Owing to this small difference of opinion, and having no wish to encourage him in his drunkenness, Benry's capacity for intoxicating fluids is yet unknown to the civilised world.

Benry's house is a palace compared to other Ainu huts. It is much larger than most of them, and boasts of a wooden floor, in the centre of which a rectangular fire-place is cut out. The hut has two windows, one toward the east, the other opening to the south; but no chimney is provided as an outlet for the smoke. A hole in the west corner of the roof answers this purpose. The rough wooden frame is thatched with tall reeds and *arundinaria*, and the roof is shaped like a prism. The different huts of Piratori vary in size, but not in type. The larger ones cover an area of about sixteen or eighteen feet square. Most of them, however, do not measure more than ten or twelve feet square. Benry's house was exceptionally large, and being such a "swell" one, two rough *kinna* (mats) were spread on the floor and a number of Japanese rice boxes and *shokuji* tables[6] adorned one side of the dwelling. Over these were hung a number of swords, knives, etc., most of them with no blade at all, or with only a wooden one. The few old blades which Benry possessed were of Japanese workmanship, probably obtained by the Ainu in their former wars with the Japanese. A few Ainu spears and arrows with bone and bamboo poisoned points were fastened to the roof.

These Ainu of Piratori have frequent intercourse with the Japanese, who get from them furs and other articles in exchange for *sake* or a few worthless beads. A few half-castes are also found at Piratori. The Piratori Ainu, with those of Volcano Bay, as we have seen, are those best known to the civilised world, as a few foreigners have travelled so far to see them. I may mention that as types the inhabitants of Piratori are a great deal better than the residents of Volcano Bay, most of whom are half-breeds; but even they themselves cannot be taken as fair specimens of their race, for they have adopted several customs and habits of the Japanese, which the incautious traveller has then reported as purely Ainu customs. For instance, the pure Ainu diet consists almost entirely of fish, meat, and seaweeds. Only occasionally are the roots of certain trees eaten. At Piratori I found that many grow and eat millet, and corn and bad rice are also sometimes procured from the Japanese. Benry has also gone so far in the way of civilisation as to invest his small fortune in buying half-a-dozen hens and a cock, with whom he shares his regal home. These hens lay eggs according to custom, and Benry and his "wife" eat them. As the Ainu language has no special word for this imported kind of bird, they are known by the name of "kikkiri."

BENRY, THE AINU CHIEF OF PIRATORI.

After the experience which I had had at Horobets I decided to be more careful with my sketching. I broached the subject to Benry, and asked him to sit to me for his portrait. At first he was very reluctant, but the prospect of receiving a present finally overcame his scruples—for he was indeed civilised in this respect, and understood the worth of his version of the almighty dollar to perfection—and, consenting to be sketched, he sat—at the outset with as much courage as docility. He produced a crown of shavings and seaweed, which he solemnly placed on his head, whilst his better-half helped him on with his regal *imi* (garments), as well as a large sword, which also made part of his regal insignia. The crown had in front a small bear's head roughly carved in wood, and the clothes were very gaudy. They were made of strips of blue, white, and red cloth sewn together. The materials used were Japanese, but they were cut and arranged in a thoroughly Ainu pattern. Though he began well, Benry was not a good sitter, and, like most animals, he did not like to be stared at. He felt the weight of a look, as it were, and it made him uncomfortable. Not many minutes had elapsed before he became openly impatient; he even showed his temper by flinging away his crown and his wooden sword. On the other hand, sketching in Benry's house was no easy matter for me. With all the respect due to the chief of Piratori, I am bound to say that his house was not a model of cleanliness. Those of his hairy brothers and subjects were no better than his, and many were a great deal worse. Fleas and other insects were so numerous that in a few minutes I was literally covered with them, each one of them having a peaceful and hearty meal at my expense, while I, for the sake of art, had to go on with my sketch and leave them undisturbed. Notwithstanding all this Benry was immortalised twice that day, and his maid, housekeeper, or wife—three words which have the same meaning to the Ainu—was also handed down to posterity while in the act of spinning the inner fibre of the *Ulmus campestris* bark, destined to form a new garment for her lord, master, and husband.

When I went out to sketch the houses and storehouses in the village Benry and another man followed me everywhere; but neither he nor his fellow-shadow seemed to take any interest in the sketching. In Japan, Corea, and China I have often been surrounded by hundreds of people attentively watching every stroke of the brush, and I have always found them clever and quick in making out the meaning of each line or brush-mark. I can assert, without fear of being contradicted, that the majority of Japanese, Coreans, and Chinese are even quicker than Europeans in that respect, owing to the fact that lines constitute for them the study of a lifetime. Chinese characters, which are nothing but a deep study of lines, are adopted by the three above-mentioned nations, and I consider this to be the original cause why this artistic insight is to be found even among the lowest classes. The Ainu have no such insight; they have no characters, no writing of any kind, no books, and it is therefore not astonishing that they are not trained to understand art, bad as it may have been in my case. Their appreciation of lines is yet in the rudest form, and they possess no more than what is instinctive with them. For instance, while I was sketching, Benry and his friend either sat or crouched down by my side like two dogs, and when my sketch was finished I showed it to them.

"Pirika, Pirika! Nishpa!" ("Very pretty, very pretty, sir!") Benry exclaimed with perfect self-assurance; but when I asked him what he thought the sketch represented, he cut me short by saying that *I* had done the picture and *I* ought to know what it was meant for; he did not. His friend agreed with him.

When my work was done we three walked back to Benry's house, my two Ainu friends being very anxious that I should get something to eat. From their conversation and gestures I caught that it seemed incomprehensible to them that I should sit in front of an Ainu hut and—to use their expression—"make all sorts of signs on a wooden panel." After a lengthy discussion the two came to the conclusion that houses in our country were so bad that I had been sent to the Ainu country to "copy" the pattern of Ainu huts!

Benry seemed excited about something, and hurried us back with curious haste and eagerness. When we left the house in the morning I saw Benry's better-half placing a few eggs in water to boil over the fire. When we entered the hut, nearly two hours afterwards, the eggs were still boiling, and no fair maid within yelling reach. In order that the fire might not go out during her absence the thoughtful girl had placed the largest portion of the trunk of a tree in the fireplace!

Taken altogether, Benry and all his Saru Ainu are very good-natured. They gradually got accustomed to being sketched, seeing that after all it really did not bring on them "immediate death."

The more one sees of the Ainu the dirtier they appear, but as dirt to a great extent contributes to picturesqueness, I was indeed sorry when Benry, exercising his authority, sent several of my sitters to dress up in their best clothes—often Japanese—while I should have preferred to sketch them in their every-day rags. I must say, for their sake, that they were never sent to wash. Being a rapid sketcher, I had recourse to a trick. I pretended to sketch one given person, who, of course, was sent at once to "dress up," and while he or she, after having returned, posed patiently for half an hour or more, I in the meantime took sketches of four or five different natives, who were not aware that they were being portrayed. As the Ainu—and they are probably not the only people—could not make either head or tail of my sketches, my trick was never found out.

One day, old Benry led me by the hand in the most affectionate manner to a hut some way off, and confidentially told me that we were going to see his favourite girl and her boy.

"This," said the chief triumphantly as we went in, "this is Benry's *Pirika menoko*" (pretty girl), "and that"—pointing to a youth—"her only son."

"And what about the old hairy lady in your own hut?" I inquired.

"That is my *Poromachi*" (great wife), said he, qualifying matters with a compliment to the elder woman, "and this is my *Pon-machi*" (small wife).

"Why should you have two wives, you old Mormon?"

"Nishpa," retorted he, "my great wife is old, and she is only fit to do all the rough work in the house and out. My hair is white, but I am strong, and I wanted yet a young wife."

Indeed, there was enough mother-wit in Benry to have made him either a scamp or a philosopher. His theories were as remarkable as they were accommodating, particularly to himself.

Returning from the house of his love, the chief was in a very talkative mood, and he related two or three Japanese stories, which he wanted me to believe to be pure Ainu legends. A learned missionary and two or three travellers before him, who had visited Piratori previous to myself, have accepted these so-called legends wholesale, taking Benry's word for their accuracy, which, as the old chief speaks very good Japanese, of course simplified the task of understanding and transcribing them. I was, however, much surprised to find that such learned Europeans could yield such ready credence to a barbarian Ainu chief.

Thinking that it would please me, Benry told me the story of a deluge and a big flood, in which nearly all the Ainu were drowned. The few that escaped did so by finding refuge on a high mountain.

"Where did you learn this story, Benry?" I asked sternly.

"Nishpa, it is an old Ainu story, and all strangers who come to Piratori write it in their books."

"Oh, no, Benry, you know well that *one* stranger did not write it in his book," said I quickly, as if I knew all about it.

"Oh, yes, nishpa; *that* was the stranger who told me the story!"

This small anecdote shows how careful one ought to be in accepting information which may sound extremely interesting at first, but is absolutely worthless in the end.

AINU MAN WAVING HIS MOUSTACHE-LIFTER PREVIOUS TO DRINKING.

AN AINU FESTIVAL.

CHAPTER IV.
An Ainu Festival.

The Ainu have few public performances, and no special time of the year is fixed for them. As it so happened, a festival—a "Iyomanrei"—took place while I was at Piratori.

The performance was held in a large hut belonging to the heir apparent to the chieftainship of Piratori. I went to the hut and asked whether I could attend the performance. The host, in answer, came to meet me at the door, and, taking me by the hand, led me in. I was shown where to sit, on the southern side of the hut, the place of honour for strangers, and my host sat in front of me and saluted me in Ainu fashion.

Benry and several old men were squatting on the floor, Benry in the middle, and he was again gorgeous in his regal clothes. Some of the others, who wore a crown like Benry's, were chiefs of the neighbouring villages, who had come up for the grand occasion.

One by one all the men present rose and came to stroke their hair and beard before me, and I returned the compliment as well as I could in Ainu fashion. The hut was gradually getting filled, and each man that entered first saluted the landlord, then Benry, then myself, and ultimately the two guests between whom he sat. Women and children occupied the darker west end of the hut, and they took no active part in the function. Other chiefs came in, and Benry was surrounded by many of them and by elderly men.

The whole group of these chiefs, with their long white beards, lighted up by a brilliant ray of sunshine, which penetrated through the small east window, was extremely picturesque.

In its savagery it was almost grand, with a barbaric quasi-animal sense of power and irresponsibility. In truth, it was a wonderful sight to see all these hairy people assembled in this small place—men, yet not men like ourselves—men, and not brutes, yet still having curiously brutish traits athwart their humanity.

The performance was simple, but really fine in its simplicity. A fire burning in the centre of the hut, and filling the place with smoke, added, by its suggestive dimness, to the picturesqueness of the scene. It was strange that the only ray of sun which came in should fall on the most interesting group. Was it chance or design? Rembrandt himself would have delighted in painting that scene.

Benry looked every inch a king, and several of the younger men were busily engaged lighting his pipe and refilling it with tobacco. He puffed away at such a rate that no sooner was the pipe filled than it was smoked and handed over again to undergo the same process.

Two large casks of Japanese *sake* were brought in, and each man produced his wooden bowl.

The host came slowly forward, and planted an *Inao*—a willow wand with overhanging shavings—in one corner of the fireplace; then muttered a few words, which implied that the *sake* could now be poured out. A Japanese lacquer rice-box was filled with the intoxicating liquid, and no sooner had this been done than old Benry, forgetting his dignity, jumped up and made a rush for it, filled a large bowl, and retired to a corner to drink it. All the men present followed his example. Benry was never selfish when he had had enough for himself. He filled his bowl again and brought it to me, saying that I was a friend of the Ainu, and must join them in the drinking.

My attention was suddenly drawn to three old chiefs, who, half drunk, stood in front of the small east window. They dipped their moustache-lifters in their bowls, waving them towards the sun as a salutation to the "Chop Kamui," the "Great Sun." There was no religious character attached to this libation offered to the sun, no more than when we take off our hats passing a respected friend in the street. It is a mere sign of respect, not of worship. Besides, it must be clearly understood that no "offerings" of wine are ever made by the Ainu to the "Great Sun," and that the "libations" offered are invariably consumed by the offerer.

I managed to get several sketches of the assembly, and every moment I expected to get into trouble again; but this time they took it most kindly.

The hut became very stuffy, owing to the large number of persons and the smoke. There were nearly two hundred people in it, packed closely together, and there was nothing in the show to interest one—certainly not the disgusting sight of this drunkenness, which, moreover, became monotonous as well as disgusting.

I stroked my hair and beard—the latter only figuratively—in sign of salute, to the host, Benry, and the other drowsy chiefs, and, carefully avoiding pushing or treading on any member of the unsteady crowd, I made my exit.

Oh, what a treat it was to breathe fresh air again!

Outside the hut the pretty *menokos* (girls) of Piratori were having a lot of fun all to themselves. They were all dressed in long yellowish gowns, with rough white and red ornamentations on a patch of blue cloth, on their backs; and each girl took a very active part in a game, or a kind of savage dance, called Tapkara. They all ranged themselves in a circle, and a child or two was sometimes placed in the centre. The game consisted in collectively hopping an indefinite number of times, calling out either the name, or the accompanying sound, of some of their everyday occupations, and clapping the hands so as to keep time. For instance, one sound was "Ouye, ouye" ("Fire, fire"), and they all blew as when making a fire, and hopped till they were nearly senseless.

Then the next was "R-r-r, r-r-r, r-r-r," and with this they imitated the pulling of a rope.

Then "Pirrero, pirrero; pirrero, pirrero," was the sound accompanying the action of rowing, imitating the squeaking of the paddle produced by the friction on the canoe.

The movement of the arms changed according to the sounds uttered, but the hopping was kept up continuously. The game reminded me much of our Sir Roger de Coverley, in a more barbarous form, but certainly not less pretty than our old country dance.

AINU WOMEN DANCING, PIRATORI.

Late in the afternoon all the men came out of the hut, and by a winding path I was taken to the valley along the river, at the foot of the cliff on which Piratori is built. Benry and all the other chiefs remained on the cliff. Bareback races formed the next and last event in the programme, and the chiefs were to witness them from their "high point of view."

PIRATORI WOMAN IN COSTUME.

There was great excitement as to who should ride the ponies. The Ainu are fond of sports, and I noticed that ultimately they were sharp enough to select their jockeys from among the lightest men. The winner of each race had a good time of it, but the other unfortunate jockeys were pulled off the ponies by the angry mob, and knocked about as worthless beings.

The evening came, and with the dying sun ended that memorable day of festivities. I retired. Distant sounds of the *menokos*, still enjoying themselves, came to me with the wind, but fainter and fainter they grew as it was getting darker.

"Pirrero! Pirrero! Pirrero!" I heard again, till at last the sounds faded away into a mere murmur, and I fell asleep.

The morning that I left Piratori, old Benry put on his regal clothes and crown to bid me good-bye.

"Nishpa, Popka-no-okkayan" ("Sir, may you be preserved warm"), said the old chief, in the Ainu fashion of bidding farewell; "I have a pain in my chest, owing to your leaving Piratori, but I shall accompany you part of the way."

I dissuaded the old chief from doing that, but he went on, with his plaintive voice: "Nishpa, you must tell in your country that Piratori is a nice place, and all the Ainu are good people. Not like the Shamo" (Japanese; also half-breeds), "for they are bad. You must return soon," he added, and, taking my hand, he pressed it to his hairy chest. He then took me to his hut again, and there renewed his farewells, and I renewed mine to him, to his *great* wife, and

- 31 -

to his house, for it is part of the Ainu etiquette to bid good-bye to the house of a friend as well as to the owner of it.

The return journey to Saru Mombets was accomplished without much difficulty.

UTAROP ROCKS.

CHAPTER V.
From the Saru River to Cape Erimo.

After quitting Saru Mombets I was altogether out of the beaten tracks. The twenty-two miles to Shimokebo were monotonous in the extreme. High cliffs towered above me on the one side, and the sea stretched into infinity on the other. River after river had to be waded, the At-pets,[7] the Nii-pak-pets,[8] and the Shibe-gari-pets.[9] The Nii-pak-pets is wide and fairly deep. Near the At-pets river the Japanese Government has established a horse farm, in order to improve the breed of Yezo ponies. A few miserable Ainu huts are scattered along the coast, and millions of scavenger crows, with their monotonous cries, seem to claim sovereignty over these shores. Near the Takae village, on the Nii-kap-pets, is an enormous perpendicular cliff, which, jutting out into the sea, bars the way to the traveller; therefore I had to abandon the sandy shore, and with considerable trouble get the ponies to climb over the steep banks, which was no easy task for them. Shimokebo is a peculiar-looking place. It is entirely a fishermen's village, and I put up at the Ogingawa Zunubi yadoya—a tea-house owned by a Japanese fisherman.

Japanese will be Japanese wherever they go, and people who have had anything to do with them know how difficult it is to satisfy their curiosity.

"How old are you?" inquired the *occamisan*—the landlady. "Where do you come from? What is your country? Why are you travelling? Have you a wife and children? Can you eat Japanese food; also Ainu food? Can you sleep in *foutangs*?" (Japanese bedding). "Also with a *makura*?" (a wooden pillow).

About fifty more personal and indiscreet questions were also asked, and all my belongings were examined with ever-increasing astonishment as one thing after another was handled and investigated. I was tired, and felt as if I could have kicked the whole crowd of them out of my room; but I was unintentionally polite to them to such an extent that the *occamisan* loudly exclaimed—

"*Honto Danna, Anata Nihonno shto, onaji koto!*"—"Really, sir, you are just like a Japanese!"

"*Domo neh!*" rose up in a chorus from the large assembly, "*nandemo dannasan wakarimas!*"—"The gentleman really understands everything!" This was a decided compliment, and I was bound to accept it as it was intended. When they heard that I was indeed "*Taihen kutabire mashita*" (very tired), they reluctantly left the room, and closed the *shoji* (sliding doors of tissue paper on a wooden frame). Each bowed gracefully, drawing in his breath at the same time. This is the Japanese polite way of leaving a room. Their conversation was resumed in the next apartment, regardless of the fact that

- 33 -

tissue paper walls are not sound-proof. Remarks on me, not quite in harmony with their courteous bearing, were passed freely about, and the politest thing I heard them say was that I must be a *lunatic* to travel alone in these inhospitable regions, and what a pity it was for a man *so young* to be so fearfully afflicted.

"Oh, those *seyono shto* (foreigners) are all born lunatics," said the voice of one who knew better.

The Shibegari River, at the mouth of which Shimokebo is situated, is also called Shibe-chari—"sprinkled salmon river." Very minute traces of gold are found in the river-sands and gravels, and also some well-developed brown garnet crystals and quartzite and phyllite pebbles. The gold, however, is not in sufficient quantity to enable it to be worked profitably. Seven and a half miles from Shimokebo the Japanese Government has another horse farm similar to that of the At-pets.

The travelling along the coast was heavy, and I could ride but slowly. I had to make the ponies go where the sand was wet along the beach, as there it was harder and they did not sink. This had its drawbacks, for the sea was very rough, and once or twice my ponies and I came very near being washed against the cliffs by some extra large wave. Instead of green banks, as between Tomakomai and Shimokebo, here were high cliffs of volcanic formation, with a narrow strip of sand at their foot.

The few Ainu along the coast were decidedly ugly. It was only now and then that in a sheltered nook I came across a hut or two of seaweed gatherers; and, still following the cliffs, I passed two or three small villages of a few houses each. After fifteen miles of this heavy track I reached the fishing station of Ubahu, where I was able to obtain some fresh horses. Prowling along the beach, I examined some of the Ainu canoes that had been drawn on shore. They might be divided into three classes—(*a*) the "dug-outs," used mostly for river navigation; (*b*) the lashed canoe; and (*c*) a larger kind used for sailing. The "dug-out" does not require explanation, as everyone knows that it is a trunk of a tree hollowed out in the shape of a boat, and propelled either by paddling or punting.

AINU LASHED CANOE.

FRONT VIEW OF LASHED CANOE.

The lashed canoes are made of nine pieces of wood lashed together with t

he fibre of a kind of vine. The concave bottom is all of one piece—a partial "dug-out"—to which are added the side pieces, of three planks each, sewn together at an angle of about 170°, and made to fit the sides of the "dug-out." Two more pieces, one aft and one forward, meet the side planks at right angles. The length of these canoes varies from 10 to 15 feet, the width from 3 to 3½ feet. Two pieces of wood are then lashed horizontally, which answer the double purpose of strengthening the sides of the canoe and, being provided with pins outside the canoe, of allowing it to be used as an outrigger when rowing. Canoes are either rowed or sailed. The oars are made of two pieces firmly lashed

AINU OARS.

together. A hole is bored in the part which is to be passed through the pin in the outrigger. One person is generally sufficient to row an Ainu canoe, and he does so standing. There is no steering gear or rudder, and when rowing the oars are used for that purpose. Ainu canoes are not decked, and therefore cannot stand heavy seas. They are alike on both sides, and in most cases the two ends of the canoe are also shaped alike. There are, however, certain canoes which, in my opinion, have been suggested to the Ainu by Japanese boats, and which are flat at the stern. These are generally larger, and used for sailing. A square mat sail is rigged on a

SAILING CANOE.

short mast forward, and the steering is done with one of the oars at the stern. The sailing qualities of these canoes, however, are not very great, and the slightest squall causes them to capsize and "turn turtle." The anchors used by the Ainu are very ingenious; they are cut out of a piece of wood,

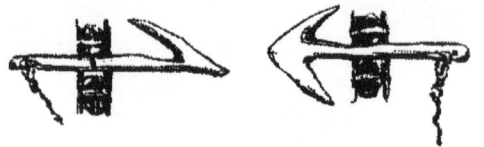

AINU WOODEN ANCHORS.

with either one or two barbs, and two stones are fastened on the sides of the stem so as to carry the anchor to the bottom. No compass is either known or used by the Ainu, and the natives shape their course by sight of land. They very seldom go long distances out at sea, as they are fully aware of the dangers of the ocean and of the imperfection of their own methods of navigation, though they are wholly incapable of making any improvements by their own judgment. The canoes are always beached when not used, and each family possesses its own. There are none which are the property of companies or are common to certain villages.

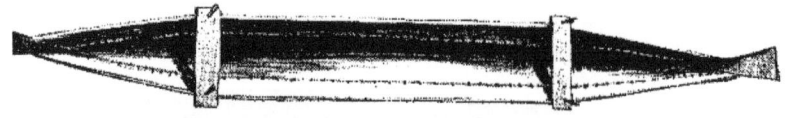

TOP VIEW OF AN AINU CANOE.

The track between Ubahu and Urakawa is rough, and the rivers are somewhat troublesome. Not far from the Mitsuashi river one has to pass a tunnel which has been made through a rock projecting into the sea. In rough weather it is difficult and dangerous to get through, as the waves wash right through the tunnel. In fair weather it affords a safe passage to the traveller.

The Matourabets (the winter fishing river) was successfully waded, and the Ikantai[10] village passed. Then at Urakawa or Urapets (the fish river) I made a halt for the night. There are many half-breeds at Urakawa, and a few real Ainu, but the small population is composed mostly of Japanese fishermen.

Seven and a half miles further, at Shama-ne—a corruption of *Shuna*, stones, and *ne*, together—there are some magnificent granite pillars boldly standing out of the sea. The sandy beach came to an end, and huge cliffs barred my way in front. I could see that the water was not very deep round these rocks, as the waves were breaking a long distance from the cliff, a sure sign of shallow water, though even then it might have been too deep for my ponies to go through. With great difficulty I got the two brutes into the sea, trying to round the large rocks for the better ground, which I hoped to find on the other side. The tide was low, but the sea was still rough, and nearly every wave as it came in went right over my ponies, frightening them, and made them extremely difficult to hold. The instinct of self-preservation made them rush for the cliff, with the only result that they missed their footing, and they and I were both swept away by the next receding wave. I was carried off the saddle, but I had sufficient presence of mind to hold on to the bridle. An awful struggle ensued between my ponies and myself. Each wave that came carried and knocked us one way, each wave that retired carried and knocked us the other. In the midst of all this danger I suddenly remembered that some years ago a lady who knew all about palmistry prophesied that I should one day be drowned.

Had the day come now? Not if energy and perseverance would avert the doom! After a long struggle, I succeeded in pulling my horses where the water was a little shallower, and there we three stood for some minutes, trembling with cold, my two ponies looking reproachfully at me with those half-human eyes of animals when forced into positions of danger which they can neither understand nor overcome. It is wonderful the amount of expression that horses have in their eyes, and how plainly one can read their dumb thoughts and formless emotions!

From the point where I was standing I could see that I had to go on but a few hundred feet more, and that then my ponies and I would be safe. Sure enough, the water grew shallower and shallower, and, to my delight, I was soon on the other side of the cliff. At high tide, and in very rough weather, it is impossible to pass by this ocean-ford.

Shamane is a picturesque little fishing village, built on the side of a promontory jutting out into the sea. From there, looking towards Urakawa, there is a lovely view of all the small islands and picturesque rocks, standing like huge jewels in the water, while on the Horoizumi side, as far as the eye can see, there are only cliffs of peculiar shapes, and marvellously rich in colour.

I got two fresh animals, and pursued my journey towards Horoizumi. Rocks, rocks, nothing but rocks! My ponies stumbled and slipped all the time, and for eighteen miles the riding was hard and intricate. I had to lead my ponies most of the way, and help them, pull them, or push them, from one rock on to another, and down the next, and so on.

The scenery all along was magnificent and grand. A short distance from Shamane a large natural archway emerges from the sea, which is called by the Ainu, Shui-shma, "a hole in stone."

Holes have been pierced through the rocks in several places, to give comparative safe passage, and to prevent wayfarers from being carried away by the waves. Over the entrance of one of these tunnels a pretty waterfall, descending from a great height, gives a poetic effect to the scene, while it obliges the unfortunate traveller to take an extremely cold shower-bath, should he wish to push forward on his journey.

As if all these discomforts combined were not enough, it is to be added that the rivers in this part of the coast, though not wide, are extremely swift and dangerous to cross. My second pony was carried away by the strong current when I crossed the Poro-nam-bets,[11] and I had great difficulty in rescuing him.

At Shamane there are a few Ainu, but from there to Horoizumi I saw none.

Sardines are very plentiful all along this coast, and long seaweeds also abound. The latter is used for export, chiefly to China. Horoizumi, a nice little village of one hundred and fifty houses, is the most picturesque in Yezo. It is built on the slopes of a high cliff, and it reminds one much of the pretty villages in the Gulf of Spezia. I arrived at sunset, and the warm red and yellow tints which the dying orb of day was shedding on the weather-beaten brownish houses, gave a heavenly appearance to this very earthly place. As I got nearer, a good deal of the heavenly had to be discarded, for the odours of fish-manure and of seaweed are two smells which can hardly claim to be classed under that heading. The inhabitants of the place themselves seem to feel the ill-effects of constantly living in that corrupted atmosphere and on a fish and seaweed diet; for, indeed, it is revolting to see the amount of horrible cutaneous diseases which affect them. One hardly sees one creature out of ten that is not covered with a repulsive eruption of some sort. Leprosy, too, has found its way among the fishermen; and my readers can easily imagine how pleasant it was for me, when I was sketching, to be surrounded by a crowd of these loathsome people, who all wished to touch my clothes and all my belongings, and who would even lean on my back and rub their heads against mine, when trying to get a better view of the sketch.

Poor things! I never had the courage to scold and send them away. It was enough that they were afflicted, and I did not like to add humiliation to their other sorrows by showing them my disgust.

I rode on to Erimo-zaki, or Rat Cape. Thick fogs are prevalent during the summer months along the whole of the south-east coast, of which Erimo-zaki is the most southern cape. It is the terminating point of the backbone of the main portion of Yezo, which extends from Cape Soya to Cape Erimo from N.NW. to S.SE. A lighthouse has lately been erected on the cliffs by the Japanese Maritime Department, and a steam fog-horn has also been provided for the greater safety of navigation, as a reef of rocks and a stretch of shallow water extend out in the sea for about two and a half miles from the coast.

The foghorn, I was informed, was only blown when the lighthouse-keeper suspected some ship was likely to make for the rocks! A likely thing, indeed!

"But how are you to know, especially when there is a thick fog on?" I asked.

"So few ships pass near here," was the reply; "and it would not be much use keeping steam up all the time to blow the horn, considering that we have fog during nearly four months in the year."

"Then," I could not help remarking, "I expect you only light the lighthouse when there is going to be a wreck?"

"Oh, no; we show the light every night."

This was just like the Japanese! Owing to the imperfectness of charts—none delineating correctly that part of the coast—the strong currents, the thick fogs, and the dangerous reefs, there could not be a more perilous coast for navigation than that which terminates in Cape Erimo. The ships which go from Shanghai, or some of the ports in the Petchili Gulf in China, to North American ports, often steer this course through the Tsugaru Strait and pass directly south of Cape Erimo. Thus the *Mary Tatham* (an English screw-steamer), while on her journey from Shanghai to Oregon, was lost in 1882, with nearly all lives on board, about two miles from this cape.

At the foot of the Erimo cliffs is a small fishing village called Okos. The sea is shallow at this place, and there are many low-lying reefs which afford abundance of kelp and seaweeds.

A short time before I arrived at Okos a man had gone out in his boat to save some nets in which a large fish had got entangled. His boat capsized, and he was drowned. His wife was in a dreadful state of mind, not for the loss of her better half, but for the more irreparable loss of the nets.

The distance between Horoizumi and Cape Erimo is seven and a half miles, and the track is exceedingly rough in many places. Nearly half-way between the last-mentioned village and the cape are the three high pillars called *Utarop*, which are represented in the illustration at the head of the chapter.

As it was impossible to take my ponies along the few miles between Cape Erimo and Shoya, following the precipitous coast, I retraced my steps to Horoizumi, meaning to attempt the mountain pass the next morning.

ERIMO CAPE.

A NATURAL STONE ARCHWAY NEAR SHOYA.

CHAPTER VI.
From Cape Erimo to the Tokachi River

The mountain pass between Horoizumi and Shoya is supposed to be very dangerous on account of bears. I rode the ten miles quietly, but failed to meet or see any. The way through thick woods is exceedingly pretty. After traversing a small valley with a dense growth of scrub-bamboo, it climbs a small hill, from the top of which a lovely view of Cape Erimo lies like a picture before one's eyes. There are only thirty houses at Shoya, and the place could not be better described than by the words "a miserable hole." The rough weather, as well as several landslips, had some time before my arrival broken all communication between Shoya and the next village east of it. There is a rough mountain trail as far as Saruru, but my ponies could not possibly get through the scrub-wood and heavy climbing, and none of the natives could be induced to carry my luggage. They all positively refused to follow me on account of the multitude of bears which they said were on the mountains.

"If the sea goes down," said an old fisherman, "you may be able to get through early to-morrow morning at low tide; and, if you are careful, you will not be washed away by the waves." The cliffs near Shoya are remarkable for their beauty. They are mostly older eruptive rocks which nature has carved into hundreds of rugged and fantastic forms. About a mile from the village is a huge natural archway, and from this point begin the precipitous cliffs, pillars, and rocks which make the journey so difficult.

At Shoya there are no pure Ainu, but some of the fishermen exhibit traces of Ainu blood. My recollection of Shoya is decidedly not of a pleasant character. I put up in the house of a fisherman, which also answers the purpose of a tea-house for the few stranded native travellers.

"We are so poor," said the landlord when I asked for something to eat, "and we have finished our provisions of rice. The other people in the village are poorer than we are, and they also have none; and as for fish, the sea has been so rough for several days that we have not been able to catch any. We ate the last scrap of fish we had just before you arrived! If you gave me a fortune, I could not give you anything to eat."

When the landlord confessed this to me in the evening, I had already been fourteen hours without food. The prospect of not getting any more for at least the next eighteen or twenty hours was not an agreeable look-out. I was very hungry, but, failing a meal, the next best thing was to try and go to sleep. Even that did not prove successful, for hunger keeps you awake, and in its first stages sharpens all your senses considerably.

The night I spent at Shoya is worthy of a description. From top to bottom the corners of my room were filled with webs, which the spiders had spun undisturbed in all directions across the room. Hundreds of flies and horseflies rose buzzing when I entered the room, and I had to engage in a very unequal war against them before I could settle down on the hard planks. In one corner of the ceiling a big, long-legged spider, too high for me to reach, was enjoying a good meal out of a huge horsefly which he had captured in his net. I almost envied the long-legged epicure. Nature will be ironical sometimes. When night came, and I was still sleepless, the planks on which I was lying seemed harder than any planks I had ever slept on before. I turned round one way, then the other, then another, till all my bones were aching. Finally, through exhaustion, I fell asleep, and even had a nightmare. In my dreams, the ghosts of all the spiders I had killed, magnified to the size of human beings, were dancing round me, while one fat old fellow—fatter than any two others put together—was gravely sitting on my chest watching the performance. His weight was such that I was nearly suffocated. Sometimes he would seize me by the throat and almost choke me, while the dancing spiders would choke themselves with laughing ... when—

"*Hayaku Danna!*"—"Quick, sir!" said a Japanese voice, waking me suddenly; "get up, or else the tide will rise, and you will not be able to get to Saruru."

I opened my eyes; the dream passed, and the monstrous spiders vanished; but the pain caused by the emptiness of my stomach was still there, and my throat was dry and aching.

It was before sunrise, and it was almost in complete darkness that I left Shoya. I was weak and chilly. The monotonous sound of the waves breaking over the shore added melancholy to *malaise*, and made me very doleful and limp. Nevertheless, as I was in for it, I pushed my way with my ponies along high cliffs and among rocks, and got on as best I could.

Where the sea had receded the stones were slippery, and my two animals were no sooner on their feet than they were down again on their knees. The hollow sound of their hoofs on the rocks was echoed from cliff to cliff, and awakened the sleepy crows from their night's repose. I had to walk most of the way, and urge on my ponies with howls, as well as stir them up with the whip. Though the tide was low, the waves often washed up to my waist. Daylight came, and I went along, following the high, rugged cliffs, through tunnels occasionally, among rocks continually. The scenery was really magnificent, seen as it was in the mysterious morning light of the rising sun. My horses were done up when I got to Saruru, and I exchanged them for fresh ones. By this time the tide had risen, and it was not possible to proceed any further along the sea-shore. I was glad of it, as I should thus be forced to try the mountain track, which I was told was not so very rough from this point. A half-caste offered to show me the way. It was a very stiff climb among thick shrub, but it was comparatively smooth work after the experience of my journey from Shoya. I came across many tracks and footprints of bears on the mountain. In some places the marks were quite fresh and of different sizes, varying in length from one foot to four inches. The half-caste told me that black bears seldom attack men unless they are hungry. They often attack horses.

"But if they hear that a man is near they will not dare to attack even the horses," he said, and then began to sing at the top of his voice. His singing, half Japanese, half Ainu, was so excruciating that it was no wonder to me that it kept the bears away.

We crossed two rapid streams before reaching the summit of the mountain range. The view from the summit was lovely. In the distance I could distinguish two headlands, while an immense stretch of stormy sea and a high mountain were in the foreground. I began to descend, and again I got into the region of thick forest and scrub. I perceived a few houses near the coast, and we made for them. It was the village of Moyoro,[12] or Biru, as it is called by others.

Between Saruru and Biru, where the mountain track sometimes descends to the shore, I found many Ainu and half-breeds, especially in the two villages of Onnito[13] and Bitatannuki.[14] They are said to be very bad, and what I saw of them, even at Biru, corroborated this assertion.

Biru is situated on a small bay, in the centre of which some gigantic pillars stand out at a great height. The rough sea dashes against them, and thousands of crows and sea-birds have chosen these rocks for their abode. Biru is not a large village. There are only forty fishermen's huts, most of which are on the high cliff surrounding the small bay; the others are down on the beach. Kelp, seaweed, and sardines are as abundant here as on the south-west coast, and maintain the staple industries of the inhabitants. The sea-weed is of great length but small width. Fourteen more miles over the cliffs brought me to Perohune.[15] There were four large deltas to cross, that of the Toyoi-pets[16] being the largest. The current in all these rivers is extremely swift.

Perohune enjoys a big name, but there is only one house in the place. I was, however, fortunate enough to get two good ponies there. The fog was settling down thicker and thicker, and I could not see more than a yard or two in front of me; but at times it lifted up for a few moments, and showed me either the dangers I was nearing or the landscape I was losing. I passed two lakes, the Tobuts,[17] otherwise called Oputs, and the Yuto. Both are divided from the sea by a narrow sand-ridge. There is but little of human interest along this deserted coast. There are no houses and no people, but many small rivers, and now and then high cliffs. My ponies, driven mad by the *abus*, the terrible horseflies of Yezo, constantly threw themselves down and rolled on the sand.

From Perohune to Yuto Lake the distance is about eleven miles, and from Yuto to Otsu it is eleven more miles, on a very easy track. I saw some large sea-birds and penguins, and I was struck by the great number of drift logs which had been washed on shore by the sea. The last thirty-eight miles of the coast was literally covered with this drift wood. During the summer months the fog is always dense along this coast, greatly owing to a cold current which comes from the Otkoshk Sea, passes through the strait between Kunashiri and Etorofu, in the Kuriles, and then turns south, following a great part of the south-east coast of Yezo. Not far from Erimo Cape it meets a warm current from the China Sea, which passes through the Tsugaru Strait, and which in all probability is the Kuro-shiwo, or Japan current. This Japan current parts from the main stream near the south-western extremity of Japan, goes through the Corean Strait, and follows the north-west coast of Nippon, passing then through the Tsugaru Strait. As will be seen later, a branch of this current runs along the north-west coast of Yezo, and through the La Perouse Strait.

IWA ROCKS AT BIRU.

AINU HOUSES AND STOREHOUSE, FRISHIKOBETS,
TOKACHI RIVER.

CHAPTER VII.
The Tokachi Region—Pure Ainu Types—Curious Mode of River Fishing.

The Tokachi River is one of the largest and most important in Yezo. Knowing that the Ainu either settle on the sea-shore or up river-courses, I formed an idea that some good types were to be found up this river. On reaching Otsu, a small settlement at the mouth of the Otsugawa—a branch of the large delta formed by the Tokachi—my idea was confirmed by the report that there were no Japanese villages in the interior. The expedition up the Tokachi River was by no means easy from the accounts I heard at Otsu. None of the Japanese ever dare to penetrate into the interior from Otsu, and, so far as foreigners are concerned, the Tokachi River was utterly unexplored. There is a certain charm in being the first man to do something, and I decided to attempt the experiment. The Japanese of Otsu dissuaded me strongly from carrying out my plan; for they said the grass and reeds were so high that I could not possibly get through.

"It is a kind of a jungle, in fact," said they, "in which yellow and black bears are plentiful. The rivers, which are numerous, are swollen by the heavy rains that have fallen lately. The natives up the river are unsociable and bad, and they will kill you. Then in the high grass horse-flies, black-flies, and mosquitoes abound."

"If you attempt it alone," said the wise man of the party, "you will not come back alive."

These reports were not encouraging, but, anyhow, I determined that, Irish as it may sound, *dead* or *alive*, if there were any Ainu up the stream I would see them. Owing to the difficulty of taking even my usual baggage, and not wishing to burden my ponies with more than was necessary, I decided to carry with me only a paint-box, many wooden sketching panels, my diary, and my revolver. I left all my other things at Otsu to wait for my return.

"Should you not come back again, can I keep all your belongings as my property?" kindly enquired the landlord of the tea-house, when I bade good-bye to him and to all the villagers who had collected round early in the morning to see me start.

I took two ponies, as usual. I left Otsu at dawn, and followed as well as I could the winding course of the river. Not far from Otsu I came to the thick jungle of high reeds and tall grass of which I had already heard. I made my way through the first obstructions; but I had not been in the jungle more than a few minutes when I was simply devoured by horse-flies, mosquitoes, and black-flies. My ponies were kicking, bucking, and trying to bolt, as they also were literally covered with horse-flies, sucking their blood and stinging them to madness. The reeds and grass were about ten or twelve feet high, so that, being higher than myself on my horse, I could not see where I was going. I kept along the river bank as much as I could; but in many places it was difficult to get through the ravines which one invariably finds along rivers, so I kept a little way off on the west side, and had the noise of the running river to guide me. For many wearisome hours I rode through this jungle, the dividing reeds continually rubbing against my face, arms, and legs, sometimes making pretty deep cuts with their razor-edged long leaves. The huge *shirau*—the horse-flies—grew more and more tiresome as the sun got warmer, and my head and hands were swollen and bleeding. The sun was by this time high in the sky, but there were no signs of the jungle coming to an end, no indications of huts anywhere near—no other noise but the sound of the crashing reeds and the running water of the river. My ponies were feeding well, as grass was plentiful; but I was faring badly. What with the exertion of keeping the ponies in order, while the densely-entangled reeds nearly dragged me off the saddle—what with the plague of mosquitoes and horse-flies, added to the sense of weakness caused by fatigue and hunger—it was really a terrible time for me—one of the worst episodes in my life. Nevertheless, I persevered, and went on and on, determined to reach my destination. I came upon two very large swamps, which forced me to make a wide *détour*. The ponies were very tired, and so was I. When darkness set in I halted, took the heavy pack-saddles off the ponies, and tied the animals to them, so that they could not bolt during the night; and wearied, disheartened, and discouraged as I was, I began to think how stupid I had been to start on such an expedition without carrying any provisions with me—without having provided myself with even a tent or a covering of any kind.

Circumstances made me a philosopher. What is the use of worrying about things that cannot be helped? After all, when you get accustomed to it, starving is really not so bad as people think. One of my ponies was of a sentimental disposition, and he seemed to understand my troubles. He came close and rubbed himself against me, placing his head near mine. It was touching, and in the solitude in which I was the sympathy of the dumb beast was as precious as that of a human being. Had he been able to speak, he might have been taken for a Christian, and a good one, too! He had been fearfully stung by horse-flies, and my petting him seemed to alleviate his pain. There is nothing like sympathy and a little personal kindness if one wants to make friends with animals. The last few rays of light were spent in putting together the notes which I had taken during the day, and which enabled me to draw a sketch-map of the river. At Horoizumi some days previously I was able to buy myself a compass from a Japanese fisherman, and on this occasion it was extremely useful to me.

By the soft, or rather shrill, music of a full orchestra of mosquitoes I fell asleep. It was poetic, but not comfortable. Strange noises woke me several times during the night. My ponies also were very restless, and repeatedly tried to get loose while I was lying down on the two saddles to which they were fastened.

It was some time after sunrise when I woke up, and with stiff bones set off again. A heavy dew had fallen during the night, and had made my clothes very damp. The reeds and grass also were saturated with water, and riding through them caused a continuous shower to fall over me, giving me an uncomfortable and by no means efficient kind of shower bath.

I rode in a westerly direction till about two or three in the afternoon, when suddenly the jungle came to an end. Not only that, but a short distance away I saw some Ainu huts. I soon reached them, dismounted, and tied my ponies to a tree. I went to the first hut, and previous to going in I called out: "Hem, hem, hem, hem!" which in the Ainu country is the polite preliminary when a stranger wishes to enter a hut. The usual practice of *knocking* at the door is dispensed with, for Ainu doorways have no doors.

"Hem, hem, hem, hem, hem!" called I again much louder, but I heard no answer; so I lifted the mat and entered the hut. It was empty. No one was there. I came out again, and went into the next hut, into another, and yet another; but nobody was to be found. I supposed that they were all out fishing. From the roof in each hut was hanging some dried and half-dried salmon. I could not resist the temptation after nearly thirty-four hours of involuntary fasting; and I stole—I mean "conveyed," or helped myself to the largest fish. I was greedily eating it—and how good it was!—when I thought I heard a groan inside the hut. I listened, and I distinctly heard some one sniffing in a corner of the dark dwelling. Had I been caught stealing? The crime I had committed would be called felony at home, but in the Ainu country it has not nearly so bad a name as that. However, felony or not, I dropped the fish, or rather what remained of it, and made for the corner whence the noise came. As I got closer I discerned a mass of white hair and two claws, almost like thin human feet with long hooked nails. A few fish-bones scattered on the ground and a lot of filth were massed together in that corner; and the disgusting odours these exhaled were beyond measure horrible.

"What the devil is that!" I said aloud in my own native tongue. I could hear someone breathing heavily under that mass of white hair, but I could not make out the shape of a human body. I touched the hair, I pulled it, and with a groan, and movements similar to those of a snake uncoiling itself, two thin bony arms suddenly stretched out and clasped my hand. As my eyes were getting accustomed to the dim light I thought I saw some almost worn-out tattoo marks on her arms. Yes, it was a woman in that corner, though her limbs were merely skin and bone, and her long hair and long nails gave her a ghastly appearance. Indeed, crouched as she was, doubled up, with her head on her knees, and the long hair falling over her face and shoulders, it was really difficult to make out what she was.

I asked her to come out, but she was apparently deaf and dumb. I dragged her out, and she made but little resistance; only she preferred crawling on her hands and knees to walking upright on her feet. There is no accounting for people's tastes, and I let her please herself in her manner of locomotion. When she was fairly out in the light I shivered as I looked at the miserable being before me. I lifted up her hair to see the face. Her eyebrows were thick and shaggy, and were joined over the nose. Her eyes were half closed, and dead-looking. The strong light seemed to affect her, and with her hands she was feeling the ground, probably in order to retrace her steps back to the dark spot. Nature could not have inflicted more evils on that wretched creature. She was nearly blind, deaf, and dumb; she apparently suffered from rheumatism, which had doubled up her body and stiffened her bony arms and legs; and, moreover, she showed many of the symptoms of leprosy. Altogether, she was painful, horrible, disgusting, and humiliating to contemplate.

I went back to my ponies to fetch my paint-box. During my absence there had collected round them half-a-dozen Ainu. They did not know what to think of the appearance of the two animals, and the few articles fastened to the pack-saddle were regarded with suspicion. When I appeared on the scene their astonishment was even greater, and it reached its climax when I saluted them in the Ainu fashion, and told them that I was a friend of the Ainu. I unfastened my paint-box and went back to the old woman. She was still where I had left her. All the Ainu present followed me, and when I squatted down they did the same in a semicircle round me. My wretched model attempted several times to crawl inside the hut, but as I was sitting close to her, I prevented her from doing so. There she sat in the most extraordinary position, with her head resting on her left hand, and the stiff fingers of her right hand pressed on the ground. One leg was bent up and the other was folded, resting on the ground and on the foot of the first. She was sniffing the wind, and making efforts to see with her half-blind eyes.

MADWOMAN OF YAMMAKKA.

It is hardly necessary to say that I did not keep my model longer than was strictly necessary, and when the sketch was finished I took her by the arm, brought her back into the hut, and led her to her favourite corner. There she crouched herself again, as I had found her; and there I left her, to bear the miseries of her life, till death, the cure of all woes, shall take away her soul, if not her body, from the filth she had lived in. She was neither ill-treated nor taken care of by the villagers or by her son, who lived in the same hut; but she was regarded as a worthless object, and treated accordingly. A fish was occasionally flung to her, as one would to a beast, and in such a condition this human being had lived, or rather existed, apparently for several years. Not a word was uttered by the villagers during the few minutes I took to paint the sketch. I turned round to inspect my new friends. Others had come up, and these men and women, hairy and partly naked, squatting down amidst filth, and driven half mad by the horse-flies and black-flies, looked just like a large family of restless monkeys. They were gentle and kind—much more so than any of their more civilised brethren; and one of them, a fine old man, came forward when I came out of the hut and wished me to go and see a big yellow bear they had captured. I went, and near the man's hut, in a rough square cage made of crossed branches of trees, was Bruin grinding his teeth as we drew near. In a sing-song monotone the man told me the story of the hunt, and how the bear had been captured. Then we went from one hut to another all through the village. Yamakubiro is the name given to the huts taken collectively, but the man took good care to explain to me that one part of the village (numbering only seven houses) was called Tchiota, and the other, a short distance away, was named Yammakka. Tchiota in the Ainu language means "dead-sand," and Yammakka is "land in behind."

Yammakka has ten huts. The hut in which I had to put up was more than filthy, and I had a sort of presentiment that my landlord was a scoundrel. He saw me giving a small silver Japanese coin to a girl I had painted. From that moment I noticed his eyes were continually fixed on my waistcoat pocket, out of which I had taken the coin. However, I did not think much of that, as all Ainu are fond of beads, metals, or anything that shines. When the evening came I tried to go to sleep on the hard planks, as usual. There is undoubtedly more *board* than *lodging* about Ainu accommodation. Myriads of Taikkis, the tiny but troublesome and uninvited guests of all dirty dwellings, did me the honour to sup off the few drops of blood which remained in my veins. I owed it to a bottle of Keating's Powder that I was not carried away bodily by them. I felt cold and feverish, and having no civilised bed-clothes to cover me, I slept with my clothes on; and this the more willingly, as I felt an instinctive mistrust of my host, and I thought it was as well to be ready for any emergency.

A few salmon were hanging right over my nose. They hung low, but they smelt high. I had been given a place in the south-west corner of the hut, and my landlord retired to the north-east corner. Though this may sound very far, my host was really not more than a few feet away from me. He apparently thought that I had gone to sleep, for I heard him creep to my side. I could not see him, being in absolute darkness, but though he was evidently holding his breath, I could feel the warmth of his face near mine. He was listening to hear if I were asleep. I kept quiet, and pretended to snore. This gave him courage, and sliding his hand gently along my arm, he came to a pocket in my coat. He began to explore it—but the Ainu are an unfortunate people even when they try to steal. He had got hold of a pocket with no bottom to it—a common occurrence in my coats. The more he explored, the more he found there was to explore. I am fond myself of explorations, and I have no objection to a fellow-being, hairy or not hairy, "prospecting" my empty pockets or my pockets which have no bottom to them. However, my host was not satisfied with the first results of his researches, and with his hand still through the torn lining of the coat-pocket proceeded to investigate the contents of my waistcoat pockets. This was a different matter altogether, and catching hold of him before he was able to disentangle himself, I swung his arm away and hit him hard on the head with my right fist.

"Wooi!" cried he in despair, and half stunned, as he scrambled away as best he could to his north-east corner. By way of apology and excuse, and with a trembling voice, the man from his corner said that he had only come to sleep on my side of the hut, as the wind was blowing strong where he had lain down, and that my side was warmer. A good excuse indeed when you are caught *flagrante delicto* pickpocketing!

The salmon which my host gave me last night for dinner and this morning for breakfast was so rotten, that, hungry as I was, I could not eat it. From Yammakka, in a westerly direction, the way begins with a gentle incline; therefore there is a complete absence of the high and troublesome reeds which I had found in the vast marshy plain I had crossed on my way here from the coast. I intended pushing on to Frishikobets, a larger village some miles off. The old scoundrel wanted to accompany me part of the way, saying that there were two dangerous rivers to cross, and he would show me where to wade them. I fancied that they were as dangerous as they were imaginary, and I started off declining his offer. I came across several Ainu huts on my way, passed the village of Pensatsunai—six Ainu huts—on the Satsunai river, an affluent of the Tokachi, and then arrived at Obishiro in the afternoon. There are seven houses at Obishiro. I entered one of them, and to my astonishment I found myself in front of an old man and a pretty woman, whose appearance and manners were as refined as those of the better classes in Japan. A younger man also came in. Their astonishment was as great as mine, as they had not seen any civilised beings since they had been there. Though the outside of their dwelling was not prepossessing, the inside was so clean that I felt as if I had dropped into heaven. After what I had gone through, this unexpected *rencontre* brought me back to life and a belief in the proprieties of a civilised existence, almost forgotten by now!

These people had a romantic history. Watanabe Masaru—the younger man—was a Japanese gentleman by birth and education, but he had no fortune. Of an adventurous disposition, clever, sensitive, and tired of the conventionalities of his fatherland, he decided eight or ten years ago to emigrate to Hokkaido, and there lead the life of a colonist. The woman he loved was as brave and constant as he. She sailed with him and her father from Japan, and after a long and perilous journey in a junk (sailing boat), they landed at the mouth of the Tokachi River. In Ainu canoes they went up the river, and established themselves at Obishiro, far from civilisation, nearly in the centre of Yezo. At first they had a great deal of trouble with the natives, but now they are loved by all. There, with two lovely children, they lead an ideal life, far from the madding crowd and noise of the world, and freed from the vulgarity of society.

I rode on to Frishikobets village, situated on the Frishiko, "old river," and in the midst of a beautiful plain. There are only twenty-eight houses, and they are scattered about in the plain at a distance of several hundred yards one from the other. Some of the huts were hidden in the forest. A peculiarity of the Ainu of the Upper Tokachi River is, that they frequently cover their dwellings and storehouses with the bark of trees, instead of with reeds, as is the custom among the Ainu of the Saru River and Volcano Bay.

I was told here again that Ainu women often suckle small bears at their breasts so as to fatten them up for the festival; and one not infrequently sees the women in Ainu households chewing food, and letting the young cub take it from their lips.

These Ainu are much more interesting as types, and also much purer in race, than either the Piratori or the Volcano Bay Ainu. A learned missionary, who has not himself visited these people, writes as follows regarding them:—"The Ainu of the Tokapchi district, in Yezo, are spoken of as having been particularly addicted to this kind of warfare (night raids against each other, in which the men were murdered, and the women stolen and used as slaves or kept as concubines), and are even now held in abhorrence by the people of some villages. They are said not only to have murdered people, but also to have eaten some of them. They were, therefore, cannibals, and I have heard them spoken of as 'eaters of their own kind.'"[18]

From my own personal experience—and I may add I am the only foreigner who has seen these Tokachi, or as others call them, Tokapchi Ainu—I came to a conclusion very different from this. I found that not only were they not cannibals, but that, taken altogether, they were the most peaceable, gentle, and kind Ainu I came across during my peregrinations through the land of the hairy people. Indeed, I am sorry to say that it is not savagery that makes the Ainu bad, but it is civilisation that demoralises them. The only place in Yezo where I was actually ill-treated by Ainu, as my readers will remember, is the village where they were said to be "very civilised."

I have no wish to force my opinion on the public as the correct one. I do but describe what I have actually seen in a district in which others who have written on this subject have never set foot, and I leave it to my readers to judge who has most claim to be heard.

The language of the Tokachi Ainu varies considerably from the language spoken in more civilised districts, and none of the natives up the river could speak Japanese when I was there.

AINU WOMAN OF FRISHIKOBETS, ON THE TOKACHI RIVER.

Unfortunately, the Ainu of this region are not very numerous, and constant intermarriage among near relations has proved detrimental to the race. However, a glance at them is quite sufficient to show the difference between them and Ainu of other tribes. They are not so picturesquely arrayed as their more western brothers, and the large Japanese brass and silver earrings, as well as the glass bead necklaces which make such a brave show yonder, are replaced here by rough bone or wooden ornaments. Men and women in summer are almost entirely naked, and all children are clad in their own bare skins only. Their winter garments are made of bear and deer skins. Some peculiar snow-sandals, made of the bark of a kind of ash-tree called *shina*, are sometimes worn over the winter salmon-skin boots or moccasins. The Ainu make their ropes out of the bark of this *shina*, though often young vine stems are used for the same purpose. River fishing-nets are generally made of young vines twisted. They are of the roughest description, and are only fit for rivers where fish is abundant, as in the Yezo watercourses. The Ainu at Frishikobets took very kindly to sitting for their portraits, and one after the other—all the best types—were immortalised either in oils or in pencil. Strange to say, I came across another old woman, a lunatic, very similar to the one I saw at Yammakka. Her face was that of a witch, her eyebrows joining downwards somewhat in the shape of an owl's beak. Her long pale hands and face, and the long wild hair covering half her face, gave her a striking appearance. She had, however, not yet reached the stage of imbecility which her Yammakka sister had attained. Lunacy is very common among the Ainu, and the unfortunate creature thus afflicted seems to lose not only the respect, but also the pity, as well as care, of all the others, and is treated by them as a worthless animal.

After crossing the Frishikobets River, some distance off, on the east side of the Tokachi River, are the villages of Upar-penai,[19] twenty-one Ainu huts, Memuro-puto,[20] sixteen huts, and Ottoinnai,[21] fourteen huts. Then comes Kinney, with seven houses; and finally Nitumap,[22] the last village on the Tokachi River, has as many as thirty-six houses.

The huts of the Tokachi region are much smaller than those on the Saru River, and near many of them is a cage, in which a big yellow or black bear is confined. The natives told me that yellow and black bears were numerous in the neighbourhood. Deer (the *yuk*, male deer, and *mowambe*, female), were formerly plentiful, but now are very scarce. A few years ago a pestilence killed great numbers of them, and since then they have dwindled away.

Not many miles from Frishikobets a huge cliff rises perpendicularly along the Shikarubets River. A landslip seems to have taken place, which leaves one side of the cliff perfectly bare and rugged, showing the strata composing the soil. It is of a light yellowish colour, and it is called by the Ainu the *Shikarubets Otchirsh*, which translated into English means "the white cliff on the bend of the river." This cliff stands very high, and can be seen from a great distance, especially in a north-east, east, or southerly direction. In winter, when the rushes and reeds are not so high in the south-eastern portion of the plain, the white cliff can be distinguished from the whole of the Tokachi valley. The Ainu themselves use the Shikarubets Otchirsh as a landmark when out hunting bears. Owing to its light colour it is visible even at night. I was anxious to ascend it, as I was sure no European foot had ever trodden on it before. Accompanied by Watanabe Masaru, I started out on horseback and crossed the Frishikobets village and river. Here we left our horses under the care of an Ainu till our return. We had to cross the Tokachi in an Ainu "dug-out," and then, proceeding for several miles in a northerly direction, we arrived at the foot of the mountain. It would have been impossible to climb it on the east side, as it is quite perpendicular; but we were fortunate in getting an Ainu called Unacharo, who said he knew a point from which we could ascend, and that he would show us the way. He had been hunting bears on that mountain, and he knew its slopes well; but as to the way which he was to show us, we had to make it for ourselves. With our large knives we were forced to break, cut, and tear the entangled branches of trees and shrubs before we could get on. We actually had to cut our way through the dense scrubwood until we reached the summit. The ascent was rather dangerous in some places, and extremely rough when going through the brushwood. We had to keep as much as possible near the edge of the cliff, for though it involved more danger if we slipped or stumbled, the entangled shrubs were not so thick on the edge as farther inland. Finally, after several hours' hard work, we reached the top, and were well repaid for our fatigues. The whole of the Tokachi valley was stretched before us as far as the sea, and almost the whole course of the winding river, with all its numerous affluents, could be distinguished like so many shining silver ribbons on the green background formed by the tall grass and reeds. As a farming region the Tokachi valley and high plains are certainly the most fertile in Hokkaido. All the requisites for successful agriculture can be found there. The absence of the mountain masses of volcanic rocks, so common all over Hokkaido, the richness of the soil, the quantity of water for irrigation or for motive power, besides the comparative facility of making roads on such flat ground, are qualities that good farmers do not generally despise. It is therefore a great pity to see all that Tokachi valley practically deserted and so much good land wasted. Hemp, wheat, corn, potatoes, beans, and all kinds of vegetables and cereals, could be grown with advantage, and the produce carried down the river to the sea without much difficulty and at little expense. At Yamakubiro the land begins to rise in a gentle slope, but only to form a plateau, of which the top is another large plain reaching to the foot of the Oputateishike mountain mass. The Otopke Mountain is the highest peak, and resembles in shape the Fujiama of Japan. On the north-east side of this mountain are the hot springs of Ni-piri-bets.[23] A kind of wood is said by the Ainu to be found near these hot springs which is good for curing wounds, cuts, rheumatism, and other ailments. These hot springs are not of much importance, and it is but seldom that even the Ainu themselves visit them. In going to and returning from these springs the Shikarubets Otchirsh is never lost sight of by the Ainu, and by the aid of this landmark they return safely to their homes.

All the Oputateishike mountain mass is volcanic, and forms the backbone of the island of Yezo. From the Shikarubets Otchirsh I was able to draw a bird's-eye view of the course of the Tokachi River and its affluents, which afterwards helped me much in delineating a sketch-map of the Tokachi region, with its complicated watercourses. The two high mountains of Satsumai and Ghifzan could also be plainly seen from there. Coming down was much easier than going up, and when we had again reached the bottom of the mountain we turned northward until we came to the Shorui-washi River, an affluent of the Tokachi. Previous to this, while following the course of the Otsu River, I saw a strange sight. When on the summit of the Shikarubets Otchirsh I had seen two Ainu "dug-outs" pass up the river, and the Ainu who accompanied us said we should soon see them coming back again. We were not far from the river banks when shouts and cries of excitement reached my ears. I hurried on to the water-side and saw the two "dug-outs" swiftly coming down with the strong current, parallel with each other at a distance of about seven feet apart. There were three people in each "dug-out," viz., a woman with a paddle steering at the prow; another woman crouched up at the stern, and a man in the middle. A coarse net made of young vines, and about five feet square, was fastened to two poles seven or eight feet long. The man who stood in the centre of each canoe held one of the poles, to the upper end of which the net was attached, and attentively watched the water.

"They are catching salmon—look!" said Unacharo to me; "the salmon are coming up the stream from the sea." The small net was plunged into the water between the two canoes, and nearly each time a large salmon was scooped out and flung into one or other of the "dug-outs," where the woman sitting at the stern crushed its head with a large stone. If a fish escaped, yells of indignation, especially from the women folk, broke out from the boats, to be echoed by the high white cliff. Both men and women were naked, and the dexterity and speed with which they paddled their canoes down the stream, working the coarse net at the same time, seldom missing a fish, was simply marvellous. On the other hand, it must be remembered that fish were so plentiful in the river, that it was really easier to catch than to miss. In wading the Shikarubets (river) I could see large salmon passing me by the dozen, and I felt quite uncomfortable when some large fish either rubbed itself against or passed between my legs. We got across the Shorui-washi—literally "very burning a place to stand"—and having then gone far enough from the Shikarubets Otchirsh to see the whole of it, I managed to take a good sketch of it. Near this river are some hot springs, called Nishibets, from which the river has taken its peculiar name. The easiest way to the Otopke Mountain is to follow the valley between the Shikarubets and the Otopke River, and then climb the mountain on the north-east side. The latter part of the journey is extremely rough and difficult. Watanabe and I returned to Obishiro. It is not often that one anywhere meets with such simple, straightforward people as these Watanabes. They have lived alone at Obishiro for eight years among savages, but never in my life have I met with more civilised, kind, thoughtful, gentle beings than Watanabe and his wife. As civilisation makes savages bad, I dare say savage life makes civilised people good! I go away carrying with me a deep affection for these gentle strangers, whose kindness to me has made them my friends.

The day came for me to return to the coast. My ponies, probably frightened by bears, broke loose during the night, and one of them ran away; and I was rather in a difficulty as to how I should get back whence I had come. Watanabe, adding kindness to kindness, allowed me to have one of his ponies, and after repeated good-byes I started on my journey back to the coast. About four miles east of Yammakka the Tokachi River receives a large affluent, the Toshibets, or "river of high swamps." The Tunnui Puto is the largest of these swamps, about four miles north of the mouth of the Toshibets. *Tunnui* means a kind of tree, probably the *Quercus dentata; puto* or *put* means the mouth of a river. The course of the Toshibets River is almost from due north to south from its source, then for about six or seven miles from north-west to south-east, and, sharply turning again from north to south, continues in this direction winding continually for eighteen or twenty miles, till it throws itself with a large body of water in the Tokachi River. On the southern side of the latter part of the watercourse are found the Ainu villages of Pombets, twenty-two huts; Purokenashpa,[24] three huts; Kenashpa,[25] twelve huts; and Beppo,[26] eleven huts. The characteristics of the natives of these villages and their habitations are similar to those already described at Frishikobets. The journey down was much the same as that coming up. Tobuts, on the north side of the Tokachi, is the largest Ainu village in the district, and has as many as sixty huts. The inhabitants are possessed of a somewhat fiery temper in this particular village, and the day previous to my going through two men were killed in a row. I felt awfully annoyed at being just one day too late to see it, as then I might have described how the Ainu die. However, I reached the other side of the Tokachi again. A way through the same tall rushes and reeds had to be forced, and the same army of mosquitoes and horse-flies had to be met and endured. It was my intention to push on and reach the coast as soon as possible. At Yammakka the natives had seen my runaway pony galloping at full speed towards the coast, but no one had caught it. Probably no one had tried.

My ponies went well. I could plainly see where I had already come through the jungle, by the long trail of crushed and broken reeds I had left behind me. Everything was calm, but for the monotonous sound of crashing leaves produced by my forcing my way through the reeds. Suddenly my ponies stopped, shied, and began to back. They sniffed the ground, then the air. Their ears were straight up, their eyes were restless, and their nostrils widely distended. They were certainly under some great excitement, and showed unmistakable signs of terror. "What could be the cause of it?" I asked myself, but all the same gave the ponies a sound thrashing to make them go. It was useless—they would not stir. The second pony came by the side of mine, and they both put their heads together, in their own way consulting and concerting. They were utterly demoralised, and were kicking awfully. It was getting dark, and this riotous conduct on the part of my ponies was annoying. Unexpectedly, and with a tremendous growl, a huge black bear sprang towards us, and tried to seize the baggage pony. However, he and the beast I was riding bolted, and ran a desperate race for life; and though Bruin followed us clumsily for some time, we soon were far ahead, and lost sight of him. It was more than I could do to stop the frightened brutes; but finally, after a reckless steeplechase of many miles, after jumping over brooks and splashing across torrents, flying over the ground and through the jungle, without omitting to anathematise a horsefly that had settled on the back of my neck, and was amusing itself by boring holes in different parts of it to find a suitable spot for feeding, finally we came to a halt. It was about time. During the violent ride the reeds had cut my face and neck and hands, and I was bleeding all over. I went on and on, and, as my ponies did not seem to be very tired, I tried to reach the coast that night. It grew dark, but the night was fine, and I let the noise of the running river guide me. Each minute seemed an hour, each hour an age. I rode and rode, and still rode, till I was nearly exhausted; and still I was surrounded by the tall reeds and rushes. "Thank God!" I heartily exclaimed, when finally, at a small hour of the morning, I found myself in open ground again, and the wind brought in waves the salt smell of the sea.

An hour or so afterwards two tired ponies were easily pulled up at the tea-house at Otsu, the landlord was roused, and a wearied and half-starved traveller was let in.

THE SHIKARUBETS OTCHIRSH.

AINU MAN OF THE UPPER TOKACHI.

CHAPTER VIII.
From the Tokachi River to the Kutcharo River.

I decided to stop a day at Otsu, so as to recover from the fatigue of my late travels and adventures, and I chose my quarters in the *yadoya* of a Japanese called Inomata Yoshitaro. I was told that he was an ex-convict. Be that as it may, he had now turned into a fisherman and innkeeper. Like all Japanese, he was an inexhaustible talker, and his politeness was so great that it became a bore.

It was about three in the morning when I reached Otsu. I had taken off my boots on entering his house—for it is an insult to enter Japanese houses with one's boots on—and I had seated myself on the soft mat in order to rest my aching limbs, when Yoshitaro made me get up to place a small square cushion under me, on which he said I should be more comfortable. I had not been on it one minute before Yoshitaro, wanting to increase my comforts, made me rise again to exchange the first cushion covered with cotton for one covered with silk—a detail to which a man is not likely to pay much attention when tired to death, and only anxious to be left alone. It followed as a matter of course that before I was allowed to go to sleep I had to sip several cups of tea, which Yoshitaro's wife had hurriedly made, and I had to relate the result of my expedition to the sleepy fishermen who had crept out of their *foutangs* at the news of my arrival. In spite of all this, when I had got rid of my audience I had a good night's rest; but when I woke up the next day at noon I found myself surrounded by a crowd of fishermen of Otsu, who had invaded the *yadoya* to have a peep at the young foreigner, while in the back yard I recognised the voices of Yoshitaro and his wife, who evidently were occupied in the exciting chase of a fowl.

A few minutes later Yoshitaro triumphantly entered the room with a large dish, on which the same fowl, uncooked, and cut into a thousand little bits, was served to me, together with pieces of raw salmon, *daikon* (a vegetable), and boiled rice. This he called a European dinner! I did my best to roast the chicken bits on the *hibachi* (the brazier); but I was never well up in the culinary art, and, as my landlord remarked, he had brought up the meat for me to eat, not to "burn."

Fowls are very scarce indeed in Hokkaido, and the few found have been imported; therefore the landlord did not fail to explain, in a roundabout manner, under what great obligation I was to him for killing such a precious bird.

I said that I had not asked him to do this, and with his perfect Japanese politeness, bowing gracefully down to the ground, he said:

"Sayo de gozarimas" ("Yes, your honourable sir"). "But," he added, "the bird was so old that if I had not killed it I fear it would have died by itself ere long." Such a sacrifice undoubtedly deserved a reward, and he assured me that we should be "quite even" if I, being an artist, would condescend to paint twelve portraits of him. I had no little trouble to make him understand that he was mistaking me for a photographic camera, but I offered to paint him a small sketch the next morning if he would leave me alone all that day.

Punctually at sunrise he entered my room. He had his best clothes on, and his anxiety to be painted was such that he had not been able to sleep all night. I painted the sketch, and Yoshitaro and his male and female friends joined in exclamations of admiration at the good result of the *abura è* (oil painting). He professed to be very grateful, and carefully packed the picture in a box, which he carried into another room.

I took advantage of his absence to pack up my traps, as I wished to leave for Shaubets that same morning. In a short time Yoshitaro came back to my room, but a different man. He was rude, and tried to bully me. He presented a bill for the sum of sixteen *yen*, equivalent to £3 in English money, which I considered exorbitant for two nights' rest, a few bowls of rice, and the "European dinner." The highest charge made by the very best tea-houses in Hokkaido never exceeds one yen—two shillings and tenpence a day—including all meals. I quietly told the landlord that he was a thief, and that I would punish him by taking the picture away from him; but he swore that he would not surrender it, and that he would fight for it if necessary.

I seldom refuse a challenge when I know that I am going to get the best of it, and as it so happened that my arms were a great deal longer than those of Yoshitaro, I caught him by the throat and shook him so violently that he was nearly strangled. His friends came to his rescue, and when I dropped him he fell heavily on the mats, and had to be carried away. Some minutes elapsed, and while I was hastily taking my heavier luggage out of the house I heard Yoshitaro in the next room call out to his wife to bring him a sword, as he wanted to kill the "*ijinsan bakka*"—"the fool of a foreigner." I entered his room. Yoshitaro, pale with rage, was sitting by his *hibachi*, and round him were eight or ten of his men. They were apparently holding a congress on what to do, and each one of them, as is usual on all occasions in Japan, had pulled out his little pipe, and was continually refilling it with tobacco as they all discussed the matter on hand. I had my boots on this time, as I wished to show the scorn I had for him, his friends, and his house. In my coat pocket— the only sound one—I had my revolver, but it was not loaded.

"Yoshitaro," I said, "deliver the picture at once."

"I will not," said he.

"Good!" said his friends in a chorus.

"Yoshitaro," I said again, producing the revolver and pointing it at him, "if I have not the picture before I count twenty you will be a dead man."

I never in my life saw a crowd of bullies so scared. Covering their faces with their hands, Yoshitaro's friends bolted in all directions, some jumping out of the semi-European window, some dashing through the violently-opened paper *shojis* (sliding doors), leaving eight or ten pipes and as many tobacco pouches scattered on the mats. The landlord, a moment ago so brave, had not strength to get up, so great was his terror. Pale as death, and with a trembling voice, he called imploringly to his wife, servants, and friends to come and deliver up the picture.

I had counted up to number fourteen, and no one had put in an appearance. Then I incidentally mentioned to Yoshitaro that time was nearly up, and enquired if he preferred to be shot through the head or the heart, at the same time cocking my revolver. Yoshitaro shuddered.

At number sixteen a little girl, the only brave one of the lot, was sent to his help.

"Dutchera Danna?" ("Where is it, sir?") she asked him, quite perplexed.

"Hatchera, hayaku, hayaku nesan!" ("It is there; quick, quick, girl!") pointing to a closet in which a pile of *foutangs* (small mattresses) were kept rolled during the day.

Yoshitaro had hidden the sketch so well in the closet that the little *nesan*[27] could not find it, and when I called out number nineteen the poor girl, discomfited, cried out, "Mi-imasen" ("I do not see it!")

Yoshitaro was more dead than alive; his lips were white, and he tried to articulate some words, but could not. His eyes, fixed on the closet, were glazed and set. His body was beginning to collapse, and every moment I thought that he would faint.

In the meantime the *nesan* hurriedly pulled out all the *foutangs* and unrolled them, and the box with the sketch fell out just as I was about to call out number twenty. She gave me the box and sketch, and I told Yoshitaro that he must now come out with me, and, putting my revolver in my pocket, I pulled the man to the entrance door.

Several villagers had collected at a respectful distance on the road, waiting for the report of the revolver. Yoshitaro's wife was the farthest of all.

I signed to them to come nearer, and seeing that the revolver was no longer in my hands, they came, though very reluctantly. Yoshitaro was beginning to breathe again; and when a sufficient crowd had collected, I compelled him to accuse himself before them all of being a thief, and to confess that he was glad to have been punished. Also I made him promise that he would not play such tricks again on any other traveller.

The Japanese are fond of a good joke, even when it is played off on one of themselves; and when I had seen all my baggage safe on my pack-saddles, I gave Yoshitaro the sixteen dollars he had asked me: "Two dollars," I said, "in settlement of my bill, and fourteen to go to your doctor for restoring you to good health after the fright you have had to-day."

To show how shabby Yoshitaro's nature was, it is enough to state that out of the sum received his munificence went to the extent of five *sen* (2½*d.*) as a present to the girl who had come to save his life!

When my ponies were ready, I showed Yoshitaro and his knavish friends how I had sold them. I brought out my revolver again, and they all saw that not a single cartridge was in any of its chambers. This done, I bade them good-bye, and left them to reflect that it is not always the quietest persons who can be imposed on with most impunity, but that sometimes such quiet persons get the best of it, even against ten bullies or more banded together. I have no doubt that a good many of my readers will think me cruel for carrying a joke so far; but, on the other hand, if placed in similar circumstances, when no redress from without is to be obtained, and one must defend oneself by main force, very few would treat such a serious imposition and offence as a joke.

In going through the village more than one fisherman came to tell me that I had done right in dealing severely with Yoshitaro, as he was known to be a scoundrel and a thief, and they all detested him.

There was little of interest between Otsu and Shaubets, with the exception of the beautiful delta formed in the low alluvial valley by the Otsu River and the Tokachi River, two large estuaries nearly two miles apart, by which the Tokachi River enters the sea. The Tokachi is a river of large volume and considerable length, and even when divided, the body of water carried by both outlets is so great as to make it necessary to cross in boats, fording on foot being quite impossible.

The Urahoro River was successfully crossed, but for the twenty miles on to Shahubets the track was flat and sandy, lying mostly under high clay banks, some of which form picturesque headlands. The country is not mountainous in the proximity of the coast, but it is of a moderate elevation all through, and wooded with deciduous trees. The formation of the south-east coast from Cape Erimo to Cape Noshafu is in many ways unlike that of the south-west coast. The south-western part is more mountainous, and is further characterised by the absence of extensive plains. The coast-line is indented, and there is a striking want of broad beaches. Precipitous rocks are also frequent along the south-west coast, and thick deposits of pumice—as we have seen—are lying over quaternary rocks, filling up the declivities of mountain lands and river shores.

In the western part the tertiaries are more tufaceous than on the south-east coast, and they are distinguished mainly by the presence of shales and andesite breccia. The south-eastern part is characterized by the almost entire absence of volcanic rocks and older eruptive rocks. After leaving the range of mountains forming the *Sparti acque*, east and west of Cape Erimo, high land is met all the way along the south-east coast. Nevertheless, pumice is found in the basin of the Tokachi River, and also in that of the Kushiro River, but it does not form the surface soil, covering large areas of ground, as in many places on the south-western portion of the coast.

The different aspect in the tertiaries of the south-east and south-west coast may be accounted for by the presence of breccia and conglomerate, shales and sandstones, on the western part, while on the eastern coast beds of lignite, coal of inferior quality, and diatom earth form the tertiary strata. If it were not for the total want of harbours, or even moderately sheltered anchorages for ships, this south-west portion of Yezo, with its agricultural resources, its milder climate, and the facilities that it offers for the construction of roads and railways, ought to support a large population. As things stand now, there are no colonists inland, and the coast is deserted and desolate-looking. As I have mentioned before, the only drawbacks are the thick fogs prevailing during the summer months along the south-east coast, and I believe that this in some measure accounts for the Japanese not wishing to settle in a part of the country so depressing to their spirits and so trying to their nerves. I have often noticed how easily affected the Mikado's subjects are by atmospheric and geographical conditions, and how, before settling to do business, they make a point of finding some pleasant spot where to cast anchor, thinking more of the amenities of physical existence than of the facilities for successful trade. I did not see a single house for twenty miles until I reached Shaubets, a village of eleven Ainu huts and one Japanese house. Thousands of sea-gulls and penguins lined the sandy shore, and I saw several large black sea-eagles. A pretty waterfall, gently descending from the high grey cliff, was decidedly ornamental to the scenery and useful to the wayfarer, as it afforded my ponies and myself a good drink of deliciously fresh water. Far off in the distance I could distinguish a long tongue of land. At Shaubets I was told that it was the peninsula on which *Kossuri*, or *Kushiro*, as the Japanese call it, is situated. I left Shaubets early in the morning, with the intention of pushing on to Kushiro, thirty-one miles distant. At Shiranuka, only ten miles from Shaubets, I changed my ponies. Shiranuka is an Ainu village, the inhabitants of which employ themselves in collecting and drying seaweed. There are also seven or eight Japanese shanties besides the Ainu huts. At the mouth of the Tcharo-bets, near the latter village, coal and lignite of inferior quality are found; but this coalfield was not worked at the time I passed through Shiranuka. The remaining twenty-one miles were monotonous and uninteresting. The long *Kossuri* peninsula was before me, increasing in size as I drew nearer; and after having gone through the two small villages of To'tori and Akan-gawa, in the neighbourhood of Kossuri, I crossed the Kutcharo River, on a nicely-built wooden bridge, and found myself at Kushiro, an important Japanese settlement on the south-east coast. From its favourable situation Kushiro is likely to become one of the chief towns in Yezo, though unfortunately it does not possess a good harbour, and is much exposed to westerly winds. The largest number of the houses are situated on a slight elevation above the reef-harbour, immediately south of the river mouth. In the proximity of Kushiro, and just beyond the range of hills which stretches for about three miles from the entrance of the harbour in a northerly, and for about two miles in an easterly direction, is a lagoon, called by the Ainu "Harutori." This lagoon is nearly two miles long, and certainly not more than a quarter of a mile wide. It is divided from the sea by a very narrow strip of sand, through which the water of the lagoon finds its outlet. On the east side of the Harutori coal has been discovered, and it seems to be of fairly good quality; and three miles further, quite close to the sea-coast, coal was dug out some years ago, but the quality was so inferior that the works had to be abandoned.

There is a considerable area of good land in the neighbourhood of Kushiro, and here again it is to be regretted that Japanese farmers do not emigrate to work it. Yezo has a very small population for its size, and I was surprised that emigration from the mainland was not carried out on a larger scale. Yezo is a rich country in many ways. Why do not all the troublesome students, the fiery *soshi* of Japan, abandon politics and futile rows and go and do men's work in that northern region of the empire? They would profit by it, and so would their country. An immense loss occurs every year simply because no one is there to take the profit; and it is a great pity, and almost a shame, to see so much waste and neglect in a region which, after all, is not difficult of access from the main island of Nippon. To the mineral products of the Kushiro district must be added the exports of fish (salmon and herrings), fish manure, and seaweed, which could be greatly increased if more practical processes were used.

The town of Kushiro itself is not picturesque. There are, I dare say, as many as five hundred houses, some built in Japanese, some in semi-foreign style. The streets are very wide, and along the main street rails have been laid to carry coal trucks from the Harutori mine down to the shipping point. Thus the town has a civilised appearance, which was artistically ugly enough, but refreshing to my eyes after my experiences along the south-west and south-east coasts. There are Ainu huts along the river banks, on the high lands, and on the strip of sand between Lake Harutori and the sea. Unfortunately, most of the Ainu here, being in the employ of the Japanese, have adopted Japanese clothes, customs, manners, and language. Nearly all the younger folks are half-castes. A select few have even gone so far as to forget their strongest national characteristic of dirt; and, to my great amazement, one day I saw an Ainu half-caste actually taking a hot bath. It may amuse the reader to learn of what this Japanese bathing accommodation generally consists. It is one of the features in nearly all fishing stations in Yezo, and it is worth describing.

When the day's work is over, one or more of the iron fish-kettles or caldrons used for extracting the oil from herrings are filled with water. These caldrons rest each on a cylindrical base of stones and clay, thus allowing a big fire of wood to be lighted under them. When the water has reached a high temperature, the bather either provides himself with an old pair of straw sandals (*waraji*), and steps in, or, placing a small board on the water, places his foot on it, and forces it down to the bottom of the caldron by his own weight. He thus avoids scalding his feet, which otherwise he would do severely. I have often seen two or three men (Japanese) placidly sitting up to their necks in the steaming water of the same caldron, with a huge fire burning under it; and several times I have been *warmly* invited by the bathers to join them, which *very warm* invitation, however, I invariably *coolly* considered and declined with thanks.

As regards the Ainu, they are not fond of bathing or washing, and they share the Chinese idea that it is only dirty people who need continual washing. They do not regard themselves as dirty, and therefore dispense with such an "uncleanly habit."

"You white people must be very dirty," once said an Ainu to me, as I was taking a plunge into a limpid river, "as you tell me that you bathe in the river every day."

"And what about yourself?" I asked him.

"Oh, Nishpa," he replied with an air of contempt, "I am very clean, and have never needed washing!"

If Kushiro is not interesting to an artist, it is decidedly so from an archæological point of view. Numerous pits, forts, and camps, flint implements, and fragments of pottery, are found in the immediate neighbourhood of the town, both on the range of hills and along the west shore of Lake Harutori. The pits are found in such numbers as to lead one to believe that the old "Kossuri" of the Ainu was once the capital of a race of pit-dwellers previous to the conquest of the whole of Yezo by the hairy race. The Ainu gave these people the name of *Koro-pok-kuru*—men of the holes. A few words on them may not be out of place, though, unfortunately, little is to be learned from the Ainu as to who their predecessors were, and it is merely by a close examination of their pits, and relics found in different parts of Yezo and the Kuriles, that we can to a certain extent trace the existence of such a race of people, and also prove that they were in no way connected with the present Ainu.

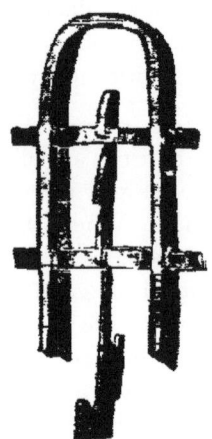

AINU HOOK FOR SMOKING BEAR-MEAT.

KORO-POK-KURU FORT.

CHAPTER IX.
The Koro-pok-kuru, or Pit-dwellers.

All over Yezo and the Kurile Islands remains of an extinct race of pit-dwellers are to be seen. It is especially near lakes and swamps or along the coast that rectangular, circular, and elliptical pits are numerous, but square pits are not so common. None of these pits have yet been discovered on the main island of Nippon, but many are still to be found as far south as Hakodate, in Yezo. On the east and north-east side of the peak, at the latter port, these pits, flint implements, and rude pottery, mostly in fragments, are met with in great abundance. The implements consist mostly of arrow-heads, stone adzes,

FLINT ARROW-HEADS.

hammers, flint knives, and round pebbles, which were used as war ammunition. The arrow-heads vary in size, length, and breadth. The larger ones I saw measured an inch and three-quarters in length by an inch and five-eighths in breadth, while the smaller were seven-eighths of an inch by half an inch. They were triangular, with the angle at the point sometimes more, sometimes less acute, or lozenge-shaped; they are chipped, and not ground. Most of the arrow-heads and a good many of the knives were made of a dark reddish siliceous rock. The adzes also, of course, varied in size and shape, some being oblong in section, others almost rectangular, while others again were oval. They were ground, and always made so that the hand could have a good grip on them. The average length from the sharp edge to the other end would be about four inches, and the sides were rounded. It is apparent that most of these adzes were not originally fastened to a stick or club, but were held in the hand. They usually have a smooth surface, while the knives, as well as the arrow-points, exhibit marks of chipping quite plainly; their edges are very sharp. Hard stones are often found on which the people of the Stone Age used to grind their implements. The knives are mostly rectangular, with very sharp edges, sometimes on both sides. Then there are some in the shape of a sword-blade, rounded at the top, and with a rounded place at the other end, where they were held. Those with two sharp edges were triangular in shape, and were held by the upper part of the triangle, which point ends with a kind of knob.

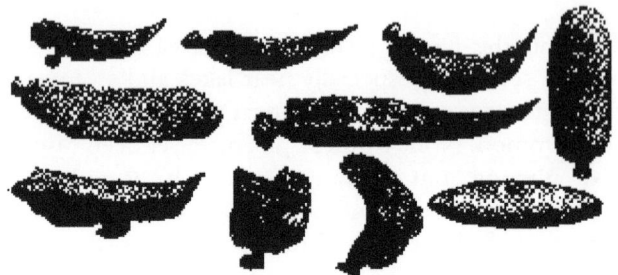

FLINT KNIVES.

It is a curious fact that bone and bamboo arrow-points—probably Ainu—are sometimes found in pits, and this would lead me to believe, either that the conquering Ainu used these weapons in their attacks upon the pit-dwellers, or, supposing for a moment that the Ainu themselves were the pit-dwellers in former days, that they had abandoned their stone implements and had adopted bone and wood, which they found easier to work. I am inclined to the first supposition as the correct one. The pits are numerous in Yezo, and, following the southern coast from south-west to north-east, we find that they increase in number towards the north. Though stone implements and fragments of pottery are numerous nearly all along the southern coast, but few pits are found either on Volcano Bay or on the south-west part of the coast as far as Erimo Cape. As we pass this cape and go north, on the south-east coast the pits become more numerous, and at Kushiro—or Kossuri, as the Ainu call it—they are found in great quantities. Further on are some at Akkeshi, and they are plentiful nearly all along that stretch of the coast as far as Nemuro, and on Bentenjima, the small island which forms one side of the harbour at that place. North-east of that, in the Kuriles, at Kunashiri and Etorofu, we have abundant evidence that a large population of these pit-dwellers once existed there. In Etorofu particularly the pits, besides being frequent, are in much better preservation than any on the island of Yezo.

The pit-dwellers do not seem to have been particular as to the shape of their dwellings, though they evidently had a certain predilection for the elliptical and rectangular forms. The pits at Kushiro are nearly all rectangular, while those from Akkeshi to Nemuro are either rectangular or circular.

The average dimensions of rectangular pits are about twelve feet by nine feet, but I have seen some as large as sixteen feet by twelve feet. The sides slope inwards, and the average depth is from three to six feet. Pits which are situated on cliffs, or at any height, are generally deeper, probably for the extra shelter required by those living at an altitude, compared with those living on the sea-level. The round pits are from ten to fourteen feet in diameter, and the elliptical have a length of about sixteen feet, and are about eight feet at the widest part of the ellipse. The pits which I found on the north-east coast of Yezo, from Shari to Cape Soya, were not so numerous as those on the southern coast; but some of them were larger in size, as probably, owing to the greater severity of the climate, more people lived in the same hut for the purpose of creating natural heat. At Tobuts, on the Saruma Lake, are three of elliptical shape. Near Abashiri several well-preserved specimens of pottery have been found, especially in the mud of swamps or lakes; but after leaving Lake Saruma, I did not see any traces of the pit-dwellers till I approached Soya Cape. When these pits are excavated, a stratum of sand is generally found, and beneath it a large quantity of charcoal in the centre of the pit. Under the charcoal the earth is burnt, showing that the hearth was in the centre of the dwelling, as it is now in the Ainu huts. This goes to prove that there was one fire, and not, as some travellers have endeavoured to show, five or six burning at the same time, round which, or, rather, between which, the pit-dwellers slept. I have often dug in different parts of pits, and have invariably come upon this burnt charcoal in or near the middle. I never saw any signs of more than one fire in the same pit. Digging in a large pit at Kushiro, I found some stag-horns, and numerous bits of black and red pottery. Some of the fragments had rough line ornamentations on them. There was also a large quantity of war ammunition, in the shape of big pebbles and round stones. Most pits contain heaps of rubbish and bones of animals. Sometimes there are heaps of oyster shells, as near the pits on Saruma Lake; and these shell-heaps are similar to those found on the main island of Nippon. In another pit on one of the forts at Kushiro I found what I thought was part of a human skull; but on a closer examination it turned out to be the skull of an animal—probably a fox or a stag. A bone arrow-point also came to light in the same pit, and several stone defensive weapons. It was interesting to note that this pit was built on the top of a small conical hill, and that the hill itself was surrounded by a ditch only a few feet wide, thus forming a kind of fort. On the side and at the bottom of the fort I saw numbers of stones, which had in all probability been used by the pit-dwellers as missiles against the attacking Ainu during a battle. Besides forts, the pit-dwellers had camps, generally situated in a commanding position above a river, a lake, or a harbour. Single pits also are found only under similar conditions.

Near Kushiro, on the Lake Harutori, which is divided from the sea by a sand isthmus, are several camps and one or two forts, the first of which overlooks the sea. Along the Kutcharo River are forts and camps. These camps are on the crowns of the hills, and each is surrounded by a small ditch. In the last, about three miles from the coast, were several square pits, larger than those on the other three forts. This last fort stands some distance back from the river, and is situated in a little plain at the summit of a detached mound, which has the appearance of having been artificially cut from the larger remaining portion of the hill itself. The shape of the fort is a broken cone, and the base measures about nine hundred feet in circumference, while the upper one is about three hundred. From the top, where there is only a small pit, the entrance of the river can easily be watched; and it must have been almost impregnable, as the walls of the fort, or, rather, the sides of the conical hill, rise nearly perpendicularly from the plain. A small stream runs at the foot of the fort.

On the Lake Harutori the range of hills which stretches from the sea for three or four miles along its eastern shores is literally covered with these pits, and on the sandy isthmus separating the sea from the lake some very large pits can be observed. The fort near the sea is called *Shirito* by the Ainu, and that at the other end of the range goes by the name of *Moshiriya*. It was in the latter fort that the well-shaped bone arrow-point was found, as well as one or two stone adzes, which were so shaped as to fit the hand, and evidently had been used as hammers, or weapons of offence at close quarters. In the same fort I found two stags' horns in good preservation, and many bones of different animals. It is doubtful whether these heaps of horns and bones were brought into the pits for the purpose of making arrow-points and other weapons, or whether the stags had been used merely for food. The bone arrow-point found in the same pit was not in such a decayed condition as most of the bones I found there, which led me to believe that it was not made out of the same kind of bone, or that the bone out of which it was made had been cured before its conversion into an arrow-point. I believe that in the neighbourhood of Kusuri—or Kushiro, as it is now called by the Japanese—there are as many as a thousand or fifteen hundred pits. In Etorofu, at Bet-to-bu, on the north-west coast of the island, nearly as many are to be found along the seashore, mostly on the plain at the top of the cliffs overlooking the sea, while the rest are situated on the banks of a narrow stream and along what appears to have been a river course. On the same island, at Ru-pets, are several pits of a similar description, and a fort.

As the pit-dwellers have disappeared from Yezo and the Kuriles, and only pre-historic remains and relics have been left behind to indicate their former existence, the questions naturally arise: Who were these pit-dwellers? Whence did they come? and whither have they gone? We can place no reliance on the accounts given by the Ainu or by the highly imaginative Japanese, who, moreover, are perfectly ignorant on this subject. Some Ainu say that Yezo was formerly peopled by a race of dwarfs, who were their enemies, and were extirpated by them after many sanguinary battles. The Ainu are very vague as to when and where these battles were fought, but according to their accounts these pit-dwellers, whom they call the *Koro-pok-kuru*—literally "men of holes"—once inhabited Yezo and the Kuriles. They were only three or four feet in height, and some semi-Ainu stories represent them as being only a few inches tall. This of course might be taken to mean that they were very small by comparison. A few Ainu, yet more imaginative than others, go so far as to say gravely that the Koro-pok-kuru were so tiny that when a shower of rain came they hid under burdock leaves for shelter. Others, however, tell us that these Koro-pok-kuru were their ancestors, and much more hairy than the Ainu of the present day. They were strong, fond of hunting, and able to cross the mountains with great facility and speed. According to Mr. Batchelor, some Ainu state that they themselves formerly lived in huts over pits, and that they changed their method of house-building on coming in contact with the Japanese; but if this were the case it seems unaccountable that they should distinguish their predecessors as pit-dwellers. Moreover, if the influence of the Japanese was sufficiently strong to cause them to make this most important change in their habitations and mode of living, how comes it that in other matters they have not adopted Japanese customs? I was unable to trace the slightest resemblance between Ainu huts and Japanese edifices of any kind, either in their general appearance or in any of the smaller details, and I was always struck by the small extent to which the Ainu have adopted the customs of the dominant race. Indeed, the character of Ainu buildings is peculiar to the Ainu themselves, and, far from constructing their dwellings over pits, they go to the other extreme, and perch their storehouses on piles or posts. It is a remarkable coincidence that on the Lake Kutcharo, not many miles from Kusuri, where the Koro-pok-kuru pits are numerous, the roofs of the Ainu huts and storehouses are not angular, but circular, which gives them the appearance of half a cylinder resting on the ground. This struck me as being in all probability the shape of structures built over rectangular pits, while the coverings of round pits must have been shaped like half a sphere, similar to the snow houses of the Esquimaux, and the elliptical like the longer half of an egg.

The present houses of the Kutcharo Lake Ainu, however, are not built on pits; and on my questioning the few inhabitants of the village, all were perfectly ignorant of the existence of the Koro-pok-kuru, and they knew nothing of their own ancestors, nor whether they had built structures over pits or not. The idea seemed to them highly ludicrous, and afforded them a great deal of amusement.

On the north-east coast of Yezo, where pits are found, some Ainu huts have round and others angular roofs; but even in the latter instance, the angle of the two sides of the roof is not as acute as with the huts on the Saru and the Tokachi River; but both slant in a more gentle way, forming an obtuse angle of about 135°. In fact, these variations in the Ainu architecture have not yet been accounted for, and whether they copied their roofs from their foes the

Koro-pok-kuru, or whether it is a mere chance that the roofs bear a certain resemblance, cannot be discovered from tradition or hearsay. I may mention incidentally my own theory, which may afford an explanation of this point. As the Saru, the Tokachi, and the Ishikari districts have no very severe weather in winter, and only a comparatively small quantity of snow falls during the colder months, the Ainu build huts with very slanting roofs, so that the snow should not remain on them in winter, while during the summer months the rain should fall off the steep incline of the roof before it could filter through into the hut. On the Kutcharo Lake and on the north-east coast, where strong winds are prevalent, the huts have round roofs, so as to offer the least possible resistance to the gales, and thus escape the danger of being blown down.

With regard to the snow, the opposite of the Saru Ainu method is practised. Instead of preventing the snow from resting on their roofs, the Ainu of the colder regions do all they can to let it remain, for by thus forming an air-tight vault it renders the hut much warmer in winter. In other words, the system is the same as that adopted by the Esquimaux, with the exception that the latter, I believe, have no frame to their huts, and the vault is entirely of snow and ice; while with the Ainu of the north-east coast the snow vault is directly over the hut itself. I invariably noticed on the north-east coast, where the Ainu have a mixed architecture, that wherever a hut was built in an exposed position it had a round roof, while those built under the shelter of a cliff or a hill had angular ones, and this is what led me to the above conclusion.

To return to the Koro-pok-kuru, they undoubtedly must have had semi-spherical and semi-cylindrical roofs over their pits, whether the vault was constructed of mud, sticks, and reeds, or simply of snow and ice, like the Esquimaux dwellings. For all that we know, the Koro-pok-kuru huts may have had conical roofs, like those of the present American Indians; but one fact is certain, that whatever shape the roof may have had, it was not supported by a central pole, for the hearth is invariably in the centre of the pit.

The curious fact already mentioned, that in every pit we find a thick layer of sand, seems to prove that it was certainly intended to render the ground less damp; and it is my own impression that these pit-dwellers, having snow or ice vaults over their heads, resorted to that expedient to keep the floor of their huts dry under the continuous dripping of the vault, melted by the heat of the fire inside. Undoubtedly Yezo was a much colder country in bygone years than it is now; and though we cannot implicitly rely on the information given by the Ainu, they are all of one opinion in believing that their country was all ice and snow in former days, and to give a proof of it they say: "Why should we be as hairy as a bear if not to keep the cold out?"

The Japanese know the pit-dwellers by the name of "Ko-bito," or "Ko-shto," the latter word meaning "men of the lakes,"[28] but they know nothing of their history.

One fact still remains to be explained, namely, who made the pottery that is disinterred in almost every pit and by the shores of lakes. The present Ainu do not know how to make pottery, and they have never been known to manufacture anything of the kind. All Ainu implements are made of wood, though of course the more civilised tribes have now purchased iron or porcelain implements from the Japanese. The question, then, is, supposing that the Ainu were formerly the pit-dwellers, have they lost the art of making pottery, or did the pottery belong to a different race of people?

KORO-POK-KURU POTTERY AND FRAGMENTS OF DESIGNS.

It seemed singular to me that, conservative as the Ainu are of their relics, even allowing for its brittle nature, no pottery of the kind found in pits is ever to be seen in any Ainu hut. Had they made the pottery themselves, surely some specimens or parts of specimens would have been preserved.

Comparing facts, we find, then, that the Koro-pok-kuru built their huts over pits, made pottery, and used stone and flint implements; while the Ainu have never been known to dwell in pits, have never made pottery, and have always used bone or bamboo implements. Moreover, Ainu traditions of internecine wars, vague as they are, and their designating the enemy by the name of Koro-pok-kuru, are further proofs that the Ainu themselves do not regard the pit-dwellers as their forefathers. As, then, the few facts collected tend to prove that the Ainu and the Koro-pok-kuru were two distinct races, it would be interesting to know who the latter really were, and what became of them. A learned missionary, Mr. Batchelor, writing on this subject, says:—"But I am of opinion that these pit-dwellers were closely allied to the Ainu in descent, and that the remains of them may now be seen in Shikotan and other islands of the Kurile Group. The inhabitants of Shikotan are much shorter in stature than the Ainu of Yezo. They are not so good-looking, and are said to be a very improvident race. The Ainu look upon the Kurile Islanders as the remnants of the Koro-pok-gurus; but this is a mere opinion, to be adopted or rejected at pleasure. That they are pit-dwellers *is quite certain*, for *they live in pits* at the present day."

Before being so certain as to what he was stating, it would have been well had the writer of the above lines visited the island in question. He would not then have committed so many blunders in so few lines. The inhabitants of Shikotan are *not* shorter than the Ainu of Yezo, and I cannot give a better proof of this than by asking my readers to compare the measurements which I took while there with the measurements of the Yezo Ainu. The medium height of the Shikotan Ainu is between sixty-one inches and sixty-two and three-quarter inches; the medium height of the Yezo Ainu is between sixty-one inches and sixty-two and three-quarters, or exactly the same. The chest inflated measures thirty-seven and a half inches with the Shikotan Ainu, and thirty-seven and a half with the Yezo Ainu, while the spinal column is only twenty-four inches with the Shikotan Ainu, and about twenty-six and three-quarters with the Yezo Ainu.

The Shikotan Ainu have the same structural peculiarity as the Yezo Ainu, namely, the length of their arms, which peculiarity, by the way, is greatly accentuated with them. The humerus is much longer than with the Yezo Ainu, while the ulna and radius are shorter; the hand is the same length. A Shikotan Ainu with outstretched arms is generally the length of one hand longer than his own height, which is more than is usually found with the Yezo Ainu. The medium foot is nine and a half inches with both Ainu. In the Ainu the tibia is rather flattened at its angular part, but the Shikotan Ainu have a nearly circular tibia. I do not know of any other existing race in the world in which such an extraordinary phenomenon occurs, and the tibia struck me also as being extremely long, while the femur appeared proportionately short. However, with the exception that the tibia is more circular than with the Ainu of Yezo, I could not see any material difference between them and the other Ainu. As we have already seen, each tribe in Yezo has certain characteristics which other tribes have not; each tribe has conformed its habits to the climate of the district in which it lives, as well as to other circumstances; and each of these tribes has adopted a slightly different architecture for its dwellings; but it is plain that all belong to the same original race. The same might be said of the Shikotan Ainu. At this point it is well to explain that the Kurile Islands not many years ago belonged to Russia; but they were exchanged for the southern half of Sakhalin, then belonging to Japan, and now form part of the Japanese Empire. The two larger islands—Kunashiri and Etorofu—are inhabited mainly by Ainu and a few Japanese, who migrate there from Yezo during the fishing season; while the Island of Shikotan is inhabited by sixty Ainu, brought there from the northern islands of Shirajima or Shimushir, and Urup, leaving thus all the islands north-east of Etorofu uninhabited.

Of Kunashiri and Etorofu I shall say no more in connection with the pit-dwellers, but a few more words on the Shikotan inhabitants may prove interesting, especially as people have been led to believe that they are the descendants of the Koro-pok-kuru, and not really Ainu.

I shall begin by saying that the Shikotan people call themselves Kurilsky *Ainu*, and that they speak both Ainu and Russian. Their features are not very massive, and their cheek and temple bones slightly project. They have strong mouths, and eyes identical in shape and colour with those of the Yezo Ainu. They are as hairy; they live by fishing and hunting; they clothe themselves in skins; and they are fond of beads and shining ornaments. Their huts have angular roofs, and are built in the same style as those of the Yezo Ainu, but on a smaller scale. The interiors are also alike, and equally dirty, if not more so. The Ainu huts at Shikotan are sixteen in number, and *not one* of them is built over a pit, thus showing that Mr. Batchelor was a little rash, when, relying on mistaken information, he drew a conclusion which is not in accordance with the facts. One thing that has misled most people as regards these Kurilsky Ainu is, that they were compelled to cut their hair and shave their beards. To the superficial observer this naturally gives them a different physiognomy from that of the Yezo Ainu, who let their hair grow long, and have flowing beards. Prof. Milne, who some years ago visited the Island of Shumshu,[29] relates that he saw there a small group of Kurilsky Ainu, who, all included, numbered twenty-two. Their dress, although made of skins, was European in form, and the upper garment, shaped like a shirt, was made of bird-skins (puffins) with the feathers inside. The back was ornamented with the plumes of the yellow puffin, and the edge was trimmed with seal-fur. The men wore garments tied at the waist with a belt of sea-lion hide. Their feet and legs up to the knee were covered with moccasins, also made of sea-lion skin, and their food consisted of a few berries, the eggs and flesh of sea-birds, seals, and other meat. They were few and migratory, and carried with them all their property when migrating. Prof. Milne, in a paper contributed to the Asiatic Society of Japan, thinks that the chief point in connection with these people is, that they constructed houses by making shallow excavations in the ground, which were then roofed over with turf, and that these excavations had a striking resemblance to the pits now found further south. I believe, however, that Prof. Milne never saw them excavating these pits, and the fact that hardly two dozen people in the extreme north-east Kuriles having temporarily adopted shallow excavations which they roofed over, is barely sufficient proof that they were pit-dwellers, and, as will be seen later, I had ample evidence afterwards that they were not. It is probable that this wandering band, owing to the scarcity or difficulty of procuring timber in those regions—the smallness of their canoes not permitting them to transport the materials for above-ground structures from one island to another—it is probable, I say, that, having come upon pits already dug, they had roofed them over and lived in them, finding them suitable to the severe climate. When I visited Shikotan (September, 1890), where not only these Shimushir people, but all the Kurilsky Ainu, numbering sixty, are now collected, and where they have built dwellings in their own style, the architecture and mode of construction were identical with those of the Yezo Ainu, and there were *no* pits whatever to their huts.

Had they been pit-dwellers, why should they have so suddenly modified their habits as to construct huts wholly above-ground without any reason for so doing? Supposing they were actually pit-dwellers, and had lived generation after generation in pits, why should they abandon this chief structural characteristic in a place where the climate is as severe as in the islands they formerly inhabited? I am willing to admit that the Kurilsky Ainu, like all barbarians, made the best of what they found in their migrations from one island to another, and that, having found pits already dug, they had lived in them simply for convenience, and to protect themselves from the cold. The impossibility of constructing their own style of dwellings, which would have required too much time and a great amount of timber and reeds—two articles scarce in the north-east Kuriles—may account for their being driven to occupy pits already dug; but I am certainly not inclined to admit that therefore the few remaining Kurilsky Ainu are in any way connected with or related to the Koro-pok-kuru. I believe that I have given sufficient evidence to prove this. At any rate, I have given such evidence as it was in my power to collect, and I have based my statements on what I actually saw, and not on what I heard people say. As others have speculated on this subject, I shall now ask the forgiveness of the reader if I am also dragged into a little pre-historic speculation as to who the Koro-pok-kuru were, and whence they came.

As I remarked at the beginning of this chapter, we find that pits are more numerous as we go in a north-east direction. Thus, few are found at Hakodate; and though none or few have been found along the south-west coast of Yezo, still, flint arrow-heads, pottery, and stone adzes collected here and there, show us that the Koro-pok-kuru had travelled along that coast, probably journeying in their canoes, landing to hunt, or to fight the Ainu.

Along the south-east coast the pits increase in number as we approach Kusuri, and at this place the largest number of pits in Hokkaido is found; then they are numerous all along the coast as far as Nemuro; and in the islands of Kunashiri and Etorofu the population must have been large, as there are numerous pits throughout. Pits are found in the smaller islands of the Kurile group, and I believe also in Kamschatka. From Nemuro, following the coast-line of Yezo, we find some along the north-east coast of Yezo, and none down the west coast until we reach the narrower part of the island near Sappro. This said, we have two points to consider:—

(1.) That the pit-dwellers moved from north-east to south-west.

(2.) That the main bulk of the population settled in Etorofu, Kunashiri, and at Kushiro. Few went further south to settle.

All evidence tends to show that they came either from Kamschatka, or perhaps more probably from the Aleutian Islands. It seems not improbable, looking at the volcanic formation of the Kurile group, that in bygone days Yezo was joined to Kamschatka, affording a land passage to the migratory people; but this we need not take into consideration.

From what one can gather of this race, the habits and customs of the Koro-pok-kuru must have had many points in common with the present Esquimaux. Very likely their pits were roofed over with a snow vault. They evidently lived by fishing and hunting, like the Esquimaux, and all that we know identifies them more with the latter race than with the Ainu.

I believe that the present Aleuts have a striking resemblance to the Esquimaux; and if this were the case, there is no reason why we should not suppose that they in former days inhabited the Kuriles, part of Kamschatka and the north-east portion of Yezo. It is a well-known fact that the Esquimaux formerly lived in corresponding latitudes on the east coast of America, and that they withdrew little by little to the more inhospitable regions of the north, and the same might have occurred here after the Ainu invasion of Yezo. The Koro-pok-kuru were apparently more civilised than their conquerors the Ainu, for they made pottery and worked stone; but owing to their retiring nature and weaker physique, and outnumbered by the savage hairy people, they became extinct. As to the Ainu, they also are undoubtedly a race of the north. Their music, their decorations, their habits, display characteristics of northern origin; but the Ainu, as we have seen from their structures and customs, were by no means accustomed to so cold a climate as their predecessors the pit-dwellers. In my opinion they did not invade Yezo from the Kuriles, but came from the continent of Asia, probably across Siberia, and descended as far as Sakhalin Island, where many Ainu are still to be found. As the Koro-pok-kuru resemble the Esquimaux, the Ainu have a striking resemblance in many ways to the Northmen of Europe, and this is what makes me suppose that they came across the northern part of the continent, and not from the northern islands of the Pacific. They made their way south, probably crossing over the La Perouse Strait, and the main contingent of them came down the north-east coast of Yezo. I base this theory on the fact that the strong current which passes through the La Perouse Strait from west to east would have made it impossible for the Ainu in their light "dug-outs" to navigate against it, or straight across from Sakhalin to Soya Cape, and in crossing they were undoubtedly drifted far south-east on the north-east coast, probably landing near Abashiri or Shari. Another evidence which made me think that the Ainu came from Sakhalin is, that all knew of another island besides Yezo, which they called Krafto, by which name they designate Sakhalin. Of the Kuriles no one knew except those in the immediate neighbourhood. At one time the Ainu are said to have inhabited the whole of Japan as far south as Satsuma. Archæologists are puzzled by the discovery in the main island of Nippon of various kitchen-middens, which include fragments of pottery identical with those attributed to the Koro-pok-kuru, and also of shell heaps, which some consider of Ainu origin, others as pre-Ainu. No pits, however, have been found near these shell heaps, nor on any part of Nippon. Thus another question is raised as to who the originators of these shell heaps and kitchen-middens were. Is it not likely that, as the Ainu proceeded south, they encountered the Koro-pok-kuru at Nemuro and then at Kushiro, and, having easily defeated them, forced some of them to retreat in the direction of the Kuriles, while the rest went towards the south? They probably fled along the coastline in their "dug-outs," those who moved south occasionally landing to hunt or to attack their pursuers. Thus we can account for the occurrence along that coast of some of their implements, but of no pits, which they were not likely to dig in such circumstances. Having then retreated as far south as Ushongosh (Hakodate), and with the conquering Ainu still at their heels, there was nothing more natural than that they should cross the Tsugaru Strait,[30] only a few miles in width, carrying with them their kitchen-middens and pottery.

The Ainu crossed after them, and, pushing the retreating Koro-pok-kuru further and further south, exterminated them, and became the masters of the whole of Japan, the Kuriles, and Sakhalin. As they were thus pursued by the Ainu, whom they knew as a warlike people, and stronger than themselves, there seems to me no cause for wonder that the Koro-pok-kuru did not dig any pits while on the main island of Nippon, first, because these pits would have been the sure means of bringing the Ainu on their track, to their certain annihilation; next, because the climate, being a great deal warmer, they had no need for them. On the other hand, it is more than probable that the retreaters carried with them their kitchen-middens and pottery, which constituted their treasures, and without which they could not have prepared their food. The barbarous Ainu then came in contact with the Japanese, at whose hands they received the same treatment as that which they had inflicted on the Koro-pok-kuru. Little by little the land so easily conquered was lost again, and the conquering Ainu were ere long in retreat towards the north. They were beaten and defeated by the more civilised Japanese, and the few who survived had to cross over the Tsugaru Strait back to Yezo. There is not a single Ainu now to be found in Nippon, with the exception of a child, a half-caste, whose mother was an Ainu, and who lives about sixty miles south of Awomori. The mother of this child was the last of her race who was born on and who inhabited the main island of Nippon.

Ainu blood can be traced in many of the Japanese in the northern part of Nippon, especially between Shiranoka to Awomori, and also some corrupted Ainu words are still in use in the dialect spoken in that part of Japan. Names of places, rivers, towns, etc., of Ainu origin, are common all over Japan. It was this former occupation of Japan by the Ainu that for some time led people to believe that the Ainu were the forefathers of the Japanese; and when pits were found in Yezo, the same hastily-judging people attributed them to the Ainu; and then, when mention was made of the Koro-pok-kuru and the Ko-shto, they affixed this name to the Kurilsky Ainu whom they had never seen nor studied.

I am not prepared to say whether or not traces of these Koro-pok-kuru are to be found in the Aleutian Islands, as I have not visited them; but it would prove interesting to trace a connection between them and some existing race, in case my supposition be not correct, though I am sure that it is nearer the mark than any of the conjectures made by others with regard either to the Ainu or the Koro-pok-kuru. At any rate, as I do not pretend to infallibility; should my supposition be wrong, the facts given above will remain, and a more successful student and investigator will be able to work on them with a decided advantage over the writer, who had to start from the very beginning, and work on information which was more of an obstacle than a help.

STONE ADZES AND HAMMERS.

AINU HUTS AND STOREHOUSES ON KUTCHARO LAKE.

CHAPTER X.
The Kutcharo River and Lake—A Sulphur Mine—Akkeshi and its Bay.

The Kutcharo River is of some importance, for though not of great length, it is navigable by small boats for nearly twenty miles from its mouth.

I left Kushiro one morning, and made my way up the river, not by boat but along its banks on horseback, so as to get a better idea of the surrounding country and its inhabitants. At Kushiro I left more than half my luggage, to be sent down to Hakodate by the first ship that happened to call, and this greatly changed my mode of travelling. Instead of two ponies, one pony would now be quite sufficient to carry my baggage and myself; and where ponies were not obtainable, I could carry all my paraphernalia on my own back with no very great difficulty, and in this way I should not be hindered on my journey.

I daresay the baggage I was carrying now weighed about forty-five pounds. It mostly consisted of painting materials, and wooden panels, on which I usually paint my sketches when travelling.

As to clothes and boots, I was beginning to be rather "hard up." No weaver's work, no tailor's garments, nor tanner's hides, can stand the wear and tear of such rough travelling as I had had, and the old saying, that a "light heart and a thin pair of breeches carry you a long way," is most decidedly not to be applied to anyone journeying to and fro on a pack-saddle in Yezo. My coat and trousers were showing signs of rapid decay, and I thought with vain desire of needle and thread, buttons and hooks. My boots were falling to pieces owing to their continual immersion in salt water. The impossibility of cleaning or greasing them added to the original damage; and, worse luck of all, they could not be replaced. Altogether, what with frayed garments, leaky boots, a battered hat, and a general out-at-elbows air, I was scarcely presentable in any society a grade above that of the hairy Ainu.

A road has been cut between Kushiro and Shibetcha, a distance of thirty miles; but though quite new, it is already out of repair, and it will not be long before it is washed away entirely. The Japanese Government does its best to open roads near the largest settlements, but Japanese officials do not seem to understand that after a road has been made it has to be kept in repair.

The country all along is good, and the soil seems rich and fertile. Nearly half-way up, on the east side of the Kutcharo River, are three lakes,—the Takkobe, the Tori Lake, and the Shirin. The Tori is the largest. Its length is five miles, its width about one mile. On the southern shore of this lake is a picturesque Ainu village, with its old tumble-down huts, and close to it is a group of Japanese houses. The contrast between the dirty and neglected old hovels of the Ainu and the clean, spruce, and somewhat finikin houses of the Japanese is very striking. In this difference we read an epitome of the way in which civilisation has travelled from primitive barbarism. The road runs through dense forests; but in several places, especially on its highest level, we come to lovely views of mountain scenery, towering over the shimmering water of the underlying lakes.

In the evening I reached Shibetcha, a nice little place, constructed on each side of a large road which rises considerably as it goes through the village. The village lies in a small valley surrounded by moderately high mountains, and is on the western side of the Kutcharo River, which intersects the valley. A wooden bridge and a three-storied Japanese tea-house are the two main structures in the place. There are sixty-eight houses in the village, and nearly half of them are houses of ill-fame, the three-storied tea-house being the principal.

At a distance of twenty-five miles from here is a sulphur mine, and the miners, after having amassed sufficient money, come and squander it at Shibetcha, thus supporting this nook of demoralization in the wilderness of these mountains. As the river becomes very shallow, the mineral from the sulphur mine of Yuzan was carried until quite recently on pack-saddles as far as here, whence it was brought down by boat to Kushiro for shipment; but a small railway, on which only a "truck train" is now running once a day from the mine to Shibetcha, has greatly simplified matters, and increased the export returns of the mine.

By the kind permission of the Mitsui Company I was allowed to travel on one of the trucks (no passenger carriages being provided), and the two and a half hours' journey was thus accomplished much more comfortably than if I had ridden the twenty-five miles on my pack-saddle. The railway took me to the foot of Mount Yuzan, and that same afternoon I made the ascent of the mountain. The most valuable sulphur deposits in Japan are found on this mountain, the quantity of the mineral being practically unlimited. The ascent was hard work, but it was interesting to see the *fumaroles*, whence the sulphur is extracted, and whence a dense smoke shoots out with great force. The whole mountain is covered with thick layers of sulphur of very good quality, and when more practical processes are employed for the extraction and carriage of the mineral there is no doubt that the sulphur trade will assume a very prominent place in the exports of Yezo. Dozens of men are employed now to carry the sulphur from the mountain to the railway, but there is work enough for hundreds and hundreds more. All the sulphur is at present carried on small wheelbarrows, which each man slings on to his shoulders when empty and he is going up the mountain. When the sulphur is reached the workman sits down, pulls out his pipe, which he fills from the folds of his tobacco-pouch, has a quiet smoke and a good rest, then he slowly fills his wheelbarrow with the primrose-yellow blocks, and comfortably wheels it down hill to the station, a considerable distance. Such a primitive fashion of carriage involves great loss of time, and a simple mechanical contrivance, by which a large quantity of mineral could be brought down at one time, would save an enormous amount of labour, and therefore expense. A cable railway would answer the purpose to perfection, and the cost of running the steam motor would be insignificant, owing to the amount of wood and coal found within easy reach. I passed through a large gorge in the mountain, and finally reached the summit of Yuzan. Walking on sulphur beds is like walking on ice, and many a time in the climb I landed on my knees. Near the summit is a huge pinnacle of volcanic rock, standing up perpendicularly, and of impossible access. From the foot of this pinnacle a lovely view of the Kutcharo Lake is obtained, and it has as a background chain after chain of thickly-wooded mountains, beyond which are visible Oakan and Moyokan, two volcanic peaks, respectively four thousand and three thousand four hundred feet above the level of the sea. On Moyokan are some hot springs and accumulations of sulphur. Both these peaks can be seen from the coast on a clear day. A small lake lies between Moyokan and Oakan, which takes its name from the latter mountain, and finds an outlet in the Oakan River. The Oakan joins the Kutcharo River not far from the sea.

KUTCHARO LAKE FROM MOUNT YUZAN.

The descent was easier than the ascent, and I put up at a small tea-house, the only one in the place. The landlord promised to get me a good pony early the next morning, but, like a true Japanese, he did not keep his promise. He called me at 5 A.M., saying that the pony would be ready in a few minutes, and at 9 A.M. the quadruped had not put in an appearance; and after numberless excuses, compliments, bows, and lies, the landlord acknowledged that no ponies were to be had. I gave my luggage to a railway *employé*, who undertook to bring it back to Shibetcha, and I started on foot for Lake Kutcharo. From Yuzan a track across the mountains goes due north to Abashiri, on the north-east coast. I went in a south-westerly direction, and as on the previous day from the summit of Yuzan I had noted the position of Lake Kutcharo, I had no difficulty in finding my way there; in fact, I came upon a small Ainu track leading to it. A delightful walk of ten miles in the forest took me to the Ainu village of Kutcharo, on the borders of the lake of the same name. The village is a miserable one; it differs from all other Ainu villages in its huts, which have semicircular roofs instead of angular ones, as is the case with the Ainu of Volcano Bay and of the Saru and Tokachi Rivers. I entered some of the huts, and in a few minutes I was surrounded by the small population—I daresay about twenty souls, all included—whom I led out into the open air to see what they were like. They appeared to me smaller than other Ainu, and their bones were less massive; they were not so hairy, and more inclined to baldness. Their garments were wretched, and resembled those worn by the Tokachi Ainu; namely, a few rags held together one could scarcely say how. Women were tattooed on their lips and arms, but less extensively than are those of other tribes, and the tattooing was not so accurately done.

Other Ainu whom I met in the forest in the neighbourhood of this village bore the same characteristics, and everyone seemed to be curiously melancholy and depressed. An Ainu existence is certainly not one's ideal of comfort and hilarity, but their gloom and melancholy seem to me to be purely racial and congenital.

The Lake Kutcharo is very large—too large to be seen to advantage from its borders, as one can see only parts, and not the whole of it at once. It has a pretty island in the centre, and on the west side is a peninsula projecting almost as far as the island. On this peninsula a small active geyser is found, which rises to a height of about twelve feet, and acts spasmodically. The high mountains which surround the lake would make the latter a pleasant summer resort were the place within the circle of civilisation. The scenery is very similar to that of Norway or the Scotch lakes. The Kutcharo River, as can be seen on the map, is an outlet of the Lake Kutcharo, into which the waters of the latter discharge themselves a few hundred yards west of the Ainu village.

SULPHUR MINE.

An Ainu pointed out to me the track leading to Tetcha, or Tetchkanga, and I directed my steps in that direction, the Ainu having informed me that it was very far, and that I could only reach it at night. I crossed the stream in a "dug-out," and found the track on the other side. I walked fast, for the most part through a thickly-wooded country, and at about sunset I reached Tetcha. The distance from Kutcharo, I should think, is about ten or twelve miles. Tetcha is an Ainu village, near which a few Japanese houses have been built. The Kutcharo River intersects it, and the sulphur train from Yuzan stops here to take water on its way to Shibetcha. The train had gone through some hours previously, and I was left the alternative of walking on to Shibetcha, twenty miles further, or of sleeping at Tetcha. I had walked twenty or twenty-two miles already that day, and I felt in very good form. I knew that it would be full moon that night; and walking through a forest by moonlight has always had a great charm for me. Watching the shadows, with their thousand different fantastic forms, running in and out through the trees and playing round them, has the same weird fascination for me as one of Tieck's tales, or the suggestive music of an æolian harp. Some of the Ainu and a Jap entreated me not to attempt to cross the forest at night, for wolves and bears were numerous, they said, and in all probability I should be attacked by them. This last announcement, which I was destined to hear every day in Yezo, and which, of course, I did not believe, decided me to go, and I started.

"But," cried after me the astonished Japanese, "*anata micci wakarimasen!*"—"You do not know the way!"

"*Kamaimasen, Sayonara!*"—"It little matters; good-bye!" was my reply; and I left him standing there perplexed, looking after me as if I had been a phenomenon.

The Japanese in Yezo and the Ainu never on any account travel far at night; and as for going through a forest alone, unprotected, and without knowing the way, they evidently regarded it as something more reprehensible than folly. Two days previously, when in the train, I had noticed that the railway described a curve several miles long, and I knew then that by cutting across I could considerably shorten my way. When I entered the forest, the sun with its last rays was casting warm tints on the tops of the pine-trees. Everything was still, and only now and then some huge owl, awakened by the noise of my steps from its day's long sleep, would fly away, starting off on its night's peregrinations and depredations. I walked mile after mile, and finally struck the rails again. On a white post I saw a cipher in Chinese characters, which brought me back to the reality that I was still seventeen miles away from Shibetcha. I followed the line of rail as closely as I could, and late at night I reached Shibetcha. I roused the people at the *Marui yadoya*, and, having eaten some salmon and water soup, I retired to my *foutangs*, between which, it is useless to say, I slept well. I had walked forty-two odd miles that day, and it had been a pleasant change from the continuous riding on pack-saddles.

The next day I rode down to the coast to the bay of Akkeshi, about forty-two miles east of Kushiro. The road is very good all the way, and has on each side woods of oak and pine trees. The traffic on it is at present very small, and the only living creatures I saw during the twenty-eight or thirty miles were a beautiful long-tailed red fox and a number of Japanese convicts led by a policeman. These were dressed in red trousers and a short red coat made of coarse material. They were walking in a row, and they were chained two by two, and, moreover, a long rope joined the chain of each couple to that of the next, so that all couples were tied together. The end of this rope was held by the policeman. Some of them wore large hats entirely covering their face; others wore no hat at all, and had their head shaved in a peculiar manner. They were mostly bare-footed, but a few wore straw sandals. The Government wisely makes use of these convicts in opening roads and other public works, and after their term of punishment is expired, these men almost invariably become fishermen. A great part of the Japanese population of Yezo is composed of exiles and ex-convicts; in other words, Yezo is nothing more or less to Japan than what Australia was to England some years ago.

Nearing the coast I passed the "Tonden" of Hondemura, a colonial militia farming settlement. A long line of new houses, all exactly alike in shape and size, and built at intervals, stretches on each side of the wide road. Each of these houses is inhabited by a man who has served his time as a soldier, and who has now his family about him, and does work as a farmer in this settlement assigned to him. These "Tondens" were established by the Government, and I believe that the farmer-soldiers give fairly good results in the zeal and industry with which they cultivate the land, and the honesty and morality of their lives. I saw most of them occupied in stubbing up the scrub, and tearing or cutting down the trees, burning the more worthless parts; but it will be some years yet before they have cleared an area of cultivable land sufficiently large for profit, as the country is very thickly wooded in that neighbourhood.

Soon after I had passed the settlement, going down a steep hill I came upon a small and dirty semi-Ainu village, and ultimately reached the seashore.

The distance from Shibetcha is thirty miles, and the riding was beginning to be unpleasant, owing to the gathering darkness, which made my pony shy at everything it passed. At the mouth of the Pehambe Ushi River I had great difficulty in getting my pony on the ferry-boat, which was to take me across the mouth of the lagoon to Akkeshi. Several drunken fishermen came on board, and were disagreeably noisy. One of these fellows had a pony, which he tied to mine when on board. The ferry was to take us across the entrance of the Akkeshi lagoon, and it was more than a quarter of an hour before we reached the opposite shore. When we were still nearly twenty feet from *terra firma*, my pony, frightened at the cries of the drunken crowd, jumped overboard, carrying with him his companion steed. The sudden shock and lurch of the boat knocked down everybody on board, and nearly capsized us. As it was we shipped a lot of water. The ponies found the water deeper than they expected, and they had to swim for it. Having landed before he came ashore, I recaptured mine, gave him a sound thrashing, and rode on to Akkeshi, a few hundred yards from the landing-place. Akkeshi lies at the north-east side of the large bay which goes by the same name, and which, by the way, is probably one of the best anchorages on the south coast of Yezo. The mouth of the bay is to the southward; it extends seven miles in a northerly direction, and is about six miles wide in its widest part. The bay is prolonged further inland by a large lagoon, called Se-Cherippe, which contains many shoals and low islands, near which are beds of oysters of enormous size, the shells of some measuring as much as eighteen inches in length. The Koro-pok-kuru, by whom this district was formerly thickly populated, seem to have relished this diet, as we find thick beds of discarded shells on the top of some of the lower hills, and in many places, especially in the vicinity of pits. These shell heaps are similar to those found on the main island of Nippon, and attributed to the Ainu. (*See* Chapter IX.)

The country round the bay and the lagoon forms a high land or plateau between two hundred and three hundred feet above the level of the sea, and the higher ground is thickly wooded, thus supplying Akkeshi with abundance of timber, mostly of evergreen trees, as Todo and Yezo-matzu, two spruces common in other parts of Yezo as well. With its good harbour, its large export of oysters, salmon, herrings, fish-manure, and seaweed, besides its seal-fishery and the quantity of good timber easily cut and transported down the lagoon and across the bay for shipment, it is not surprising that Akkeshi has become, after Hakodate, the most important centre on the southern coast. It is nearly half as large again as Kushiro, and has as many as nine hundred Japanese houses, besides sixty or seventy Ainu huts.

The Ainu were formerly extremely numerous in this district; but few of them are left now, and those few are indeed poor specimens of their race. They have nearly all become bald, and they seem to suffer very severely from rheumatism. Thick fogs are very prevalent along the coast, and it is but seldom that one can obtain a view of the whole bay. These fogs naturally render navigation unsafe, and are one of the great drawbacks to the prosperity of the place. However, our good Londoners could tell us that greater evils than fogs can exist. I have no doubt that at some future date we shall hear of Akkeshi as being the most important port in Yezo, when a railway to join it to Shibetcha shall have been constructed. The sulphur of Mount Yuzan will probably then be taken direct to this place instead of Kushiro, owing to the safety of its harbour, an advantage which Kushiro does not possess. The Akkeshi Bay is also interesting from a picturesque point of view, when fogs give one a chance of seeing the surrounding scenery. Some fine headlands are found near the town of Akkeshi, and also on each side of the opening of the bay into the ocean. On the eastern side, the two islands of Daikuku and Kodaikuku, joined to the mainland by the low reef, slightly under water-level, which goes round the bay, are of some importance for an artist. This is especially true of the larger island of Daikuku, which rises at a considerable height above the sea, forming majestic cliffs, beautiful in shape and colour, on which myriads of seagulls, albatrosses, and penguins have chosen their abode, finding in these almost untrodden and picturesque cliffs a safe place in which to lay their eggs and rear their young. Here they live undisturbed, save for the dashing waves of the ocean, which make the earth tremble and the rock crumble to pieces, but only meet with a blithesome welcome from the screaming, light-hearted, fat, and lazy-winged inhabitants, to whom those waves bring good stores of daily food.

AKKESHI IN A FOG.

AINU MAN AND WOMAN ON HORSEBACK.

CHAPTER XI.
From Akkeshi to Nemuro—A Horse Station—Nemuro and its People.

The road in the proximity of Akkeshi was extremely muddy and slippery, owing to the continuous fogs and rain. A north wind was blowing hard the day I left for Kiritap, and it drove the mist and drizzly rain right through one's skin into one's bones. The fogs, which are prevalent all along the coast, seem to excel between Akkeshi and Kiritap; so much so that the Japanese in the neighbourhood make them answerable for their baldness, and the local Ainu say they are so scantily hirsute because of the everlasting dampness in which they live. They clinch their argument by reminding you that when their forefathers came to this part of the coast they were as hairy as the bear, so what can have caused their own comparative smoothness but these everlasting fogs? I believe that to a great extent they are right, for when, after a day's wet ride, I have sat near a fire even for some hours, I have felt as if my skin were soaking with wet—as if I had been too long in a bath—and neither rubbing with cotton towels nor the warmth of the fire seemed thoroughly to dry it; and perhaps such an extraordinary dampness, constantly saturating the pores of the skin, may have an injurious effect upon the hair, and cause it to decay and fall off. It was in a thick fog like this that I had to find my way to Riruran, the next horse station, about eight miles further east. The road soon became a mere track, running through an undulating country, chiefly pasture land. As luck would have it, I had hired a pony which belonged to the Riruran station, and the beast was as anxious to get there as I was. He knew the way and I did not, so I let him guide me. Now and then, when the wind blew with increased strength, the fog lifted for a few minutes, and disclosed some pretty bits of landscape. The country all around was grassy, with the familiar densely-wooded hills in the background. It somewhat resembled the slopes and high lands of Cornwall, without, however, the herds of sheep and cattle, which in our country are connected with green fields; without the trim fences and stiles, the ploughed fields and meadows, the trim hedges and park-like trees, the bye-lanes and well-kept roads.

Hill after hill was ascended and descended, the sturdy little pony going well towards his former home; but as yet I had come on no signs of any living creature. No labourers are here to work and plough the dark rich soil. Potato fields; cottages with their plots of vegetable grounds; cows and sheep scattered over the green pastures—all signs of vigorous and successful husbandry—are things that an intending traveller to Yezo will miss. Everywhere are solitude and monotony. Still, even solitude and monotony are not always to be abhorred, and if they have their drawbacks they also have their advantages. You can go undisturbed for mile after mile; you can think; you can dream; you can sing; you can keep to the track or go across country; you can go fast or slow, and there is no one to object, to obstruct, or to comment. You breathe air that no one has breathed before, and you quench your thirst in a limpid stream unpolluted by sewage, chemical refuse, or poisonous dye-stuffs. You lead a simple life, and, what is more, an independent life. Many a time, when I woke up to the real state of my new condition, I could not help laughing at our civilised conceptions of what constitutes a free man in a free country, viz. that he can have a voice in choosing which of two men shall be sent as a member to Parliament.

Absorbed, now in my own thoughts on many subjects, and now in gazing at the monotonous scenes, which, as if reflected from a magic-lantern, suddenly appeared and as suddenly faded away, I had not seen how far my pony had hurried on, when, rapidly descending a steep hill, I discerned through the grey fog a solitary shed in the small valley below. The neighing of my steed, responded to by the neighing of his compatriots in the valley, told me that I had reached the horse station of Riruran, and a few minutes later my baggage and pack-saddle were removed from my steaming quadruped, and a fresh animal was burdened with my possessions. These horse stations generally consist of one shed, in which the owner and his family live; near it is a rough enclosure formed of branches and trunks of trees laid down horizontally, and strengthened at intervals by poles stuck in the ground. The ponies are kept in this enclosure during the day, but are let loose at sunset, when they go for their food wherever they can get it—generally on the near hills. Early in the morning one or two Ainu employed in the stations start off to recapture the ponies, and after a struggle bring back the herd to the paddock. My readers, who may not be well acquainted with the habits of semi-wild horses, will wonder that the ponies, once free in an unenclosed country, do not bolt away altogether inland, thus making it impossible to recapture them; and, moreover, these readers will think what a difficult task it must be for the Ainu horsemen to recover all the ponies, each one of which, they probably imagine, has bolted in an independent and different direction. This is not the case. When a herd of ponies is let loose they invariably all go together in one direction, generally following those of the older animals which have bells hanging to their necks. When they come to a proper feeding-ground they all graze within a few yards of one another; and the chances are that the herd will not go a step further than is necessary, as they are terribly afraid of bears, their most dreaded enemy, by which they well know the more distant hills are infested. When their hunger is satisfied they shoulder up together and form a circle, in the centre of which the young colts are placed, these being thus well protected from bears, who would find a sturdy resistance in the hind hoofs of the outstanding guard should they come to close quarters. The Ainu are good trackers, and have little difficulty in finding in which direction the herd has moved. When this preliminary is ascertained, the horseman, mounted on a swift pony, which he has taken good care to keep behind, starts from the station about an hour before sunrise, so as to allow himself ample time to reach the herd before the sun is up. He finds the ponies in this circular position of defence. With a long stick he breaks their ranks, and by shouting, and wildly galloping to and fro, drives them on in front till the station and the pen are reached. When they have all entered the latter, a heavy wooden bar is rested on two biforked poles, one on each side of the entrance, thus barring their way out; and there they are kept all day, waiting for such native travellers or traders as may require their services along the coast.

Most of the stations are owned by Japanese and by Ainu half-castes. Some have large numbers of ponies; some only a few, according to the wants of the neighbourhood.

The average market value of a beast is between five and ten *yen*, or about fifteen to thirty shillings in English currency.

At stations where the ponies are but little worked, good animals can sometimes be obtained for a small sum of money; but at stations near large settlements—where trade with other villages is carried on entirely by pack-ponies—they are mostly sorry beasts, with their backs one mass of sores, produced by the friction of the rough pack-saddles. Moreover, the cruel habit of letting colts follow mares for long distances—sometimes forty or fifty miles—is as painful a sight to witness as it is injurious to the breed. The Yezo ponies are characterised by their long hair and mane. They are short, sturdy, punchy brutes, not more than ten or twelve hands high, with a rather large and massive head, and thick, crooked legs. They are by no means fine-looking animals, nor are they well groomed—in fact, they are not groomed at all—but they serve capitally for the rough tracks and precipitous wastes of Hokkaido. They have none of the good qualities we require in our horses, but they possess others which fit them for the country they are in. Their enormous power of endurance, and the wonderful way in which they can go over the steepest tracks—almost unclimbable on foot; their sure step when going along precipices; and the marvellous manner in which they pick their way over rocky coasts, which the waves would seem to make impassable, and where none of our good horses could go without breaking their legs, are all endowments which I feel bound to quote in honour of the Yezo ponies. They are not shod, and they can hardly be called trained. Indeed, if a traveller be a good rider, it is advisable to obtain a perfectly unbroken animal, as from my own personal experience I can say that, though the riding was a little more exciting, I could invariably make better time with a totally unbroken beast, than with one of the worn-out, sore-backed "quiet ponies," which needed any amount of thrashing to make him go.

A curious method is adopted for directing the animal. It is as simple as it is ingenious. The necessary "bit" by which we control our horses is dispensed with, and it is replaced by two wooden wands about twelve inches long and two inches wide, tied together at one end, allowing a distance of three inches between them. In the middle of these wands a rope is passed which goes over the pony's head behind its ears; while the wands themselves, thus supported by it, rest one on each side of the pony's nose. Another rope, five or six feet in

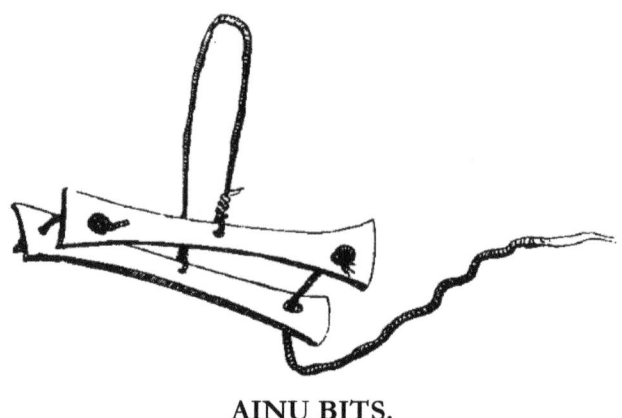

AINU BITS.

length, and acting as a rein, is fastened at the lower end of one of the wands, and passes through a hole in the other, thus allowing this simple contrivance, based on the lever principle, to be worked exactly in the same way as a nut-cracker, the pony's nose being the nut. The disadvantage of the system is, that having only one rein, this has to be passed over the pony's head each time one wishes to turn to the right or to the left, as by pulling the rope hard, and thus squeezing the animal's nose, its head is turned in the direction in which it is pulled, and it is soon taught that this is the way it must go. Furthermore, should the pony bolt, it can be stopped by pulling its head close to its haunches, thereby making it impossible to continue its race. In the latter case it often happens, especially with an untrained pony, that it will spin round, trying to stretch its twisted neck by pushing its head away from the side of its body, and the result is generally a bad fall of horse and rider.

Another thing of which one ought to be careful is to keep one's legs out of the reach of the brute's teeth; for it is not infrequent that instead of the man punishing the animal, the animal revenges itself on the man; and the incautious traveller realises Sydney Smith's position, and finds that to a Yezo pony, as well as to an English cart-horse, "all flesh is grass."

From Riruran, for about fifteen miles, the way is merely a mountain track; and I dare say that in fine weather the scenery along it is picturesque. Unfortunately, when I went through, the fog had become more and more intense, and I saw very little of the landscape. At places the track led down to the sea, and then mounted up again over cliffs and high lands. As the mist, which came in gusts and waves, deepened or lightened in intensity, the rugged precipitous rocks, formed mostly of conglomerate, sandstone, and breccia, took all sorts of fantastic forms. Along the coast were many Ainu huts inhabited by half-castes and by Japanese. The Ainu were once very numerous in this district, but few of them are to be found now. The few remaining ones have yielded to the more civilised Japanese, and have become their servants. They are used as menials in most of the fishing stations, always acting under the directions of Japanese masters. Very frequently they are employed as tenders of horses, and in some places as guides for traders and travellers from one station to another.

Not far from Riruran the mouths of two lagoons have to be crossed, the larger of which is called Saruffo-Ko, or "Lake in a grassy plain." Cranes, swans, and ducks are numerous in these lagoons.

The track continues mostly over cliffs and mountains till Birvase, a small village of seaweed gatherers, is reached, and the next two and a half miles are along a sandy beach as far as Hammanaka. A short bridge joins this place to the island of Kiritap, which is separated from the mainland by a channel only a few feet wide. Towards the evening the fog lifted, and I caught a glimpse of the village.

The ponies of the Kiritap village had just been let loose, and were running over the small wooden bridge with great clamour. The houses, which number about a hundred and twenty, are all poor and dirty. There is a main street, and most of the houses are on each side of it. The people are fishermen, seaweed gatherers, and small traders; for Hammanaka Bay, being a good anchorage for junks and small craft under the lee of Kiritap Island, is a place of some importance for its export trade of seaweeds, fish-oil, and herring guano; these products being sent down to Hakodate.

If a few Ainu have adopted the Japanese language, clothes, and customs, there are also many Japanese who have taken up the Ainu language and ways. I noticed this more particularly in this district, where the Ainu have almost entirely disappeared. The older Japanese and many of the younger folks have Ainu features; and not only have they adopted a great number of Ainu words, but when talking Japanese they speak it with the peculiar intonation and accent pertaining to the Ainu. This is not surprising, nor yet peculiar to the Japanese or the Chinese; for we find that almost all English residents in Chinese ports adopt many of the words of our pig-tailed brothers, and have thus formed a kind of local English, besides the "pidgeon-English"—a corruption of "business English"—which almost constitutes a language of its own.

The Ainu, like the Scotch or the French, give a rolling sound to the "r." Thus, for instance, if I had written the word "Riruran" as it is pronounced I should have spelt it "Rrirrurran." Then the Ainu almost sing their words—the women in a falsetto voice, ending in a singularly mournful kind of cadenza. On his return from a journey, a hunt, or a fishing expedition, the Ainu squats down cross-legged in his hut, and, after the conventional introductory ceremony of rubbing the palms of his hands together and then repeatedly stroking his hair and beard, proceeds to relate the adventures that have befallen him during his absence. This he does by singing out his story in a sort of monotone, or sometimes chanting it. When conversing with Japanese the Ainu have slightly modified this habit, which gave rise to much mirth to the light-hearted sons of the Mikado's empire. However, like all people who are ready to laugh at everything novel, the local Japanese have now themselves fallen into that same manner of speaking, which, after all, has its charms, as it is rather sentimental in spirit, and so far pleasant to the ear. What is more, they have also acquired the slow ways of the Ainu.

All along the beach between Hammanaka and Hattaushi, a distance of nearly twenty miles, there are fishermen's and seaweed gatherers' huts; but none of them is inhabited by Ainu. Men, women, and children are all occupied in the seaweed gathering industry; and it is when the sea is stormy that the largest quantity of kelp is collected. The numerous reefs and rocks all along the shore-line afford suitable ground and bottom for its growth and production; and during a stormy sea quantities of kelp float on the breaking waves, to be finally thrown on shore. The industrious gatherers seldom wait for this "jetsam," as the long weeds, after they are washed off the rock, and before they are finally swept on shore, are apt to be damaged by the waves, and are therefore of less value for the export market than when long and fresh; wherefore, each gatherer provides himself with a long pole or hook, and from morning till night these half-naked "toilers of the sea" can be seen running to and fro in and out of the waves dragging bunches of long ribbon-like seaweeds, which are then carefully disentangled, stretched on the sands to dry, and, after several days of exposure, are packed for the market.

Some huge cliffs towering over the sandy beach make the track interesting; and here and there, scattered in the Hammanaka Bay, are some oyster-banks before reaching the single shed of Hattaushi. The following twelve miles were on an extremely bad track, partly over steep hills and partly on tiresome soft sand. Then I arrived at Otchishi—without exception the loveliest little spot in Yezo. It lies in the centre of a small bay, on the two sides of which are magnificent headlands with precipitous cliffs and rocks of volcanic formation. On a pretty bit of green grass in the foreground, only a few feet above the sea-level, were a shed and a storehouse. A reef and shallow water closed the entrance of the bay to the foaming waves of the Pacific. In the sheltered water, which was as smooth as a mirror, the dark rich colour of the overhanging rocks, caressed by the last warm rays of the dying sun, was reflected with absolute fidelity and almost increased loveliness. A cold whitish sky, and the *white horses* breaking on the reef, completed the *ensemble* of that lovely scene; and it was with great regret, after having attempted a sketch, that I was told my horse was ready, and I had to leave this poetical and exquisite scene.

On the slight elevations near Otchishi, and in the valley, pits are still to be seen, showing that the pit-dwellers were once numerous in this district. They are found both along the coast as well as slightly inland by the side of small rivers, and on the shores of the Saruffu lagoon. A well-kept road begins at Otchishi, and goes on to Nemuro. At first it runs over hilly ground and through an oak-wooded country, then through thick forests of spruce trees, the trees standing very close together. About four miles from Nemuro a military settlement—"Hanasaki"—similar to the one on the Shibetcha-Akkeshi road, has been established by the Japanese Government. Here, again, I was struck by the difficulty and the amount of labour involved in clearing the trees off the ground. It will take many years before the industrious farmers will have any return for their hard labour. I do not know what the object of the Japanese Government may have been in starting these two militia settlements in spots so unfit for cultivation, but it seems a great pity to see the Tokachi region, which has all the requisites for successful agriculture, quite deserted, while hundreds of men are wasting their strength and time at other places, where it will take several years to open enough ground for even a kitchen-garden.

Past the long row of houses at Hanasaki the road descends gently, and I arrived at Nemuro, a thriving place of about fifteen hundred houses, on the south-west coast of the plateau-like peninsula ending at Cape Noshafu. The general elevation of the plateau is between sixty and one hundred and twenty feet above the sea-level, and the high land is covered with undergrowth and stunted trees, such as scrub bamboo, oak, birch, and alder, the east winds and fogs no doubt preventing the latter from attaining a larger growth. Some low islands and reefs lie north and south off Cape Noshafu, and make navigation very unsafe for the small coasting crafts which sometimes during the summer call at Nemuro for sea-weed, herring, salt, salmon, and herring guano; the first exported chiefly to China, the others to Tokio and Southern Japan. Herrings are caught in large numbers during the spring and summer, and the export of fish-manure would be considerably increased if the harbour at Nemuro could be safely entered by larger ships. As it is now, though well sheltered by the small island of Bentenjima, it can only harbour small ships, as, besides not being deep, its entrance is narrow and of difficult access during the thick fogs of the summer. In the winter and part of the spring the harbour and the coast as far as Noshafu Cape are blocked with drift ice, thus stopping navigation altogether. The trade from the adjoining coast and the Kurile Islands concentrates at this port, and as a farming region the small portion of available land north-west of the town has given fairly good results. Horse-breeding has proved a success for the local wants, but hardly so in producing a fine breed of horses. Cattle-breeding, on the other hand, has been a failure all through, owing to the severe weather in winter, which the imported animals could not stand. In spite of strong easterly winds, heavy fogs, ice, and snow, fair crops of *daikon*, potatoes, turnips, barley, beans, wheat, and hemp are successfully raised here, as the soil is of extremely good quality. As to the town itself, it is prettily laid out, the streets crossing each other at right angles, while some of the houses are built in semi-European style, to meet the severity of the climate. A Shinto temple is erected on the high level; and from this is obtained a fine bird's-eye view of the harbour and town, with the numerous storehouses overlooking the sea.

As I have given a short description of the town—uninteresting save from a commercial point of view—I feel that I owe a few lines to its go-ahead inhabitants. Belonging, nearly all, to a young and adventurous generation, they reminded me of the same type of Englishmen who have abandoned their fatherland and settled in America and Australia, striving, and often succeeding, in making a fortune. Such men are invariably of a different "make" from that of the young fellows who are satisfied to drudge for life in a bank, a merchant's office, or a shop—vegetating rather than living; following their day's routine in a mechanical sort of way; grumbling continually, but never bold enough to attempt any improvement of their position. As one is born an artist, a musician, or a literary man, one has to be born a colonist to be a successful one.

The young Japanese whom I met at Nemuro impressed me as being thoroughly different from any I had come across in my one year's stay in Southern Japan; and I was agreeably surprised when I found that I was dealing with a lot of young, clever, and serious men, willing to improve their country and themselves, and anxious to accept any practical hint that would enable them to accomplish this in the shortest time possible. In other words, they had lost the slow, phlegmatic way of transacting business of the "stay-at-homes," and had accepted the quick perception of the true colonist, who is always ready to catch all the chances which will help him to get on in life.

I had been struck with this energy, this go-ahead faculty, several times along the south-west and south-east coasts, when conversing with the Japanese with whom I came in contact; but I was never so much impressed as at Nemuro, where, indeed, the men are of a superior class, well-educated, and belonging to good families, while most of the Japanese at fishing stations along the coast are taken from the scum of the towns. They are often escaped or ex-convicts, or else people who found it advisable to abandon the livelier shores of Nippon, leaving no trace of themselves rather than end their days in a prison cell.

Nemuro is a progressive place in every way, and had it been built five miles further west it would have been intersected by the Onnetto River—a short outlet of the Onnetto Lagoon, which would have formed a larger and safer harbour than the present Nemuro anchorage. As it is, prosperity showed itself in the usual way, by the number of eating-houses for all classes, a theatre, numerous *guechas*—singers and dancers—and a whole street of houses of light morals, in which, behind a wooden grating similar to a huge cage, dozens of girls are shown in their gaudy red and gold embroidered *kimonos*, with elaborate *obis* round their waist, and expensive long tortoise-shell hairpins artistically surrounding their heads like a halo. There in a line the pretty girls sit for several hours on their heels in front of a *hibachi*—brazier—smoking their diminutive pipes. They are fair game for now the compliments and now the jokes of the crowd promenading up and down the street in the evening. Every now and then, when an admirer approaches the cage, one of the girls gets up, refills her tiny pipe with tobacco, and offers it to him, not forgetting to wipe the mouthpiece with the palm of her hand before so doing. He (the admirer) puffs away, and returns the empty pipe with thanks, shifting on to another cage to have his next smoke. Japanese men cannot live without *guechas*, and it follows as a matter of course that Nemuro, being a prosperous place, there are many of them.

A *guecha* is a singer or dancer (posturing), or both, and one or more generally attend dinner-parties and festivities of any kind. Some sing with self-accompaniment of *shamesen;* others display their wonderful powers of mimicking and posturising, in which grace is never lacking. A long *kimono*, a carefully-arranged *obi*, and a pretty pair of white *tabi*—short socks with split toes—make up the graceful and simple attire in which they appear in the house. Their hair, plastered down with camelia oil, is a veritable work of art. It is carefully combed, oiled, and flattened behind the ears. A metal fastener at the lowest point of the curve keeps it in this flat position, and it is then raised again and fastened at the back of the head, first in a most elaborate twist, and then rolled up in graceful curves. A pretty, tasteful *kanzashi*—a long hairpin—is placed on the left side of the head, thus completing that part of a *guecha's* toilette.

The sallow complexion characteristic of the race is despised by the womankind of Japan, and all women are given to "painting" themselves. With us such a custom is not uncommon, but it is disregarded by most sensible women. In Japan it is part of the ordinary woman's daily toilette. A thick layer of white chalk is first smeared with a soft brush over the face, neck, shoulders, arms, and hands; then the pretty *mouseme*, dipping her first finger in red paint, gently rubs this on her cheeks, her temples, and over the upper eyelids. The middle finger is the "black brush," and adds sentiment to the expression by blackening under the eyes; and sometimes when the eyebrows are not shaved it is also used to accentuate them. A piece of burnt cork is often used as a substitute for black paint. The fourth finger has no occupation, but the little finger is for finishing touches, brightening up the mouth with carmine, and adding a bit of gold on the lower lip. A *guecha* paints herself to a much greater extent than other women, and with brighter colours. As to her moral qualities, a *guecha* is usually not immoral enough to be called "fast," yet too fast to be qualified as "moral." Their music and posturing have a great charm for Japanese; and when money is made, a good quantity of it goes to keeping up these feminine musicians and their establishments.

To show how enterprising and Americanised the Nemuro people are, I shall ask the reader's forgiveness for again relating a personal experience which at the time greatly amused me.

I was in the midst of my simple Japanese dinner in the Jamaruru tea-house, when four youths entered my room and offered to shake hands with me—a most unusual thing with Japanese. One of them handed me his card, on which I read, "K. Sato, *Nemuro Shimbun*" (Nemuro newspaper).

"Oh," I said in Japanese, "you have even a newspaper at Nemuro."

"Yes," answered in English one of his friends, a Mr. Yuasa, handing me his own card.

"You speak English, then, Mr. Yuasa?"

"Yes."

"Can I offer you and your friends anything to drink or to eat?"

"Yes."

"What will you have?"

"Yes."

"Will you have some *sake*?"

"No, no; I come to speak to you."

"Thank you."

"No, no; I come to *take your life* in Nemuro newspaper. Please speak where come? How old? Where go?"

When I had sufficiently recovered from the shock of his announcement that he had come to take my life, and understood what he meant by it, I had a most pleasant conversation in English with him, and in Japanese with the others. Mr. Yuasa's English improved as his shyness wore off, showing that he had a very fair knowledge of the language. The interview lasted many hours, continually interrupted by the *nara honto* and the *sajo deska*—"really" and "indeed" of my visitors—while notes were taken by the editor and his staff. They finally departed, and early the next morning I received the following letter:—

> "SIR,—I long that you will correspond to me any events wherever you have met them in your journey when you are not so awful busy, as I have to translate and write on the Nemuro *News*. I meet the first time here, and I hope to have your friendly favor hitherto, and thanks for your kindness I have received ever, believe me, your humble servant, F. YUASA."

The same afternoon the editor and his staff called again, accompanied by the two Mr. Nakamuras, the richest merchants in Nemuro, and they insisted on giving me a European dinner. After my experience at Otsu as regards European cooking by Japanese, I was rather loth to accept their kind invitation, but I had to yield. The feast began with biscuits and jam,[31] and the soup was brought immediately after; then vegetables were followed by roast chicken, and the latter by salad and fried fish. With the exception of the somewhat inverted order of the courses, this time it was actually a European dinner, and even well-cooked; but my hosts were seen at a great disadvantage when using a knife and fork. As for the anatomy of the chicken, that was decidedly their weakest point. Those of the party who were shy gave up the carving as a bad job; the bolder only fought bravely; and every now and then a knife gave a terrible squeak on the plate, and half a leg, a wing, or a carcase was fired right across the table into one's plate, if not in one's face, or on one's lap.

"*Honto taihen muskashi*"—"Really it is very difficult"—said the wit of the party, helplessly putting down his knife and fork after trying to separate the two parts of a wing. "This bird's bones have lost all their joints in the cooking."

My hosts were extremely kind, and were, besides, so clever and bright that I enjoyed their good company immensely. At the same time I gained from them valuable information as regards the neighbouring country and the Kurile Islands.

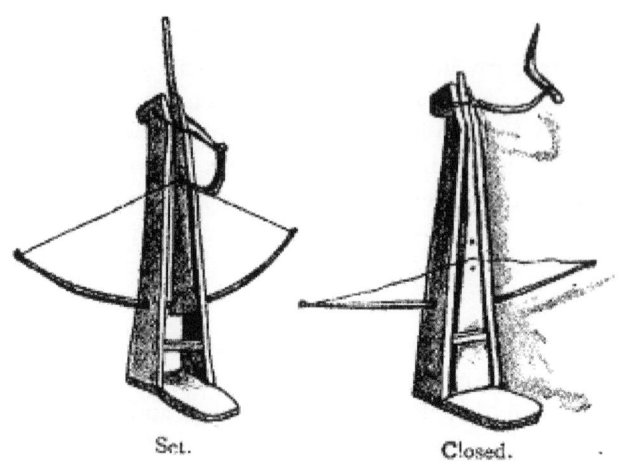

Set.   Closed.

SEMI-AINU RAT TRAP.

AINU WOMAN OF KURILE ISLANDS.

CHAPTER XII.
The Kurile Islands.

From Nemuro I put to sea in a miserable little Japanese craft—a kind of tug-boat—which once or twice a year goes to the principal islands of the Kurile group, and brings back their products to Nemuro. It is needless to say that I was the only passenger on board, though it is fair to add that the saloon was large enough to "accommodate" two, but not more. As for the only cabin, it had two berths, one over the other, but no available space for dressing or undressing, which therefore had to be got through outside, unless it was to be done by instalments, lying down in the berth itself. I shall spare my readers a minute description of this "ocean clipper," her tonnage, and horse-power, and I shall not attempt to narrate the many disadvantages of travelling in a ship engaged in the fish-manure, dried-fish, and sea-weed trade. These three very strongly scented articles speak for themselves without the need of words.

The Kuriles are the islands which stretch like a row of beads from the most north-easterly coast of Yezo to the most southerly point of Kamschatka. They extend from 145° to 158° longitude east of Greenwich, and between 42° and 51° latitude north.

The archipelago forms part of the Japanese Empire, having been exchanged by Russia not many years ago for the southern half of Saghalien Island, then belonging to Japan. This group of islands is characterised mainly by the great extent of its volcanic rocks and tertiaries, showing marked evidence that it is only a continuation of the volcanic mountain-range forming the backbone of Yezo, and extending from Yubaridake, in the upper Ishikari province, to Cape Shiretoko; which volcanic region embraces a large portion of the Tokachi, Kitami, and Nemuro provinces. In this chain of islands there are many beautiful volcanic cones, especially in Kunashiri and Etorofu. Iron, copper, and other metal veins are found in small quantities in tuffs and andesites, but more important here, moreover, are the large sulphur accumulations near and in craters, both extinct and active; as on Mount Rahush, in Kunashiri, and the Ichibishinai, in Etorofu, the largest island of the Kuriles. At Pontoo, in Kunashiri, sulphur bubbles out from the bottom of a volcanic lake, which is probably an extinct crater.

Beside being rich in minerals, the larger islands of the Kuriles abound in game; but fishing is the main industry practised by the sparse population of these rugged regions. The origin of the word "Kuriles" is not certain, but in all probability it is from the Russian *kuril*, smoke, as there are many active volcanoes in the islands. The more poetical Japanese call them *Chishima*, or the "Thousand Islands," meaning that they are numberless, and the *nonchalant*

Ainu of Yezo profess entire ignorance as to their existence, and only some of the better informed give them the name of *Krafto*, by which they really mean Sakhalin. The hairy people are emphatically poor geographers, and have but little faculty for locating islands or any other places. In fact, how could they, having no maps, and no idea even of what a map is? The Chishima group and the island of Yezo, with all the smaller islands along and near its coast, when taken collectively, are called by the Japanese "The Hokkaido." The nearest of the Kuriles to Yezo is Kunashiri, and south of it lies the smaller island of Shikotan; then comes Etorofu, the largest of the group; then Urup; after this a number of unhabited islets, reefs, and rocks form a barrier separating the Otkoshk Sea from the Pacific Ocean. Shimushir, at the south-western end of this barrier, and Onekotan, at the north-eastern, are the two largest, Shimushir being about thirty miles in length and four or five wide, and Onekotan about twenty-five miles long and eight wide. Paromushir (a corruption of the Ainu words *poro*, large, and *mushiri*, island) is the last island of the group. It has a large reef on its south-east coast, and is divided by a channel six or seven miles wide from Cape Lopatka, the most southern point of the Kamschatkan peninsula. Paromushir is about twice the size of Urup, and is very mountainous, with rugged cliffs of volcanic formation, and high picturesque peaks, bearing the same characteristics as the scenery in Etorofu and Kunashiri, and also of Kamschatka. I have mentioned this last island, as it is of some interest, being the most northern point of the Japanese empire; and also to a certain extent it is interesting from a geological point of view, but, as far as I know, it is not inhabited now, and the few Kurilsky Ainu who formerly lived there migrated further south from one island to another, till Shimushir[32] and Urup[33] afforded them a more hospitable home. However, they were not to live there for long, for the Japanese Government, asserting that subjects of the empire who chose to live so far could not be properly looked after, sent the small ship on which I was now travelling on a mission with orders to bring them all down to the formerly deserted island of Shikotan. The orders had to be obeyed; and reluctantly setting fire to the huts which they were about to abandon and never to see again, ninety souls, all that remained of that nomad tribe of Ainu, were embarked and carried into exile at Shikotan. The quiet life on the Shikotan rocks little suits the roaming disposition of the Kurilsky Ainu; and though even formerly they were rapidly dying out, the rate of mortality has increased since their exile. Having thus verified the fact that of the "Thousand Islands" of the Chishima group only three are inhabited, I shall avoid giving a monotonous description of each bare-looking islet and rock, and I shall land my readers at Shikotan, on a visit to the Kurilsky Ainu, who are important to us in connection with the Ainu of Yezo.

It was early in the morning when I looked out of the porthole, and by a fine moonlight saw that we were close to the coast. Huge cliffs and peaks, ending in a sharp point, some converging towards one another, some standing upright against the whitish cold sky, were reflected in the smooth water under the lee of the island. The moon, surrounded by a yellowish halo, shone bright over the rugged scene, giving delicate bluish tints to all the shadows; while the water, disturbed and cut by the prow of our craft, rose in gentle waves, pursuing one another, as if running for a place of refuge in the mysterious dark shadows of the cliffs. So weird, so enchanted and wild was the scene, that I jumped out of my stuffy bunk and went on deck. There I stood, notwithstanding the cold, gazing at the gigantic overhanging black rocks, at the precipices, crevices, and natural openings through which now and then the radiant moon peeped, covering the dark green water with a long undulating streak of silver dashes. There I stood, listening to the voices of the waves, which rippled on the shingle, contemplating this strange and poetic work of nature. I am certain that if sirens there ever were in this world, their home must have been among the whimsical and *bizarre* rocks of Shikotan Island. The old "tub" on which I was "ploughing the waves" moved slowly through this heavenly spectacle of ever-increasing beauty. When the sun rose, enchantment was added to enchantment. The cold bluish colour of the rocks became gradually warmer; and, as the light grew stronger, the tops of the cliffs turned into a mass of brilliant colours. Nature was waking slowly from her torpid sleep, and, in the freshness of the morning, a light breeze, caressing the shore, brought with it the smell of land.

The captain, a Japanese, informed me that we should soon enter the harbour of Shikotan, and, pointing to some huge pillars, said that was the entrance. We drew nearer and nearer to it, and the nearer we drew the more I became convinced that the captain was under an hallucination. I could only see rock after rock, huge pillar after huge pillar; but no entrance whatever.

"We are just going in," said the captain, laughing at my astonishment, and he gave orders to the quartermaster at the wheel to steer straight for one of the pillars. We were but a few yards from it when our craft was made to swing rapidly on her starboard side, and we turned round a gigantic shoulder of rock, to find ourselves in a narrow channel. One minute later we were in a pretty circular harbour, surrounded by high peaks—in fact, a kind of "fiord." The access to this harbour is certainly difficult to find, but when you are fairly in, it is seen to afford a well-sheltered anchorage. It has more the appearance of a small mountain lake than that of a sea-harbour; and undoubtedly it is a submerged crater. It is perfectly circular, and very deep, but not of large capacity. Directly opposite the entrance, on the shore, is a small narrow valley, on which is situated the village of the Kurilsky Ainu. Four men rowed me ashore, and I went to the village.

When the Japanese imported these Kurilsky Ainu to Shikotan, they allowed them to build their huts in their own way; but this done, a railing with a gate was erected, closing the entrance of the valley which overlooks the harbour, thus preventing the poor wretches from abandoning the island to resume their migratory habits, and return to their more northern homes. Inside this gate two rows of huts, exactly similar to those of the Yezo Ainu, have been constructed by the exiles. There are sixteen huts altogether, and not a single one of them is built over a pit. In Chapter IX, I have fully explained the characteristics and mode of living, which leaves no doubt as to these people being proper Ainu, and not pit-dwellers, as some have asserted; though of course their type is slightly modified by external conditions—a common occurrence in all races. Take a Londoner, a provincial, and a seaman, and though they be all three Englishmen, one will have a washed-out look, the other will be healthy and strong, but not so sturdy, wiry, and weather-beaten as the sailor. The same natural process is at work with this tribe of Ainu. They conform their life according to circumstances and places; and though they possess the same general characteristics as the rest of the Ainu, in some small details they cannot but differ from them.

Shikotan was a deserted island previous to these poor wretches being transplanted there by the Japanese Government. It does not abound in game, like Shimushir, Urup, or Poromushir, whence they were taken.

SHIKOTAN AINU.

The story of this tribe of Ainu is a sad one. Hunting, sealing, and fishing were their only aims in life, their only pastimes, the only things they lived for. At Shikotan they have none of these things. There is no big game; the only animal found being a beautiful species of white long-tailed fox. There are no large rivers at Shikotan; there is hardly any vegetation, and the whole island is nothing but a mass of barren rocks.

The food of the Kurilsky Ainu consisted chiefly of meat of bear and seals, berries, and eggs of sea-birds. They were a migratory people, and in their small cranky canoes they often crossed from one island to another, carrying with them all their property, consisting of skin garments and fishing and hunting implements, these latter the same as those employed by other Ainu. The dress of the men is shaped like a short tunic, made of sea-birds' skins, with the feathers inside. Some of the smart ones are trimmed with seal, and they are worn fastened round the waist with a girdle of sealskin or a belt of sea-lion hide, often ornamented with molten lead buttons or Chinese cash. The women's garment is much longer, and reaches nearly to the feet; it falls loosely, and has long sleeves covering the hands; it is fastened with a girdle in bad weather, and the gown is then pulled up to the knee, showing the long yellow boots. When carrying water or working this is also done, as it gives greater freedom to the limbs, making walking and all movement much easier. A red, yellow, or brightly-coloured handkerchief, of Russian manufacture, is tied round the neck and another round the back of the head, and this makes the women look like Italian peasants. As the gown is worn usually loose it has the identical shape of a dressing-gown; it is ornamented with yellow feathers of puffins round the neck and the edge. Both men and women wear either moccasins, or long boots made of sealskin, with the fur inside, or else they wear salmon-skin boots, like the Ainu of Yezo. No woman that I saw at Shikotan had a moustache tattooed round her lips, or any tattoo marks on her arms. Very few of them wore earrings, though all had the ears bored for that purpose, and had worn them. The earrings which they possessed were mostly strings of coral beads and metal ornaments of Russian manufacture, which, like the brightly-coloured handkerchiefs, they had received in bartering with the crew of a sealing schooner. Since they have been at Shikotan the men have been presented with old caps and overcoats, similar to those of the Japanese police. Previous to this, however, when the Kuriles were under the rigid Russian *régime*, the Kurilsky Ainu men were compelled to trim their hair and beard, which was the first step taken by the priests of the Coptic Church in Christianising these nomadic barbarians. When this hair-dressing order was complied with, as the first link of the chain, the Coptic creed was enforced on them, and the barbarous Kurilsky Ainu became well-trimmed orthodox Christians.

At Shikotan, as it is, fishing on a small scale is their main occupation, praying the next, and Jacko, the chief of the village, is the high priest. Jacko's predecessor, in fulfilling the duties of this high post, was a man who had dropped his Ainu name, and had been baptized as Alexandrovitch. His house is now occupied by Jacko. It is the first on the right-hand side when the village is entered from the harbour side, and it is larger than any of the others; it is built of wood instead of rushes and reeds. The interior is divided into two rooms, and in the second are three stands, the middle one of which has a cross on it. On each of these stands is a Russian Bible, with images hanging on the page-marks. Several rough stools and a couple of benches are placed in rows in front of these stands, and on the walls hang two or three Russian religious images. Taken altogether, and compared with other Ainu huts, Jacko's chapel had quite a stately appearance.

Just as the Ainu of Yezo have partly acquired the Japanese language, the Kurilsky Ainu have learned to talk Russian, besides speaking an Ainu dialect.

On Sundays, or on any day which Jacko thinks is a Sunday, the chief reads the mass before a congregation of the other fifty-nine hairy Christians of the Russian Orthodox Church; he does not spare them a sermon, which sometimes lasts half the day, and his audience are most attentive and well behaved. None of them would think of leaving church before service is over; but one detail in which these hairy Christians are not yet fully Christianised is, that no collection plate is ever sent round! The Kurilsky Ainu have undoubtedly accepted the form of their adopted religion, but I rather doubt whether they have fallen in with the principle. Their former barbarian ideas and superstitions are still well rooted in their brain, and each individual was a curious and enviable combination of a perfect heathen and a thorough Christian, according to what suited him or her better at the time being. In other words, they believed in two diametrically opposed principles, one of which fitted in with every phase of their life when the other was deficient.

As many as ninety people, all told, were landed at Shikotan, but thirty had already succumbed when I visited the island. A graveyard on a hill on the west side of the village was indeed a sad reminder of this fact. It will not be long before all the others will pass away, for consumption and rheumatism have a great hold on most of the wretches. In ten years from now, I dare say, not one of the Kurilsky tribe of Ainu will be left on this earth. It is pitiful that the last remains of these independent people will end their days secluded and in exile on the barren rocks of Shikotan.

As it is, they seem to take life easily, and, with a characteristic proper to all nomadic peoples, they make the best of what they can get. They are not shy, and they have dropped the formalities and grand salutations of other Ainu. They are, however, as dirty, especially in their homes. The women dress their hair in small tresses.

 The children wear long gowns similar to those of the women, and one or two of the children I saw had very fair hair. As will be seen by the illustrations, some of the men and women possess good features, more resembling those of European races than those of Mongolian type. They are gentle and quiet, like all other Ainu. They are submissive, and resigned to their sad fate.

The island of Skikotan is almost circular in shape, and it has one or two small anchorages on its north coast. I judged its diameter to be about twelve or thirteen miles. Etorofu and Kunashiri, though much larger in size, are of less interest to us in connection with the Ainu, as most of that race found there migrate from Yezo during the fishing season; therefore, nothing is to be added about them.

Etorofu is a long, narrow, but irregular island, over one hundred miles in length, and varying in breadth from five or six to twenty miles. It is very mountainous, and has some bold, rugged scenery, owing to its volcanic formation. Etorofu is by far the largest island of the Kurile group, and it possesses many safe anchorages, especially on its north-west coast, where several mountainous capes branch off the narrow strip of land, and afford small ships a fairly safe harbourage from west and south-westerly winds. Unfortunately, however, they are open to northerly and north-east gales, during the prevalence of which, should a ship happen to be cruising about in those latitudes, she would have to run for a shelter to the south-east coast. The south-east coast is not peopled, with the exception of a very few huts near Moyorotake, or "Bear Bay," at its most south-eastern point. A better shelter, however, is to be found in the bay, nearly in the middle of the island, on the shores of which are a few huts at Onembets and Imotsuto. Most of the coast is deserted, and the south-east portion is very rocky, huge cliffs, with high richly-coloured mountains in the background, ending like an impassable wall into the sea. Where the island is narrower there are some low terraces with scrub bamboo and stunted trees. Larch is found in Etorofu, while it is seldom found in Yezo. Heather-like plants are also indigenous in Etorofu, and cranberry bushes are frequent near the coast. From Betoya or Bettobu Bay down to its most south-western point Etorofu is all mountainous, with the exception of a small valley near Rubets. It is along the banks of the Bettobu River, in that small valley and on those terraces, that the numerous pits of the Koro-pok-kuru are found, and also at Rupets, further south on the same coast. This, however, I have already explained in connection with the pit-dwellers. The two small fishing-stations above mentioned are respectively under the lee of the headlands ending in Cape Ikahasonets and Notoro Cape. On the first headland the mountain of Tsiriju rises to a great altitude. The largest fishing-station is at Shana, on the western side of this headland, and further north, besides Bettobu, is the small station of Shibets. South-west of Shana one finds Rubets, Furubets, Oitoi, and Naibo, the latter in the bay of the same name. There are five lakes in Etorofu, two of which are between Shana and Bettobu, one near Rubets, the other close to Naibo; the fifth is a very small one, fifteen or sixteen miles north-east of Bettobu. The country has a rugged look, and in some places, as near Rubets, where the volcanic mountain masses leave space for low terraces the scrub-bamboo is very thick, as in Yezo, and small and stunted trees form the chief vegetation. Larch is more common on the north-west coast than on the south-east. Good timber is rather scarce in Etorofu, but a fair quantity of it is to be found inland, and also at the south-western portion of the island about Naipo.

Accumulations of sulphur are found at Ichibishinai, and there is an active volcano south-east of Bettobu, besides the beautiful volcanic cone of Atzosa, three or four thousand feet above sea-level. All this volcanic mountain mass, with its warmly-tinted peaks, bears the characteristics of the central portion of Yezo; and there seems to be little doubt that all this row of islands, with the frequent submerged craters and volcanic cones, is nothing but the continuation of the volcanic zone in Yezo. The main resource of Etorofu is the fishing. Four different kinds of salmon and salmon-trout are found, one similar to the salmon common in Yezo, the others somewhat differently marked. Salmon is extremely plentiful, and in July and August enormous catches are made, especially at the mouths of the rivers, where the fish are closely packed together.

The Pico Strait, between Etorofu and Kunashiri, is about fourteen miles wide, and a strong current from the Okhotsk Sea passes through it, causing the sea to break in heavy tide-rips and overfalls similar to those observed in the La Perouse Strait, between Yezo and Sakhalin. Similar tide-rips are observed also in the channel between Etorofu and Urup, but, being much wider (about twenty-four miles), they seem there less formidable.

Kunashiri is the next largest island in the Kuriles after Etorofu. It is about sixty-five miles long, and very narrow; varying from three to eight miles in width. The north-east portion is somewhat wider, and extremely mountainous. The highest peak of this mountain range is the Tcha-Tcha-Nobori (the old-old-mountain), which is said to be about seven thousand five hundred feet above the level of the sea. From this volcano starts a chain of hills—some pyramidal in form, others somewhat rounder at the top—which forms the backbone of the island. Two more active volcanoes besides the Tcha-Tcha are on the south-west portion of Kunashiri, but they do not rise to a very great altitude. On Horanaho or Rausu volcano sulphur accumulations are found, and at Pontoo (small lake) sulphur bubbles out from the lake bottom, and seems to be worked with profit. The Tcha-Tcha-Nobori is curiously shaped. It is like a large cone cut about half-way up in a section, to which a smaller cone has been attached, leaving a wide ring right round. It is extremely picturesque, and a worthy finish to the strange outline of Kunashiri Island.

Vegetation and products are the same as in Etorofu. Salmon is plentiful, and a few fishing-stations are spread out here and there at long intervals on the coast. As in Etorofu, the population of Kunashiri migrates there from Yezo during the fishing season, and leaves the island almost deserted in winter. The strait separating it from Yezo is only ten or twelve miles wide. Bears and foxes are said to be very numerous in all the larger islands of the Kuriles, and seals are captured in large quantities during the winter months, more especially in the islands nearer Kamschatka. Small game, as ducks, snipes, and sandpipers, is abundant. Besides the ruggedness and strange aspect of its numerous volcanic peaks, the bareness and the loneliness of the coast, there is nothing in the Kurile group to entice the sightseer and the pleasure-seeker to a cruise among the islands. The geologist and zoologist, however, would find in the Kuriles a very rough but very interesting field for their investigations, and a "good shot," who does not mind a self-sacrificing and lonely life, would find some good sport among the bears, especially in Kunashiri and Etorofu.

WOMAN OF THE KURILE ISLANDS

ABASHIRI ISLAND.

CHAPTER XIII.
On the East and North-East Coast—From Nemuro to Shari-Mombets.

I did not remain long at Nemuro after my return from the Kuriles; in fact, I remained only a few hours, and again my baggage was lashed to the pack-saddle, again I was perched on the top of this instrument of torture, and soon was rapidly moving north towards the inhospitable coast of the Okhotsk Sea.

The first few days of the lonely life of a peripatetic Robinson Crusoe are unmistakably disagreeable, but after that initiation there is no doubt that it is a fascinating life. I was more than glad when the gay Nemuro was out of sight, and the noise and rumble of semi-civilisation out of hearing. The editor and seven gentlemen of Nemuro accompanied me for a few miles—then I was left to myself and my own resources. Crossing the Onnetto River, the outlet of a large lagoon of the same name, I passed through Nishibets and then Bitskai, where in former days the Japanese had established a salmon-canning factory, which proved a failure, owing to the incapacity of its directors and workmen. Salmon is very abundant in the Nishibets River, and a well-managed canning factory would be a great success. About ten or eleven miles north of Bitskai a peculiar peninsula stretches out from north-east to south-west, which affords a shelter for small junks from northerly winds. It is called Noshike, and is not more than a few feet above the sea-level. The soil all along is very marshy, and the numerous little rivulets and rivers are extremely troublesome to cross. My pony was continually sinking into and struggling out of mud-holes, into which it had fallen when wading across these small watercourses, sometimes not more than a few feet wide. I pushed on as far as Shimbets, where there are only a shed and a couple of Ainu huts inhabited by half-castes. I had to put up here for the night, and by the light of a wick burning in a large oyster-shell filled with fish-oil I wrote a few notes in my diary. The fleas in that house were something appalling. The next morning I had some fun with a wild pony, which I received in exchange for the tired animal I had brought.

"Nobody can get on him," said the Ainu half-caste, "but if you think you can ride him he will go like the wind."

It took all hands in the small village to get the pack-saddle and baggage on to his back, and after we had tied him to a post and lashed his fore legs together I mounted. By instalments he was untied, let loose, and then afforded us some real fun. He revolved, bucked, kicked, stood on his hind legs, and did his very best to bite my legs and knock me off the saddle. A small fence was kicked and smashed into a thousand bits, and he even attempted to enter the huts—anything to get rid of his rider; but he did not succeed. His next trick was to plunge into the river close by, and when he reached the middle to shake himself violently. He then came out on the other side, and, turning his head, saw as well as felt that I was still on his back; then he neighed as if in great distress, and bolted. He galloped along the small track, and really did go "like the wind." As a punishment I made him keep up the pace even when he was tired of his contumacy, and in less than no time I reached Shibets, ten miles distant from where I had started.

Shibets is a village of one hundred Japanese houses and twenty Ainu huts. The Ainu here have almost altogether adopted Japanese clothes, as well as something of the Japanese style of living. The river which goes by the same name is notable for the quantity and good quality of salmon caught in it, and it is the best salmon-fishing river on the north-east coast of Yezo. Herrings are also abundant, but not to the same extent as on the south-east coast. A peculiarity of the river is that before entering the sea it turns sharply south and runs along a bank of sand and mud, which is growing larger every year, which shows that a current from the Okhotsk Sea must travel down in that direction through the strait between Kunashiri and Yezo. The same peculiarity is noticeable in nearly all the rivers of the north-east coast.

From Shibets to Wembets the track is fairly even, but from Wembets round Cape Shiretoko it is in many places impassable even on foot. The Peninsula, ending in Cape Shiretoko, is a mass of high volcanic mountains towards the interior, while scabrous cliffs and huge rocks fringe the line of coast. However, from Shibets there is a small mountain track inland which brings the traveller across to the north-east coast near Shari. The track was through beautiful forests of pine trees, oak, birch, and elm, and during the first few miles it is on almost level ground. After that, hill after hill is ascended and descended, and one goes ever onwards at a higher altitude, until Rubets, a small shed, is reached. From here the track follows a zig-zag direction till it reaches the summit of the mountain range, and one then begins to descend on the other side. From the summit there is a lovely view of beautiful blue mountains in the distant west, one of which is called Oakan, and the other Moyokan. The mountainous part of the track from Igiani, three miles from Shibets, as far as the north-east coast, reminded me much of the scenery in Switzerland, with its rapid and limpid fresh-water rivers, thickly-wooded country, and green grass, which last was replaced here by an undergrowth of scrub bamboo. When I went across this mountain pass the rain was pouring in torrents, and the road, such as it was, being very slippery and heavy, I only reached the north-east coast at dark. The moon would not rise till late, there were heavy black clouds, and I was more than puzzled how to find my way.

To add to my bad luck, my pony this time was a sorry beast, with his back a mass of sores. I was simply drenched with the rain that never ceased. Now and then, by the blinding flash of lightning, I could see a long stretch of sand

and a line of sand-hills; I could also see the reeds bending low under the squalls, and then everything was darkness again. I was leading my tired beast, and dragging him along as well as I could. Every few yards the wretched creature collapsed, and it took a lot of petting, caressing, encouraging and beating to make him get up again. I had ridden and walked about fourteen hours in the rain, and was nearly frozen to death.

Since I had got out of the forest a bitterly cold north wind chilled me through and through, and added the last touch to my weariness and discomfort. Again the pony fell, and all my efforts to make him get up were useless. The storm, if anything, seemed to increase in violence, while my own strength was decreasing every minute. I lay down by the side of the pony, trying to warm myself by his heat, and, shivering and rattling my teeth together, I tried to go to sleep.

A couple of hours were spent in this way, and when the moon rose I could see a little clearer. I climbed with hands and feet on to the sand-hills, and I fancied I saw some dark spots in the distance. Could they be Shari? First one end of my whip, then the other, was reduced into pulp on my pony's back, and with a great effort he again stood on all four legs. I had to support the wretch all the way, as you would a drunken man, and we went at the rate of less than a mile an hour. The spots grew bigger and bigger, and took the shape of huts.

"Hem, hem, hem, hem!" I called out at the first hut, while three or four dogs barked furiously and went for my legs. "Will you let a stranger sleep here to-night?"

"This is no house for strangers; go elsewhere!" answered a drowsy hoarse voice from inside.

"May you be kept—hot!" said I, in pure Ainu fashion, though in my heart I attached quite a different meaning to the sentence from that which the hairy people give it; and wearily I pulled myself together and passed on.

A shadow crept out of one of the huts, and thanks to that shadow I found a shelter for the night. There are fifty Ainu huts at Shari, and ten Japanese, with an Ainu population of about one hundred souls. The Ainu here have adopted Japanese clothes, and many of them eat Japanese food when they can get it. The Ainu women of Shari are exceedingly pretty, as they do not tattoo the long moustache across their faces, like other Ainu. Some of them have a small semicircular tattoo on the upper lip, which is not very displeasing to the eye; and in some cases is even becoming. The girls have also given up tattooing their arms. The men are much taller than the Ainu men of other regions, and they seem to be rather ill-natured. Japanese blood can be detected in many of them, and that may account for it. While the women are prettier, the men have repulsive faces, possessing all the characteristics of purely criminal types.

One young fellow who sat for me was the very image of Robespierre in his worst moments, and an old man who sat for me afterwards would, according to Phrenology, prove to be a murderer of the first water. This gentleman was a troublesome sitter, and excelled in making the most awful faces, which were accompanied by sounds imitating those of wild beasts. The Shari Ainu build their storehouses with cylindrical roofs, similar to those of their brethren on the Kutcharo Lake.

After the heavy storm of the previous night the weather cleared up for the rest of the day, and the sunset, reflected in the limpid waters of the river, was simply magnificent. On the other side, sheltered by the sand-hills, were a few Ainu huts standing out against the brilliant red and yellow sky, and here and there a large fish jumped out of the water, leaving circle after circle of concentric rings to break for the moment the reflection in the water.

From Shari to Abashiri the road is for some distance among trees, mostly fir and spruce, and then the Tobuts Lake is reached, half of which is a mere marsh. It is picturesquely situated, and I followed its borders for about three miles, having the sea on one side, the lake on the other. The track was easy and mostly on sand. At the outlet of the lake into the sea is the Ainu village of Tobuts, access to which is to be had only by boat, as the river is extremely deep, and its current very swift.

In the proximity of Tobuts another and smaller lake, the Opoto, with its short and winding estuary, is on the left of the traveller, while a long way ahead the Abashiri rocks stand high on the horizon. A few Ainu huts are scattered along the coast, and some of them have peculiarly shaped storehouses. They are small, built entirely of wood, and roofed with shingles. Some have two floors, and in this case, though built on piles, the first floor is only a few inches above the ground. The "mat" was supplanted by a wooden door at the entrance of the storehouse.

The Abashiri cliffs are grand, and from a distance have all the appearance of, though they are not in reality, basaltic rocks. They are scarred, riven, and fractured in all directions, as if by excessive heat. The upper portion of the cliffs is of a beautiful grey-whitish colour, blending into yellow and red at their warm brown bases. The small cylindrical islet which I give in the illustration is on the north side of this cliff, and is of the same volcanic formation. It has certain traces of sulphur as a further evidence of its origin. Flocks of sea-gulls, penguins, and cormorants have chosen this island for their abode.

Abashiri is the only place on the north-east coast which may eventually be of some importance, as it has a fair anchorage for small craft under the lee of the islet and outstretching cliff. No other place on the north-east coast possesses such an advantage. On the Shiretoko Peninsula sulphur accumulations are found at Itashibeoni; but, unfortunately, the want of a safe harbour, the ruggedness of the coast, and the lack of drinkable water in the vicinity, are all facts which make it improbable that it could be worked with profit for some years to come. The Ainu at Abashiri are repulsive creatures, especially the men, and have more the appearance of wild beasts than human beings. Their faces are almost square, the mouth large, with narrow lips, the ends of which converge towards the ears. The nose is short and stumpy, they have very heavy eyebrows, and the eyes are almost lost under the shadow of their projecting forehead.

Ponies are scarce and bad along this coast, and the further north one goes the more difficult the travelling becomes; the huts are rarer; the human beings more uncouth and solitary. The north-east coast is a region of swamps, lagoons, and quicksand rivers.

Not far inland from Abashiri there is a large lagoon, the Abashiri-ko; then, a few miles further north, another as large—the Notoro-ko. The Abashiri Lake finds an outlet in a river which goes by the same name of, and falls into the pretty Bay of Abashiri; but the Notoro-ko, as well as the larger lagoon of Saruma-ko, which one comes upon after having passed the two villages of Tukoro and Tobuts, open directly into the sea. The strong current and the tide often block the entrance of these lagoons, and the rising water finds an outlet in a different spot. These lagoons are separated from the sea by a long and narrow strip of sand-hill; and crossing the outlet always involves great danger if the unwary traveller does not choose the right moment. The tide creating a great inequality of level between the sea and the lake, it follows that at the opening of the lagoon the water either throws itself from the sea into the lagoon, or *vice versâ*, according to the ebb or flow, and makes a kind of whirlpool. The Saruma Lake being much larger than any of the others, while its mouth is much smaller, and underlaid with quicksands, the danger is even greater, and the safest way is always to get across in a boat at slack water. The Saruma Lake is about fifteen miles in length and from two to three miles wide. Its water is salt, and large oyster-banks are found in it. It is also a favourite resort for seal and mallard. In winter they can be killed in great numbers, but in the warmer months they are shy, and very difficult to approach. The south-western shore of the lake is thickly wooded, and has as a background a long range of high mountains with smaller mountains in front of it.

AN AINU BELLE.

At Tobuts, a small village of a few huts, situated at the mouth of the Saruma lagoon, I halted for the night. There was a change in my diet that day, and I was entertained, or rather I entertained myself, to an oyster supper. They were enormous oysters, similar to those found at Akkeshi, but not very palatable. However, I was in luck that day, and not only did I have this oyster supper, but I actually was the hero of a tender little idyll. In this country surprises never come alone, and while I was sketching in the twilight to pass away the time, a tall slim figure of a girl came out of one of the huts. She had slipped her arms out of her robe, leaving the latter to hang from the girdle, and her breasts, arms, and the lower half of her legs were uncovered. She was pretty and quaint with her tattooed arms and a semicircular black spot on her upper lip. She walked a few steps forward, and when she saw me she stopped. She looked at me and I looked at her. Hers, with her soft eyes, was one of those looks which a man feels right through his body, notwithstanding all the self-control he may possess. There she stood, a graceful silhouette, with a bucket made of tree-bark in one hand and a vine-tree rope in the other, her supple figure almost motionless, and her eyes fixed on me. She was the most lovely Ainu girl I had ever come across, and not nearly so hairy as most of them. Indeed, in that soft twilight, and her wavy long hair blown by the fresh breeze, she was a perfect dream.

"Wakka!" ("Water!") cried an angry old voice from inside the hut, interrupting the beginning of our romance, and she sadly went to the brook, filled her bucket with water, and took it into the hut. It was only a few seconds before she reappeared, and came closer, and I finished the sketch somewhat hurriedly.

"Let me see the tattoo on your arm," I asked her, and to my surprise the pretty maid took my hand in both her own, gave me one of those looks that I shall never forget, and her head fell on my shoulder. She clutched my hand tightly, and pressed it to her chest, and a force stronger than myself brought her and myself to the neighbouring forest. There we wandered and wandered till it grew very dark; we sat down, we chattered, we made love to each other; then we returned. I would not have mentioned this small episode if her ways of flirting had not been so extraordinary and funny. Loving and biting went together with her. She could not do the one without doing the other. As we sat on a stone in the semi-darkness she began by gently biting my fingers, without hurting me, as affectionate dogs often do to their masters; she then bit my arm, then my shoulder, and when she had worked herself up into a passion she put her arms round my neck and bit my cheeks. It was undoubtedly a curious way of making love, and when I had been bitten all over, and was pretty tired of the new sensation, we retired to our respective homes.

In the evening, as I was writing my diary by the light of one of the oyster-shell primitive lamps, somebody noiselessly crept by my side. I turned my head round. It was she! She grew more and more sentimental as it grew later, and she bestowed on me caresses and bites in profusion. Kissing, apparently, was an unknown art to her. The old woman, in whose house I was, slept soundly all through this, as old women generally do on such occasions. By the mysterious light of the dying wick, casting heavy shadows, which marked her features strongly, with her jet-black wild hair fading away into the black background, with her passionate eyes, and her round, statue-like arms, the girl was more like a strange fairy than a human being.

I sketched her twice in pencil, and the wick—that wretched wick!—grew feeble, and, for the lack of oil, began to dwindle away. I persuaded her to return to her hut, and with a few "bites" my hairy maid and I parted.

The morning came, and I was up early. In the vicinity of the huts I found three Koro-pok-kuru pits similar to those we have already seen; and previous to arriving at Tobuts I also found a fort belonging to the pre-Ainu race. From Tobuts, continuing my journey north, on the stretch of sand between the water of the sea and that of the Saruma lake the travelling was fairly easy but monotonous. The long chain of mountains on the other side of the lake was magnificent in the morning light. For twenty-two miles this went on; then I had to cross the Yubets River in the picturesque spot where its waters divide before again uniting close to the sea. North of this river there are three more lagoons—the Komuki, the Shibumotzunai, and the Yassuchi, the first two of which have direct estuaries into the sea, generally blocked by drift-sand, and both are as dangerous as the Saruma lagoon when the water unexpectedly overflows. Owing to the heavy rains on the mountains the level of the lakes had risen considerably when I went through, and crossing the mouth of the first in a flat-bottomed boat, I was nearly swamped. The Ainu who was ferrying me across did not lose his presence of mind, and after a long struggle and violent efforts we reached the opposite shore. Yubets is a village of eighteen Ainu and three Japanese huts. The Ainu along these shores are extremely hairy, and some of them have red beards, while others are bald. Near some of their huts you may see cages where foxes and eagles are kept in captivity.

The women, all the way to Soya Cape, the most northern point of Yezo, have given up tattooing a long moustache and their arms. A small semicircular spot, similar to the tattoo of the Shari women, is nevertheless not uncommon. Bears, yellow and black, again are said to be in huge quantities on the thickly-wooded mountains at the back of the Saruma and other lagoons.

The coast is most desolate-looking. One may travel mile after mile without seeing a hut or meeting a single human being. Now and then, when I came to a lonely fisherman's hut, I was civilly treated; and, riding from morn till night, I reached Shari Mombets, where there are forty Ainu huts and about the same number of Japanese fishermen's shanties. It has a small anchorage for small junks only; but, unfortunately, it is not well protected, as the reef of rocks which runs in a north-east direction does not extend far out to sea. I was roughly treated here at first, for some Russian convicts, who had escaped from Sakhalin in an open boat, had been drifted by the current down this coast, and previously to my arrival had landed in the vicinity of this village. They were half starved, and could not speak a word of the language. They had no money and no clothes, and none of the natives seemed willing to help them in any way. Now that the long-wished-for freedom was obtained after years of servitude and chains, the four brave men, who had suffered agonies for days, and had almost miraculously escaped death in the treacherous currents of the Otkoshk Sea, were certainly not to be outwitted by a handful of hard-hearted Japanese or by a pack of hairy Ainu. They begged for food and could not obtain it, so they stole it, and ill-treated some of the natives who interfered. They then disappeared towards the south. When I put in an appearance, all alone and almost in rags, leading and dragging my tired pony, it is not astonishing that the first thing that struck them was that I must be another escaped Russian, "or bad man from Krafto,"[34] as the Ainu called me.

The reception I received was pretty stormy; but when I understood what the matter was which caused the rioting, I set their minds at rest, and, speaking in their own language, told them that the "bad men of Krafto" were my enemies as well as theirs, and that, should I find them, I would punish them. Not only that, but, to make them perfectly at ease, I gave them some little present of money, which turned them at once into friends. As to the Russian convicts, there was no possibility of my finding them, for they were travelling towards the south from this point, and I was moving towards the north, so I was perfectly safe in passing myself off as a kind of supreme judge.

Shari Mombets is a miserable place. In the house where I put up I was received by a young man, but the owner of the house did not show himself. The next morning, however, as I gave much more money than they expected, the landlord was brought to my room to thank me. The poor man suffered from elephantiasis—the wretched disease by which the head and all the limbs of the body assume gigantic proportions. His head was swollen to more than twice its normal size, and had lost its shape; his body was piteously deformed and inflated, his eyes nearly buried in flesh. The weight of his head was such that the cervical vertebræ were scarcely strong enough to support it erect; and when he bowed down in Japanese fashion to thank me and bid me good-bye, I had to run to his help, for he could not get up again. Poor man! And when we reflect that in more civilised countries many people think themselves very ill and suffering when they have a pimple on their nose, or a cold in their head!

SARUMA LAGOON.

AN EAGLE-DISPLAYED SABLE.

CHAPTER XIV.

Along the Lagoons of the North-east Coast—From Shari Mombets to Poronai.

I proceeded north. The Ainu scattered here and there on the coast seemed to be hairier and uglier than any of their inland brethren. Two or three women had already put on their winter fur garments, as the cold weather had begun; and they looked extremely picturesque in them. Most of the huts were uninhabited, and had been abandoned by their owners. The sky was whitish and cold, and here and there along the beach some huge bones of whales had been washed on shore by the tide. Some distance off an outcast horse was attacked by thousands of famished crows. It is not an uncommon occurrence in Yezo. The black scavengers generally attack very young animals, and, flying on the pony's head, peck out its eyes. The pony, frightened, and driven mad by pain, bolts, and in his blind and reckless race either falls down a precipice and is killed outright, or else is driven to the coast by these daring wretches, which continue to peck at him with cruel and ceaseless avidity. There, with its way barred by the waves, tortured to death, and neighing desperately, the helpless beast succumbs, and affords the hungry birds a good meal, while hundreds gathered thick on the body, peck the poor brute to death. Thousands of others sit screaming in long rows round the scene of the fight, attentively watching for the final result, when they too can join in, and experience the joys of sated hunger. Nature can indeed be cruel.

I stopped at a hut. My host was decidedly peculiar. For convenience we shall call him Omangus, which only means a "gone man," or a lunatic. I had heard of him further south, and I was anxious to make his acquaintance. I had not been five minutes in his hut before I perceived that he really was a lunatic. His head was of an abnormally large size; his skull was well developed at the back, with those prominent bumps behind the ears which show great love of eating. His forehead was high, and very slanting; the upper part was wider than near the eyebrows, which were so thick and bushy as nearly to cover the eyes. His nose, with its large nostrils, was stumpy and covered with hair, while his enormous projecting eyes were restless and fierce. His luxuriant moustache and beard matched the thick crop of long black hair which covered his whole body. His legs were short, wiry, with stiff and swollen joints, probably owing to rheumatism. His arms were very long, and his toes were also abnormally long. Altogether he had the appearance of a large orang-outang more than that of a human being. All his movements resembled those of a wild beast, and now and then, when pleased or dissatisfied, he would groan in a way not dissimilar to the growling of a bear. In fact, he was labouring under the belief that he was a wild beast of some sort, and apparently he regarded himself as a "bruin." I never heard him speak or utter words, but whether he was actually dumb or not I was not able to ascertain, as every time I tried to examine his mouth he attempted to bite me. His biting, however, was of a different nature from that of the sweet girl on the Saruma shores, and when he did bite he bit well. One day in a struggle I came off nearly minus two joints of the third finger of my right hand.

I several times attempted to take measurements of his skull and bones, but with no success. Once, as I had got hold of him and was feeling the "bumps" on his skull, he managed to disentangle himself, and grabbed me by the hair, which led to a conflict, and caused me a "très mauvais quart d'heure." We fought desperately, and I was thoroughly "licked"; not, however, before having found out that he had no bump of sensitiveness and none of philoprogenitiveness. He was pleased with his victory, and the hostilities ended. He hopped away cautiously, and I saw him climb on his hands and feet over the cliff near his hut, where he disappeared.

Some hours later I saw the monomaniac stealthily creeping back among the rocks. I was some way from the hut, in a place where he could not see me. He came slowly forward, watching the hut suspiciously, as he evidently thought I was still inside. When he got near he stopped to pick up a large stone, and with it in his right hand he sneaked along towards the hut. He listened, and crept in. I followed immediately after. He was furious when I entered, and tried to escape, but I barred his way. He retreated into a corner, crouched down groaning, and showed signs of impatience. I could see that he was frightened, and I went to him and endeavoured to soothe him; not without success, for he became quieter, and I once more noticed the great power that a stronger will can exercise over a weaker one. As long as I was staring at him he never dared to move, and I could "will" him to do almost anything I wanted by thinking hard that he should do it; but when once I turned my eyes away I had no more control over him.

This is just what happened that day. Thinking that he would keep quiet for some minutes, I got out my palette and brushes in order to take his likeness. I had till then relied on my power of "willing" people, when my host, seizing the opportunity of my turning my head away for one moment, grabbed the stone which he had picked up, and threw it with great force at me. I was hit in the ribs, and was hurt sufficiently to lose my temper. I went for him, and gave him a sound thrashing, which sometimes has more effect than all the "willing" in the world. He became docile after that, and I took him outside and forced him to squat down.

MY HOST, THE MADMAN.

He was restless while I was painting him, and hundreds of half-starved crows, which seemed to be on good terms with my sitter, gathered round him, chatting in their incomprehensible and noisy language. Some of them even flew on to his back and shoulders, and he touched them without their flying away.

I was astounded at the familiarity which existed between the madman and the birds. They seemed to understand each other, and had I only been sufficiently imaginative I might have asserted that I even saw them kissing him. Unfortunately, when the first astonishment was over I understood the reason of the affection on the part of the scavengers, and the whole mystery was unveiled to me. Like all mysteries, the apparently extraordinary friendship between the madman and the black birds turned out to be a plain bit of literal prose, and, I must add, a very disgusting bit. The maniac was covered with vermin, and the affectionate kisses of the crows were not kisses of love or sympathy, but only mouthfuls of parasites, which they found among the thick hair of his body.

Two or three times the maniac crawled up to me, and seemed anxious to touch the colours on my palette, and also to put his fingers on the sketch. He saw that he gained nothing by being a foe, so he became a friend. He even became a great friend when I presented him with a shiny silver coin.

Though Omangus was undoubtedly insane, he was a very practical person. As will be seen by the illustration, his attire was simple, and no allowance was made for pockets. He looked at the coin, turned it over in his hands several times, and grinned; then he placed it in his mouth for safe keeping. His mouth was apparently his purse. As I saw that he was fond of silver coins, I gave him one or two more, and all of them were religiously kept in the same natural pocket, except at night, when he hid them under a large stone. At sunrise they were collected again and placed back under his tongue or in one of his cheeks.

I cannot say that my host was by any means brilliant, but, like most lunatics, he was a good soul apart from his little peculiarities. It was unfortunate that he had lost the power of speech, or I might have learnt some strange things from him.

Omangus was generally restless at night, and while asleep he seemed to suffer from awful nightmares. Most Ainu as a rule do not. One morning at dawn, as the first rays of light penetrated the hut, I watched him. He had been groaning frightfully all night, and I had not been able to sleep. He was lying flat on his back breathing heavily, and now and then he had a kind of spasm, during which he ground his teeth together with violence. It was during these spasms, or nervous contractions, that he groaned most fiercely. As he was so stretched I noticed how extraordinarily long his femur was compared to his tibia. I gently placed my hand over his heart, and found it was beating rapidly and irregularly. His forehead also was feverish and abnormally warm. He did not wake up, but as soon as the nervous strain was over he fell into a lethargic state. He appeared to have lost all strength, and it took me some time to awake him; but he finally opened his eyes, and, drowsily getting up, yawned to his heart's content, and went to fetch the hidden coins.

The more I saw of Omangus, the more he puzzled me. His faculties were defective; still, he seemed to possess a fairly good memory. If not, how could he remember the concealed treasure? Although he was not able to form ideas of his own, he could retain those which had grasped. His hearing was extremely acute, and his inability to speak must have undoubtedly been caused by paralysis of the tongue and vocal organs. Several times he made violent attempts to utter words, which he would not have done had he been born dumb.

After the second day of my pleasant stay in Omangus' ten feet square sea-side residence my host became more genial and even affectionate. Instead of constantly running away from me he sat opposite me, attentively watching all my movements; and if I happened to be whistling, he slowly crept nearer, grinning with delight. Occasionally he crouched himself by my side, even resting against me. I did not approve of the latter proof of affection, not so much for his own sake as on account of the "large company" which he carried with him; but I had to put up with it until I found a counter-action in loud singing, which frightened him away.

Omangus had a quantity of last year's salmon, which he had dried in the sun, and which was now hanging from the roof of the little hut. The first day or two of my stay there I had but little to eat, owing to his belligerent behaviour. He rebelled every time that I attempted to touch his provisions, and what I had to eat was generally appropriated while my host was out. Afterwards, however, he became generous, and gave me more than I wanted. He took good care to draw the three coins out of his mouth while he was eating, but once, during a nervous fit, to which he was often subject, he swallowed one of them.

One morning, weary of my lunatic friend's company, I packed all my traps and went to fetch my pony. Omangus seemed aghast, suspecting that I was about to leave. He was restless, and followed me, moaning, from the hut to the pony and back, and, with a forlorn look in his eyes, watched me bring the baggage outside and lash it to the pack-saddle. I gave him a couple more silver coins, which I thought would make him happy; but he dropped them in the sand. I bade good-bye to him and left; and there poor Omangus stood motionless, gazing at me until the winding shore took me round the cliff. He was out of sight for some minutes, but he soon reappeared on the summit of the cliff itself, on to which he rapidly climbed, and from this point of vantage he could see the coast for several miles. There standing, a black figure against the rising sun, the hairy Ainu became smaller and smaller as I moved away from him, until nothing but a black spot could be seen against the sky; then even that spot disappeared. It was the last I saw of my host the madman.

The rivers were troublesome all along this part of my journey, and as most of them had quicksands, the safest plan was to cross them in a boat, when this was obtainable. However, as I went further north the boats became scarce and more scarce, and the small villages, few and very far between. I seldom came across a human being with whom I could exchange a word, and the constant solitude induced in me the bad habit of talking to myself, to animals, or to inanimate objects. My unfortunate pony was often lectured on different subjects, and the millions of seagulls and penguins all along the coast were asked questions of all sorts, which, however, they invariably left unanswered. It was strange to see the myriads of birds stretched in two or three lines along the shore. Like the "beasts which roamed over the plains" in Alexander Selkirk's lament, they had seen so few human beings as to be indifferent to me and my pony, and I could walk among them without disturbing them or causing them to fly away. The penguins were my greatest source of amusement, with their fat bodies and their funny way of lifting up one leg as I was approaching, in order to get enough spring to raise themselves from the ground had I attempted to capture them. I was soliloquising, according to my then custom, while watching these droll birds, when not more than two hundred yards ahead I saw two large eagles. One of them was perched on a low cliff, the other was flying about, now and then returning near to its mate. I dismounted, with my revolver in my hand; I had a pocketful of cartridges. I crept stealthily from rock to rock, keeping well out of their sight until I came close to the pinnacled rock on which they stood. I was then about fifty yards from them, and it was useless my firing at such a distance with a revolver. I peeped over the rocks, and one of them saw me and flew away, while the other remained where it was, stretching its neck in my direction. Its piercing eyes were fixed full on me as I was approaching; it understood that danger was imminent, and it seemed ready to resist the attack. I drew nearer and nearer, and when about four yards away I fired two shots, both of which went through its breast, and the eagle, with its widespread wings, fell from its lofty pinnacle and came down heavily on its back.

In its last convulsions it made desperate efforts to clutch me with its long sharp claws; but a couple more shots finished it. The male bird, which meanwhile had been describing circles high up in the sky over my head, plunged down on me with incredible velocity. I emptied the last chamber of my revolver into him, just as the wind of his large wings made my eyes twinkle; and to evade the grip of his outstretched claws I had to cover my face with my left arm. The report stunned him, and flapping his wings, he rose again, to resume his circling over my head, leaving a few of his feathers floating in the air. I reloaded quickly, and each time he attacked me he was received with a volley. Another bullet went through his wing, and his flying became unsteady; he flew on to a distant cliff, and there he remained. I seized this opportunity of carrying the dead bird away and lash it on to my saddle; but while I was so engaged the male eagle flew back to the pinnacle where I had first seen the two together, and stretching his enormous wings to their full width, screamed as if in despair. On the pinnacle was their nest and young, and that was why the female had kept watch and ward over her eyrie, and also why she had not abandoned it even when I approached.

I mounted my pony and away I rode with my prey. The male bird followed me for miles and miles, and now and then I had to fire to keep him at a respectful distance. Ultimately he left me, and my delight was immense when, instead of seeing him over my head, ready to plunge on me at any moment, I saw him disappear behind the cliff, flying rapidly but unsteadily back to his eyrie.

As I now made sure that he had no intention of pursuing me any longer, I dismounted, and proceeded to skin the eagle I had shot. It was decidedly a magnificent specimen. It measured seven feet from tip to tip of wings, and its claws were nearly as large as a child's hand. The semicircular nails measured two inches, and were extremely pointed, which fact made me feel very thankful that I had just escaped the grip of its male companion. The beak was enormous, of a rich yellow colour, the upper mandible overlapping the lower. The feathers were black all over, with the exception of the tail, which was white. I believe that this kind of eagle is generally called the "black sea-eagle," and is found in Kamschatka, Yezo, and also along the Siberian coast of the Japan Sea and Gulf of Tartary.

I found a sheltered spot, and with my large Ainu knife proceeded to dissect the bird. Each minute seemed as long as hours, for I feared the male bird might reappear on the scene as I was thus occupied in stripping the skin from the carcass of his beloved helpmate. There is no knowing what effect anatomical researches might have on a Yezo eagle. My heart bounded with joy when the operation was successfully completed, and I went to wash my hands in the sea. I came back to the bird, or rather its skin, and I was indeed proud of my work, when a horrid idea struck me. How was I to get the skin dried? I should be moving day after day, and it would not be possible to pack it in that condition among my sketches; I had no arsenical soap, and unless I dried it in the sun it would certainly rot, and get spoiled.

I resorted to a trick. I fastened two sticks crossways, and having stuck one up the eagle's neck, I fastened the two opened wings to the two side branches of the cross. The skin was thus kept well opened, and with two additional strings, one at each wing, the frame was fastened on to my back, the feathered side against my coat, while the inside was exposed to the sun and the wind. In wading a river I saw my own image reflected in the water, and I must confess the appearance was strange. A few hours after a group of Ainu were able to certify to this. I was riding slowly along the shore, when I saw a few of them not very far ahead. Two men were the first to notice me, and they seemed terror-stricken. As I approached they stood still for a minute, shading their eyes with their hands so as to make out what kind of winged animal it was they saw riding on horseback. When they discovered that the black wings were on a human being, the two brave Ainu fled, crying out, "*Wooi, wooi!*" the hairy people's cry of distress.

As I got nearer the village, dozens of wild dogs came to meet me, and, barking furiously, followed my pony, while the few inhabitants, frightened out of their wits at such an unusual sight, hid themselves inside their huts. Two or three hurriedly launched their "dug-outs" and put out to sea. When I passed the first hut some large salmon were thrown at me from inside, probably with the idea that I might satisfy my appetite on them, and spare the lives of the trembling donors. Food was not over-plentiful along that coast, so I dismounted and picked up the provisions so munificently provided by the scared natives. I tied them on each side of my pack-saddle, not sorry to be thus saved from the danger of dying of starvation—at least for the next two or three days.

As I was so occupied, a little child about four years old, evading the vigilance of his parents, ran out of one of the huts. I took him in my arms; whereat he cried bitterly, and when the people inside heard it there were screams of indignation and despair.

Maternal love is occasionally strong even among Ainu women, and while I tried hard to quiet the shrieking baby, his mother, as pale as the dirt on her face allowed her to be, came out trembling, and, offering me another large salmon, begged me to accept it in exchange for her child, who, she said, was not good to eat! It is needless to say that I was magnanimous enough to accept her offer, and thereupon handed the child over to his mother, who fled with him back into the hut. Then I took off my wings and went in after her, explaining to the frightened natives what I really was. It took them some minutes, however, to overcome their first impression, and then the men were pretty hard on the women for having given all the salmon away. The same scene was more or less vividly repeated when I came across any other natives during all the time that I wore the eagle-skin on my back. I have related this small anecdote, as, a few years hence, when some worthy missionary or imaginative traveller visits that barren coast of Yezo, it is not improbable that he may hear of some additional Ainu legend, which, the good missionaries will say, proves that the Ainu are fully aware of the existence of heaven and hell.

"A heathen child," the legend will very likely run, "whose parents had not embraced our Christian faith, was one day plainly seen by his mother in the arms of a black-winged devil. The devil was seen by many, and he came from the lower regions on an unknown animal with huge side paunches, in which he kept the heathen children he had eaten. The mother, who, through her wickedness, saw herself deprived of her child, gave offerings to the gods, some through the eastern window for the sun-god, and some through the door for the other gods. The offerings were accepted, but none of the gods came to her help, and the child was nearly lost. Her guiding star appeared to her in that supreme moment, and inspired her to reach down from the roof the largest salmon in store. She walked out of the hut and offered it to another god, whom she knew not before. Instantly the child was restored to his mother. (That the god took the salmon would probably be omitted in the legend.) The black-winged demon vanished, and the hut was visited by a white being (freely translated, "the guardian angel"), with a halo (my white terai hat) round his head. He rewarded them, and from that day the family has been happy in the faith which they learned in such a miraculous manner."

"Does not this legend speak for itself?" the good missionaries will tell us. "Does it not show that the savage Ainu are Christians without knowing it?"

I have given these two versions of the same story, as they show the reader how easy it is to garble accounts and misrepresent facts. It is a good illustration of what I say in my chapter on the Ainu beliefs and superstitions, and I must be forgiven if I have ventured to make fun of the missionaries. It is not because I dislike them, for I gladly admit that some of them out in the East have done good work; but, unfortunately, most of them will not take an open-minded view of facts. They are so wrapped up in their good work of converting people to Christianity that, outside of that, they occasionally have a tendency to tinge with their own preconceived ideas, facts which to a less biased mind appear simple enough.

SARUBUTS, SHOWING RIVER-COURSE ALTERED BY DRIFT SAND.

CHAPTER XV.
On the North-East Coast—From Poronai to Cape Soya.

It was late in the evening when I arrived at Poronai.[35] Saruru, the last village I had passed, had only six Ainu and three Japanese huts, and the nine or ten miles between there and this place were most uninteresting. I was taken across one of the quicksand rivers in the ferry by a lovely Ainu girl of about twelve years of age. I have never seen a more picturesque being than she was. She was partly dressed in skins, but half her chest was bare; her wildly-curled black hair fell over her shoulders, and while gracefully paddling across the ferry she occasionally threw back her head, thus shaking back the hair that the wind had blown over her eyes.

I have often noticed how supple the children of savages are, and how like in ease and grace and unconscious rhythm their movements are to those of wild animals. Sometimes, to be sure, they have the jerky, quick, and ungraceful movements of monkeys, but as a rule their actions are unconsciously graceful. Of course, with our children such unconscious grace is rare at any time, even when found at all, as from the day when they are born we train them to artificiality of all kinds, and this artificiality becomes in a sense second nature, overlaying, if not destroying, the original impress. And yet that impress is probably not wholly destroyed, for, so far as my own experience goes, I, who had from my birth led a civilised life, now that I had been for some months among barbarians had so little conventionality left in me as to be quite happy, or even happier than before, in leading a perfectly uncivilised existence. In the absence of chairs and sofas, instinct and the example of the natives taught me to squat as they did, and when I had once got into the way of it I found the position much more restful than any of our European so-called comfortable ways of sitting. It was the same thing when I had to sleep, either in the open air or in Ainu huts, where there was no more bedding than sofas or easy chairs. To protect myself from the cold I almost invariably slept sitting on the ground, with my head resting on my knees, just like the apes in the Zoological Gardens. I am sure that a good many of my readers, who have never gone through such an experience, will put me down as a "crank;" others will say that I am a worthy companion of my friend the hairy lunatic, and the most charitable will think that, bearing the name of "Savage Landor," I am only indulging in a new edition of "Imaginary Conversations," without the literary merits of the old. Such is not the case. I have mentioned these facts, not to amuse the reader, or merely for the sake of paradox, but to show how shallow is the veneer of civilisation which we are apt to think so thorough, and how a very short time spent unaccompanied by men of one's own stamp, and alone with "nature," rubs the whole thing away, and brings us back to instinct rather than education. I am willing to admit that not many people would care to follow in my footsteps, and live as I lived for months among the Ainu in order to prove whether I am right or wrong. Many who have only sat in comfortable chairs or slept in soft beds will hardly think my statements credible; but as the experiences, besides being of great amusement, were of great interest to me, I shall pass them on to my readers, no matter what opinion they may form of him who has written them.

Another quality, merely instinctive, which I developed in my lonesome peregrinations was the power of accurate tracking. Most people are astonished at the wonderful tales told of the tracking abilities of the Australian black fellows, and of savages in general; but few ever think that if when young they had led the same life as these savages they would be as good trackers as the best. As there were absolutely no roads, and I travelled with no guide, servant, or companion, the power of discovering traces became invaluable to me. It was instinctive in me, developed rather than acquired, and therefore I mention it in connection with the other facts relating to animal and human instincts. Furthermore, I may assert that, until I was thus compelled to make use of that faculty, I was not aware that I possessed it.

We find that horses, bears, and most animals are good trackers. Dogs, the nearest in intelligence to men, are better than any other quadruped. Then come savages, who are the masters of tracking among human beings; but as we rise in the scale of civilisation we find that this faculty of following a slightly indicated track hardly exists. Does, then, intellectual education destroy our instincts instead of improving them?

Tracking on sandy or tufaceous ground is an easy matter, as of course the foot leaves a well-marked print; but where I found real difficulty was over rocky ground, until I got used to it, and knew all the signs and what I had to look for. However, with a little practice, even over rocks which the sea has washed, it is not impossible to know if such and such creatures, human or animal, have passed that way.

One of the first things in tracking is to look for marks where they are likely to be; and this is just where the instinct comes in. Next to this, a clear knowledge of the person's or animal's way of walking and general habits is necessary. For instance, when I tried to discern tracks of Ainu, I invariably looked for them along the sea-shore, and failing that, on the adjoining cliffs, as I well knew that if any Ainu had passed by there he would have kept either along the coast or not far from it. By examination it is easy to see if the ground has been in any way disturbed of late. Sometimes a small stone moved from the place where it had been for years shows a difference in colour where it has been affected by the weather and where not, thus giving a distinct clue of some passer-by, man or brute; and when once you have found what the characteristics of the tracks are, the most difficult part of the task is accomplished.

On weather-beaten rocks the trail is more difficult to strike, and more difficult still on rocks over which the sea washes. "For," say the simple people, "how can you see tracks on hard stone? The foot certainly does not leave a print on rocks as on sand; and even supposing that the feet were dirty, the sea would wash away the marks, and you could not see anything."

In my case I limited my search to bare-footed marks, as the Ainu generally go bare-footed. Everybody knows that dogs track by scent, and this is a sure proof that every footmark must have a certain special odour, however infinitesimal. When we remember that the act of walking makes the feet warm and perspire, it is easy to understand that this perspiration, which is a greasy substance, leaves a mark on the stone—though to be sure it is sometimes almost imperceptible, especially when quite fresh. But most of us, when children at school, have noticed that touching a slate with moist fingers leaves a greasy mark, which could not be rubbed off again. The same thing happens when we tread on stones with bare feet. If the sea washes over the stones after the greasy impression has been thus made on them, it does nothing but accentuate these marks, and show them more plainly, as the salt water acts in one way on the untouched parts of the stone, but in a different way where the grease has been absorbed. These marks are generally very faint, and it requires some training before they can be discerned; but when the knack is once acquired, they become evident enough. To an observant eye, and with a little practice, it is not difficult to perceive whether one or more persons have tramped on a given place, and in what direction they have travelled. The marks on stones which are washed over by the sea are usually of a lightish colour.

I could almost invariably distinguish the footmarks of an Ainu from those of a Japanese, as the Ainu take longer strides, and their toes are longer than those of the Japanese. Moreover, with the latter, when walking the greater pressure is forward under the foot, and their toes are turned in; while in Ainu footprints the whole foot rests on the ground, and they keep it perfectly straight, moving the two feet parallel to each other.

I have given these few points on tracking, as it will explain to the reader how I was able to find my way from one village to another miles apart, to steer for huts where I had never been, and to overcome great difficulties, which I could not have surmounted if I had not learnt the art of tracking, and so far developed my natural powers. My ponies were also to a great extent my teachers; and by a close examination of their instinct I learned that I myself possessed it, and improved on it.

Between Sawaki, or Fujima, and Poronai there is a beautiful forest of oak and hard-wood trees on the hills and firs on the higher mountains, while the shore above the sea-wash is covered with thick scrub-bamboo, which reaches a height of about ten feet.

On the sandy beach, besides a large number of whales' bones, there is any amount of driftwood.

At Poronai, which consisted of only eight huts, the Ainu had adopted an architecture for their storehouses different to that of other tribes. The walls and the roof were made partly of wood, partly of the bark of trees. Heavy stones were placed on the roof to prevent it from being blown away during the strong gales so frequent along that coast.

The natives described the winter weather as very severe, especially during northerly winds, and they told me that some years the sea all along the coast is frozen for some eight or ten miles out, besides the drift-ice which sets in from the north and works its way along the coast as far as Cape Nossyap, in the neighbourhood of Nemuro. At the beginning of the winter this ice, probably drifted across from Sakhalin by the strong current in the La Perouse Strait, sets in from the north and works down all along the north-east coast of Yezo, filling up all indentations in the coast-line, and forming a solid mass on the surface of the water.

Seals are very plentiful on these shores as far as Abashiri, but the greatest number are found on the Saruma lagoon. In winter it is not difficult to come within reach of them, but even in September I saw many of them. They were, however, very shy, and when they caught sight of me instantly disappeared under water.

A few miles from Poronai I came to a headland, and about one mile from it lay the small island of Chuskin.

The coast again, instead of being sandy, showed traces of its volcanic formation, forming beautiful cliffs and a rugged outline, rising in terraces at places, or cliffs of clay and gravel sediments, with reefs extending far out to sea, while below them stretched a beach of coarse sand or pebbles, strewn with enormous volcanic boulders. These terraces are wooded mostly with alder, Yezo fir, and beech.

Soon after crossing the Porobets River I came across the wreck of a sailing ship, which lay flat on the shore disabled and dismasted; and at last I reached Esashi. There I again noticed a curious fact, which may be of some interest to anthropologists; namely, that Yezo is mostly formed of Tertiaries and volcanic rocks, and that the Ainu are mostly to be found in regions of Cainozoic or Tertiary formation. In volcanic districts they are very scarce. This is curious, for it is a well-known fact that the typical life-form of

Tertiaries is anthropoid apes, and it is a remarkable coincidence that we should find ape-like men populating the same strata.

From Esashi the coast is extremely rough and rocky for about eight miles. I had to take my famished pony up and down steep mountains rising directly from the sea in places where the beach was impassable. Owing to the lack of grass my wretched beast had but little to eat; and what with the danger of riding, and the miserable condition my pony was in, I had to walk most of the way and lead him. Shanoi, about thirteen miles further, came in sight—a group of wretched fishermen's huts; and from here the coast was somewhat better. The scenery all along is beautiful, especially looking back towards the Shanoi Mountains. I saw one or two abandoned huts blown down by the wind, but no people.

Near Shanoi the eruptive rocks and granitic cliffs suddenly come to an end, as well as the mountainous character of the country, and for fifteen miles, till one comes to Sarubuts, the country is pretty flat and swampy, with a thick vegetation inland of spruce trees. There is a small lagoon formed by the Tombets River, and which often has its mouth blocked by the quicksands, which cause it to overflow.

I left Sarubuts in pouring rain, following the trail along the beach. The river forms a long narrow lake similar to that of Tombets, and at the back of it are terraces and high lands, but no very high mountains. Another wreck of a large boat lay in fragments on the sand, and after fifteen miles of very uninteresting scenery I arrived at Chietomamai, a group of four or five fishermen's huts. Here again the coast was rough, but my pony did not sink in the sand as it did on leaving Sarubuts, but it stumbled among large pebbles and stones as pointed as needles. Further on were grey and brown steep cliffs, which were extremely picturesque. The Mezozoic nature of this coast shows more distinctly between Chietomamai and Soya Cape, and a large rock emerging from the sea is both peculiar and picturesque with its numerous square sections. It is from this point that one gets the first view of Soya Cape. Going round a bay one passes a few fishermen's houses, and on the cliffs above them has been erected the Siliusi lighthouse. I cleared the Cape and rounded the bay on the other side, where I saw another wreck of a sailing ship dashed upon the rocks, making the scene a sad one. I still went on, and went round two or three smaller headlands, when the melancholy sight of a fourth wreck stood before me. This last ship had her stern out of the water, and a Turkish name was painted on it. Her appearance also was Turkish, and I was more than once puzzled as to what a Turkish ship could have been doing in the La Perouse Strait. Many months afterwards, on my return to Yokohama, but too late to be of any help to them, the sad story of the survivors of that ship was revealed to me. The mission of the ship in those far-off seas was a mysterious one. No one ever knew exactly whence she came, or whither she was bound. No one ever learned whether she had been disabled in a typhoon in the Chinese Sea, and had been drifted so far north by the strong currents, or whether the careless Turkish master had mistaken his course and had met his fate in the dangerous currents of La Perouse Strait. Only four of the crew survived. There they were on that deserted coast, with no clothes, no food, no money; but the few natives treated them kindly. Two of them wore "*Tarbouches*" (red caps), the only things they had saved from the wreck. The natives on the north-west coast told me of these men who were tramping their way south, unable to make themselves understood, continually asking for "*Sekhara,*" or "*Sakhara,*" which, I believe, in the Turkish language means tobacco or cigarettes. After months of privations, half starved, and worn out with fatigue, they reached Hakodate, where, having no passport, and not being able to explain themselves, they were duly arrested and sent down to Yokohama. Unfortunately for them, at that time the "Entogroul," a Turkish man-of-war, had come to Japan, a voyage which took her two years, to bring some decorations which the Sultan had bestowed on the Mikado. Osman Pasha, the Admiral, had the poor devils brought before him, and they told him their sad story, what they had suffered, and how they had lost their ship. The story was too true to be believed, or too strange to sound true!

"Impostors!" said Osman Pasha, and declining to listen any more to their tale of woe, which he called "pure lies," had them "put in irons," in which condition they were to be taken back to Constantinople. None of the foreign residents in Japan believed the story of these wretches, and all were glad to see the miscreants punished. "Impossible," said everybody, "that a Turkish ship should have been up there!"

As it so happened, the "Entogroul," on her return trip to Constantinople, was herself caught in a typhoon, and, steaming full speed to resist the force of the wind and the waves, her boilers burst, and Osman Pasha and nearly all hands on board were blown to pieces or drowned. If I remember right, over three hundred and sixty lives were lost, and no doubt the four men, whose prison, I was told, was near the boilers, thus found a tragic end to their life of misery.

When I arrived at Yokohama all this had already happened, and my evidence, which probably might have saved the life of these men, was therefore useless.

But let us return to Soya Cape, where we have left the wreck.

The rapid current which comes through the Strait gives a horrid look to the water, and I have never seen the sea look so vicious. The natives of the small Soya village told me that it is impossible to cross over to Sakhalin, the high mountains of which, covered with snow and glaciers, I could see distinctly. The distance from land to land is about twenty-eight miles, but no small boat can get across without being swamped. They told me also that often dead bodies of Russians are washed on shore, probably unfortunate convicts who found their death in attempting to obtain liberty. H.M.S. "Rattler" was wrecked in 1868 on one of the numerous reefs near this Cape, so the record of Soya could hardly be more mournful.

After the Cape has been well rounded one finds oneself in a bay opening due north. In the winter time this bay is completely blocked with ice, but the Strait itself is never entirely frozen, owing to the strong warm current from the Chinese Sea, which the Japanese call by the name of Kuroshiwo.

Soya village is a wretched place of thirty or forty sheds. A few planks, badly joined together, and with a kind of a roof over them, made my shelter for the night. Soya Cape is the most northern point of the north-east coast, and before we abandon it to move towards the south, along the west coast, it is important to mention the peculiar and conspicuous characteristic of the marked bending of watercourses in a south or south-easterly direction. They are forced that way by the drift-sand travelling along the coast from north-west to south-east with the Kuroshiwo current, which drift-sand is in such quantities as often to block altogether the mouths of some rivers, and form the large lagoons so common along this coast. The lack of harbours or sheltered anchorages, the inhospitable and unfertile shores, the quicksands, and the severe climate, besides the danger of being swamped and carried away by the overflow of a lagoon or lake, make this coast of little attraction for intending settlers or for pleasure-seekers.

Herrings are plentiful all along the coast, but fishing stations could not possibly pay, even if any were established, owing to the difficulty and expense of carriage and freight, and the risk that ships would run in calling at such exposed and unprotected shores.

AINU VILLAGE ON THE EAST COAST OF YEZO.

MASHIKE MOUNTAIN.

CHAPTER XVI.
From Cape Soya to the Ishikari River.

From Soya the coast forms a large bay, which opens due north, and which ends in Cape Soya on the eastern side and in Cape Nossyap on the western. Almost in the middle is the small village of Coittoe, and from this place, towering beyond the flat Nossyap peninsula, one can see Rishiri Island. Near the western part of the bay are some small hills, covered mainly with fir-trees. Wakkanai, a Japanese village, is on the west coast of the bay, and north of it is Cape Nossyap. From this cape is a lovely view of Rishiri and Repunshiri Islands. Rishiri is a volcanic cone 6,400 feet above the level of the sea. It has the identical shape of the famous Fujiama in Southern Japan, and rising as it does in graceful slopes directly from the sea, has the appearance of being higher than it really is. Repunshiri is hilly and partly of volcanic formation, but none of its peaks rise to a higher altitude than five hundred feet.

Rishiri is almost circular at sea-level, and it has no well-sheltered nor safe anchorages; but Repunshiri has one good anchorage on its north coast. Rishiri is about six and a half miles in diameter and twenty-five miles distant, directly west of Cape Nossyap; Repunshiri is eleven miles long, about four and a-half wide, and eleven miles distant to Ikaru, its nearest point east on the Yezo coast. As the Kuriles are a continuation east of the volcanic zone of Yezo, there is no doubt that Rishiri and Repunshiri are the terminus of the same volcanic zone at its north-west end.

From Wakkanai a new horse-track has been opened to Bakkai, on the north-west coast. The ride for the first eleven miles was uncomfortable, as my pony, a worn-out brute, sank up to its belly in the mud; but in due course I came to the hilly part, and after having gone up one steep pitch and down another for a considerable distance, I rapidly descended a precipitous bank, and followed the soft sandy beach till I reached Bakkai. Here there is a large and peculiar stone, which the Ainu say resembles an old woman carrying a child on her back. It stands perpendicularly out of the ground at a great height, and it is of a rich dark-brown colour. If the north-east coast was barren and deserted, the western shore of Yezo was even yet more desolate. For thirty or forty miles, as far as the Teshio River, the beach was strewn with wrecks and wreckage. Here you saw a boat smashed to pieces; there a mast cast on the shore; further on a wheel-house washed away by the waves; then the helm of a disabled ship. It was a sight sad enough to break one's heart, with all the tragic circumstances it suggested.

Between Bakkai and Wadamanai especially, I do not think that one can go more than a few yards at a time without being reminded by the wreckage which is strewn thick on the coast of some calamity. A white life-boat, with her stern smashed, lay on the sand helpless to save, and as a kind of satire on her name; and at Wadamanai, a large Russian cruiser, the "Crisorok," dismasted and broken in two, lay flat on the beach half covered with sand. Her bridge had been washed away and her deck had sunk in. Some of the bodies of her gallant officers and crew had been washed on shore by the sea. No one knows in what circumstances the ship was lost, but it is probable that during last winter, when she came to her ill-fated end, her rigging and sails got top-heavy with ice, and that she capsized. Some of the wreckage one finds on that coast has been drifted there from the Chinese Sea by the Kuroshiwo current; and then, owing to the La Perouse Strait turning so sharply to the east, has been left on this last portion of the coast. Here and there a rough tent made with a torn sail, or a deserted shed knocked up out of pieces of wreckage, is a suggestive reminder that some unfortunate derelict seafarer had suffered and striven for life on these forlorn sands. An enormous quantity of drift-logs, and here and there some bones of whales, are strewn all along the beach.

At Wadamanai there is a mere rough shed under the shelter of the sand-hills. When I left this place, moving south, a strong gale blew, which made the travelling most unpleasant. It was getting fearfully cold, and now that I needed clothes so badly mine were falling altogether to pieces. My "unmentionables," which reached down to my feet when I left Hakodate at the beginning of my journey, had long since been trimmed and reduced to a kind of knickerbockers. Then the knees got worn out, and they became more like bathing-breeches; and finally I dispensed with them altogether, and made use of them to protect my sketch-book and diary, round which I wrapped what remained of the ex-garment. My boots, of course, were a dream of the past, and little by little I was getting accustomed to walking barefooted. Thus, dressed in a coat, a belt ... and nothing else, I moved along this inhospitable coast, half frozen, but not discomfited.

The mouths of some of the small rivulets were extremely nasty to cross, as my pony sank in the quicksands. I had to help him out, and that meant a cold bath each time. From Wadamanai I kept a little more inland, still steering for the south, and every now and then I again struck the beach. Still the old sad story of wreckages strewn all over the shore, sailing boats smashed to pieces, junks disabled and half buried in sand, met me at every turn, creating in my mind a very monotony of melancholy.

Late in the evening I reached the mouth of the Teshio River, a broad deep watercourse, one of the three largest rivers in Hokkaido, the other two being the Ishikari and the Tokachi. It has a long course in a general north-westerly direction, and then sharply turns southward, running parallel with the coast for about four miles, and forming a kind of lagoon at its outlet, which seems now to be working towards the northward again. All the other rivers on the west coast tend northward owing to the drift-sand which the current brings north. It is strange that the Teshio should partly be an exception to this rule, though we have ample evidence, even in this watercourse, of the movement of the sand, for the bar at its mouth almost entirely blocks its entrance, and rapidly works in a northerly direction. Thus there is no doubt that the sand travels towards the north all along the west coast.

Sea-trout is abundant in the Teshio River, but salmon, with which this stream formerly abounded, are now less plentiful owing to the sand-bar which blocks the entrance.

A gale was blowing fiercely when I crossed the lagoon in a small Ainu "dug-out," and my pony was made to swim across. Two or three times we nearly capsized, and we shipped a lot of water. It was just like sitting in a bath with water up to my waist; but the Ainu, who had as much as he could do to paddle me across and tow the pony as well, comforted me by saying, "Now that his 'dug-out' was full, we could not ship any more water, and that his skiff, being made of wood, could not sink!"

After a long struggle we got safely to the other side, and the Ainu boatman guided me for a mile or so to the fishing village at the mouth of the river. It has but ten huts, all more or less miserable. The pony was so done up that he was hardly fit to carry my traps, much less could he have borne my weight. I could not get a fresh animal, so I had to push forward walking, and dragging the beast on as well as I could. This had the advantage of keeping me warm, which I needed badly, for what with the cold and my dilapidated costume I was more nearly frozen to death than was pleasant. The track was heavy in the soft sand, and the dangerous and numerous quicksand streams were enough to make a saint swear—if swearing would have done any good. How unspeakably desolate it all was! Not a soul to be met; not a hut to be seen! Here and there more wreckage and drift-wood on the shore, telling of storms and death, and the absence of all human aid. At last I came in sight of an Ainu hut; but as I drew near I found that it was abandoned. My meals, never very plentiful, were now specially scanty—few and far between; and, taken altogether, this part of my travels in Ainuland was somewhat lacking in cheerfulness.

The cliffs near Wembets have the strange appearance of so many cones at equal intervals along the coast. On the Wembets River there were as many as two huts; and here again I had to cross in a boat, the stream being too deep to ford on foot or horseback; then again along the sand, dragging my pony, while I myself could hardly stand on my half-skinned feet, I went on and on, wearied of the monotony of my miserable experiences. The track grew narrow, and always worse. The high grey cliffs of clay-rock began, and the rough sea washed up to the foot of them, making progress more than ever unpleasant and dangerous. Each wave that came brought the water up to my knees, often up to my waist, and for about ten miles I was continually in and out of water. On a cold day my readers can imagine how pleasant it was! About sunset I came in sight of the two flat islands of Teuri and Yangeshiri, about fifteen miles off the coast. It then grew dark; but the moon came to my help, shining brightly on the greyish cliffs. The tide had risen, and in several places I had great difficulty in getting across on account of the furious waves dashing against the cliffs, and making a picturesque and living sheet of foam.

Late at night, as I had almost given up all hope of finding a shelter, I came upon a shed on the Furembets River, where I put up for the night.

My wretched pony was nearly dead with fatigue, and I let him loose so that he might get a feed of grass. The next morning, after the inmates of the hut had volunteered to go and bring him back to me, I heard them on the distant hills calling, "*Pop, pop, pop, pop!*" the Ainu way of approaching and calling horses. After a time they came back hopeless, saying that the brute had bolted, and there was no hope of getting him again. He could not be found anywhere! I was in the most awful dilemma, for had that been the case I would have been forced to abandon all my impedimenta, consisting of sketches and painting materials, and proceed as best I could on foot. Under other circumstances I could have carried the baggage on my back easily; but as I was half-starved, and had my feet badly cut, I was hardly able to carry my own weight; therefore this was not possible now.

As incredulity is one of the useful qualities I possess, I went to look after my pony myself. The shed was protected by a sand-mound at the back, and a small space was left between the mound and the wall of the shed. I do not know what made me go and look there, but sure enough there was my pony lying flat, and almost too weak to get up again. This was no horse-stealing ruse on the part of the Ainu; simply the wretched animal's own idea of good stabling and likely fodder. I dragged him out of his involuntary prison, and after having done what I could for his comfort and well-being, we set out once more on our melancholy travels. This may sound cruel to some who in the course of their life have never travelled in out-of-the-way places, and who are ready to condemn anyone who is the means of letting an animal suffer. It may sound cruel in our humane country, where animals are protected and prize-fights tolerated and enjoyed; so to avoid misunderstandings it might be as well for me to say, that as regards this tired pony it was simply the matter to push on with him as far as I could or lose all the valuable materials I had collected during months of sufferings and privations. No ponies were to be got for any money along that deserted coast, for there were none in existence. I did my best to alleviate the poor animal's sufferings by undergoing myself a considerable amount of pain, walking most of the way with my feet a mass of sores; and as winter was rapidly coming on, I was more than anxious to make my way south with all the speed I could, to prevent being blocked up with snow and ice and forced to spend the winter on this inhospitable coast. Consequently, I was, as a matter of fact, more cruel to myself than to my animals; to the others, those who will still cast the first stone at me, I can wish no better punishment than to be placed in the same position I was then. The trail became somewhat better, as it led over the cliffs for about three miles; then again it was on the beach. The high cliffs varied from a very rich burnt sienna colour to a nice warm grey, and in some places they are perfectly white, like the cliffs at Dover. Conical mounds frequently occur, and give a curious aspect to this deserted shore. Ten miles further on, at Chukbets, I found a couple of huts; then I walked and dragged the pony on the cliffs for about four miles; then again I resorted to the beach; and finally I entered Hamboro, a small village, or rather a picturesque group of sheds and huts, and a capital fishing-station. *Shake*, salmon, *mashe*, and herrings are caught in abundance at the mouth of this river. A short distance from here hundreds of carcasses of seals were scattered on the beach, whence emanated pestilential odours. On account of the slowness of my pony I had to-night a modified repetition of last night's experience, but neither was the sea so rough nor the trail so narrow at the bottom of the cliffs; and though my wretched animal was naturally in a worse condition than before, I was able to push on to Tomamai that same night, where I arrived at a small hour of the morning.

At Tomamai, the coast, which had described a long curve, the two ends of which are Ikuru north and this point south, turns sharply in a southerly direction, running straight for many miles from north to south.

From Tomamai southwards the coast is not quite as deserted as it was further north, for here and there are villages of fishermen's houses. The population, however, is a migratory one, and when I went through, the herring-fishing season was over, and consequently most of the houses were abandoned and the people had migrated south. The winter weather is very severe, and the houses have to be barricaded with thick piles of wood as a protection against the strong westerly gales. The boats had been drawn far on shore, where they were well fastened to posts, and rough sheds thatched with grass built over them.

Along the coast there was a string of these habitations, hut after hut, storehouse after storehouse, but hardly a soul to be seen. It was like going through the city of the dead. Many of the fishermen's huts were built on the side of the rugged cliffs, and they stood on piles about fifteen feet high, the back of the house resting on the cliff itself. Twelve and a half miles further another row of houses, similarly deserted for the winter, stood along the shore-line at Onishika. In this part of the coast salmon are very scarce, and the chief industry is the herring fishery. There are no Ainu to be found either at Tomamai or Onishika.

I continued my lonesome ride in the pouring rain, and soon came to a peculiar long tunnel, natural and partly excavated, between this place and Rumoi, a village prettily situated on the slope of a hill fifteen miles further. This place possesses a small anchorage at the mouth of the river, which is now only fit for junks and small sailing-boats, but could be considerably improved. Good coal has been discovered some way up the river. There is a track on the cliffs leading to Mashike. All along the coast are any number of fishermen's houses, but they were all closed and barricaded. Ultimately, descending from the cliffs in a zig-zag fashion, after another ten miles' ride I found myself at Mashike, the largest Japanese village in the Teshio district. Close to the tunnel there is a small Ainu village, where the natives let their hair grow very long, and then tie it up in a kind of knot, similar to the Corean fashion of head-dress, while the women have given up tattooing altogether. The fishermen at Mashike seem to suffer greatly from "*Kaki*," or rheumatism, and cancer, while consumption, malarial fever, and typhus are in a small proportion.

I had to stop over one day at Mashike, for the river was swollen by the heavy rains, and it was impossible to get across. On the other side of it stood Mashike-san, a huge volcanic mountain rising sheer from the sea, and forming Cape Kamuieto, under the shelter of which lies Mashike village; and further south Cape Uhui projects into the sea. It is the end of a mountain range which here runs north and then south again, in the latter part forming one side of the upper basin of the Teshio River. Mashike is the largest settlement either on the north-east or west coast of Yezo. Its population is partly migratory, but not so wholly as is the case with the villages I had previously passed. I was delayed still another day owing to the condition of the river; for the rain, instead of decreasing, poured down to such an extent that the stream could not be crossed, the current being too swift and the water too deep. The sea was also too rough to allow of my leaving Mashike in a canoe.

On the third day I rose early, and decided to attempt this much-desired crossing of the river. It had not rained during the night, and the waters seemed to have slightly diminished. As the stream runs down a very steep incline on the slopes of Mashike Mountain, the current rushes with tremendous force. It was about five in the morning when I took my baggage to the river bank. It was made up in two bundles, which I tied together firmly with a leather strap. Some of the natives who had collected round me entreated me to give up this foolish idea, for they said I should infallibly lose my life if I attempted to wade across the swollen river.

I saw at once that my pony would never be able to cross, so I left him, and, taking the baggage on my head, and passing my hands through the strap, I went into the water. The current was indeed so strong that, weak as I was, I could hardly stand against it. I had nearly reached the middle, with the water up to my mouth, when I fancied I heard the anxious crowd scream to me, "*Abunai! abunai! abunai!*"—"Look out! look out! look out!" Startled and alarmed at this piercing cry I turned my head, and saw within a few yards of me a huge trunk of a tree coming swiftly down with the current. There was a bump, and I saw nothing more. Half a minute later I was violently thrown on the opposite bank, and in trying to stand up on my feet in the shallow water my right foot unfortunately got jammed between two stones in the river bed; I was knocked down again, and broke my heel-bone just under the ankle. Several natives came to my rescue and I was lifted out of the water, half-stunned, half-drowned, but still holding fast to my load. I was nearly frozen, and trembling like a leaf from cold. When I tried to stand my right leg collapsed, and I had to lie down on the ground. What with the blow which I had received from the floating wood, what with the muddy water I had involuntarily swallowed, it took me some minutes before I could quite understand my situation, or what had befallen me. When I did I felt a terrible pain in my right leg. I looked, and there, on the sand, under my foot and leg, which were swollen up to an enormous size, was a pool of blood; the broken bone had penetrated the skin, and was exposed to the air. When I recovered my senses well enough I got a man to tear the wet lining of my drenched coat, and with it and a few improvised splints I proceeded to set my own broken bone. It was hard work; but with the help of some natives I bandaged it up as well as I could, and with the extra help of a coarse flaxen rope I made a fairly good surgical job of the whole thing.

Stopping there till I grew better would have been foolish, for winter was setting in; everything would soon be frozen and snowed up, and, far from all my friends, as well as from anything like civilised life or elementary comforts as I was, I should probably have died. As long as I had a spark of life left in me I decided that I would struggle and push on, come what might. Two men undertook to carry me over the Mashike Mountain, which rises to an altitude of 3,600 feet above the sea-level. The mountain is thickly wooded, and the trail is steep, heavy, and in many places dangerous, and when we reached a sufficient altitude the trail was merely in the bed of a rivulet composed mainly of huge stones. Travelling in the state in which I was, was something like going to one's own funeral. The jerking and the cold were excruciating; the continuous stumbling and unsteady walk of my men over the rough and slippery slopes did not improve my condition; but finally we reached the summit. What a lovely view! One could see far along the Teshio coast on the one side and down towards the Ishikari on the other, and towards the east rose up a picturesque chain of thickly-wooded mountains. Rising from the sea stood the fine Cape Airup, near Moi; then far beyond, dimly seen in the mist, was the towering outline of Shakotan. We went down the other side, and my men, poor fellows, did their best to cheer me up. One of them told me a cheering story of a grizzly bear—which, by the way, he said were numberless on this mountain—that had killed and eaten two children, and also their father when the latter went to their rescue. The other told me of the many men who had perished in crossing the mountain; some had been overtaken by a snowstorm, others had lost their way and fallen over precipices, while others again had been killed by avalanches in winter.

Listening to this lively conversation, shaken and suffering, I arrived late at night at Moi, having been carried over a distance of twenty-five miles, to do which occupied about eighteen hours. There was no possible way of getting across the mountains between here and Atzta, as the high granitic perpendicular cliffs are unscalable, and I was bound to entrust my life to a small Ainu canoe. Two other passengers, a Japanese woman and a man, asked if I would allow them to travel in the boat with me; and then we three, rowed by an Ainu man, put out to sea. The sea was rough outside, but as the large bay was well protected by the Aikap Cape, all went right at first; but in rounding the point we went too near the rocks, got caught in a breaker, and shipped so much water that the canoe began to slowly sink under the additional weight. The Ainu was pretty smart, and he put his skiff on the rocks. Between him and the two passengers I was helped out, and while the Ainu emptied the canoe, the two Japanese undressed entirely and spread out all their clothes and underclothes in the sun to dry.

We got on board again, and, coasting more carefully, passed several small fishing villages, of which Gokibira is the largest and most important. It is backed by high mountains ranging from twelve hundred to seventeen hundred and more feet above the sea. One of the mountains—the highest— is called Okashi-nae-yama.

Atzta is a long narrow village, of which almost all the houses are built against the cliff. From here I had to begin riding again along the bad and stony coast, among drift-wood, and up and down cliffs. Anyone who has ever had any broken bones will appreciate the tortures which I had to go through. Owing to pain, exhaustion, and fatigue I had no control over my pony, and could hardly stick on to the saddle. I took the precaution of tying the bridle to my wrist, for should the pony knock me off, he could not bolt away; but, unhappily, sometimes this was the means of his dragging me mercilessly on the ground for dozens of yards before he would stop. Then I had to wait for some charitable passer-by to help me into the saddle again, for I could no longer mount by myself. Day after day of this wretched life made me feel almost unconscious that I had a pain. I took things as they came, and I went on. Now that I sit here in a comfortable chair writing this by a cosy fire, I am myself astonished at my own perseverance. If I were called upon to go through the same experience now I could not. But in truth there are many things that one does not mind doing for motives of pleasure which one would never dream of attempting under the compulsion of an external will. Kutambets is picturesquely situated in a large gully formed by a break in the red-tinted cliffs. From Kutambets to Moroi the track is slightly better, and from this to Ishikari it is quite easy. The latter river, a very large one, has to be crossed by a ferry, as the habitations are on the south banks of the stream.

ISHIKARI KRAFTU AINU.

THE KAMUIKOTAN RAPIDS.

CHAPTER XVII.
The Ishikari River.

On the north side of the mouth of the Ishikari River is an Ainu village called Raishats. Its inhabitants are not natives of this island, but were imported by the Japanese Government from Sakhalin when it was exchanged with Russia for the Kuriles.

At the entrance of the river, and close to this village, another wreck—of the "Kamida Maru"—a schooner, ended the mournful list of disasters on this inhospitable coast.

The Ainu of Raishats are different in some ways from the Yezo Ainu proper. They call themselves Kraftu Ainu, "Kraftu"[36] being the Ainu name for Sakhalin. Their skin is of a lighter colour; but the principal difference is in their eyes and eyebrows. The Kraftu Ainu have eyes of the Mongolian type, though larger, while the Yezo Ainu have not; and their eyebrows have a very pronounced curve near the nose. Most of the women seemed to suffer from consumption, and the men also did not seem as strong as the other Ainu. The women tattoo on their lips a small square pattern instead of the long moustache, and most of them have now adopted Japanese *kimonos*, or else wear gowns similar to those of Russian peasants. Some also wear skin gowns similar to those of the Kurilsky Ainu, ornamented with feathers and bits of molten lead sewn on them. A velvet cap or a kind of tiara is their head-gear, and this also is ornamented with gold and silver or red beads, or else is embroidered in bright colours.

The children are arrayed in more gaudy colours than their elders. They have bright red embroideries round their necks, and the whole gown is full of spangles and beads, the proceeds of parental barter. A peculiar paunch-suspender, which I saw here for the first time, was ingenious, and answered a great want in the Ainu country. As will be seen later, the majority of Ainu children have huge paunches, mostly due to the inability of the hairy people to tie and secure properly the umbilical cord at the child's birth. This not only produces great discomfort to the child, but often causes its death. The belt which I saw was made on the principle that the weight of the paunch, under which passed a kind of net made of strips of skin, was supported by braces going over the shoulders, and by this contrivance, if the original lesion did not get much better it did not get worse, as it does when not taken any care of at all. Neither men nor women wore earrings; but the fair sex wore a kind of velvet ribbon necklace round their neck, and on this ribbon were sewn ornaments of molten lead, silver, and other metals.

The habitations, storehouses, and customs of these Ainu are similar to those of the others. As I slowly rode along the banks of the river just before sunset, retracing my steps towards the Ishikari village, I saw a hidden trail, which apparently led to the woods. I made my pony follow it, and shortly afterwards I came to a graveyard. As I have said, the Ainu are extremely jealous of their burial-places, and they resent strangers, even Japanese, going near them. It was nearly fifteen days since the accident to my leg had occurred, and though I could neither walk nor stand on it, still I was beginning to be accustomed to the agony, and with great trouble and pain I could dismount from my tiny pony. Strange to say, mounting was not so difficult, for I could pull myself up with my arms, lie flat on my stomach on the saddle, and then swing round, and it did not jar me as much as coming down. I had my paint-box fastened to the saddle, and I unlashed it to take a sketch. The tombs were so many trunks of trees cut and carved, and with one branch left on one side (*see* Chapter XXI.). One tomb particularly was more ornamented, and it had a flat-shaped monument, roughly but well carved at its head. An object resembling the bottom of a "dug-out" covered the body, and this was also carved. At each of the four corners a wooden blade was stuck in the ground. From the stench I should think that the body was only a few inches underground.

Fate had punished me so severely of late for faults which I never committed that I thought myself now entitled to commit a fault for the sake of squaring accounts. One of the small wooden blades, nicely carved, would just go under my coat. I decided to steal it. To my mind it was hardly a big enough crime even to balance the last accident I had had.

I turned round to see that no one was looking. I put down my paint-box, crawled to the grave, took the blade, put it under my coat, and, ashamed of myself for committing the outrage—though with prepaid punishment—I scrambled up on my pony as well I could, and hurriedly left the place. I rode back to the ferry, a long way off, and went across to Ishikari, and catching a moment when no one was watching me, I quickly passed the carved blade from under my coat into my baggage.

"What a good thief I would make," I thought to myself, when to my horror I remembered that in the hurry of leaving the graveyard I had forgotten my paint-box in the very same spot from which I had taken the blade!

If any Ainu had gone to the graveyard and found it, I would get into a nice mess! During the night I felt more than uncomfortable about it, and at dawn the next morning I got the tea-house man to bring my horse and set me on it, for I said, "I wish to go and see the sunrise from the other side of the river."

The landlord thought it rather funny, and funnier still when he saw me coming back a couple of hours later with a paint-box lashed to my saddle, while he said he was sure I had started without one.

"Did you not see it this morning?" said I with assumed innocence.

"No, your honourable," said he, drawing in his breath.

"You did not look for it in the right place," said I, and up to this day the landlord does not know where the right place was.

The Ishikari is one of the great salmon rivers of Yezo. About the end of September the salmon enter the river to spawn. They are in such abundance then that the stream is crowded thick with them, and it is quite sufficient to have a hook fastened to a stick to pull out a large fish each time it is dipped into the water. Millions of fine salmon are caught within a few days, and the banks of the river are packed with dead fish, while the whole population is occupied in splitting open each fish, taking out its inside, for preservation.

The same method of netting as is practised for sardine fishing is employed for salmon. Eighteen or twenty excited men vigorously row the boats out into mid-stream, and after describing a semicircle, return to the bank. The nets are hauled in, the fish flung out on the river banks, and the same process begins *de novo*. A man in a "dug-out" watches when the salmon are more or less plentiful, and signals for the boat to start, while he himself spears them with a harpoon. At the right time of the year as many as 1500 or 2,000 and more good fish are caught each time the net is hauled in. This grand take of course only lasts a few days.

Though good, the Yezo salmon has none of the fine qualities of the salmon of northern European rivers, and it is not quite so good as that of the Canadian rivers. It does not keep so well, and in colour is much lighter than our salmon.

The Ishikari River opens to the north, and runs parallel to the coast, leaving a flat tongue of sand between it and the sea. Following the course of the stream against the current, it goes winding south, then sharply turns to the south-east, following this direction for about fourteen miles. Then again it winds up to the north, and then to the east for a distance of over one hundred miles, where its source lies in the very heart of Yezo.

The Ishikari carries a large body of water, and it is nine hundred and twenty feet wide near its mouth. Its "drainage area" has been estimated to be over three thousand square miles, including mountain slopes, while the actual valley does not, in my opinion, exceed eight hundred square miles. The river receives many affluents, of which the most important are the Rubeshibe, Chupets, Piegawa, the Sorachi River, and the Toyohira on its south side, and the Uriugawa on its north side. Near the coast the valley is wooded mainly with scrub oak, but further inland its banks are heavily timbered. The Sorachi River is the most important affluent on the south side. It is navigable for "dug-outs" and small sailing boats for some considerable distance. At Sorachi one strikes the new road which leads from the Poronai coal mines to Kamikawa, where the site has been chosen for the intended new capital of Hokkaido.

The road between Sorachi and the latter place not being metalled, was exceedingly bad owing to the heavy rains, and my pony continually sank in mud up to his belly. The road follows the course of the Ishikari River more or less; and in the woods is a military settlement like those we have seen near Nemuro and Akkeshi. At Otoyebukets the traveller must change horses. About eight miles further on one reaches the Kamuikotan rapids, a poetic spot: huge rocks in the water, violently rushing between and over them, form pretty waterfalls. The Ainu occasionally shoot down these rapids in their "dug-outs," and remains of these are to be seen here and there smashed on the rocks. From this point the road rises almost all the way, and the wayfarer must cross over the hill range, from the top of which the whole plain of Kamikawa can be seen, in the upper basin of the Ishikari, which, winding like a silver snake, intersects the flat valley.

Descending the hill on the other side, I reached the future capital of Hokkaido. It is indeed a town of the future, for at the present moment there are only five houses, if I may call them so. The site of this embryo metropolis is by the Chubets River; and on the hill called Nayosami I was told a palace for the Emperor is to be erected. However, they were not certain about it yet. It is a pretty hill, almost in the centre of the large plain, and from the top of it one gets a lovely view of a volcanic cone standing in front of you to the south. Near this hill the new road turns sharply almost at a right angle, and two miles further some *Tondens* have been begun (*Ciuta Hombu*). Hundreds of convicts, who, by the way, have made the road between here and Poronai, were at work continuing the same road towards the east. I believe that eventually it will be prolonged to the north-east coast, where it will end near Abashiri. In my opinion the scheme practically will be a failure, for Kamikawa will never be a flourishing place, as there is nothing to support a large population. From a strategic point of view of course Kamikawa has the advantage of being in the centre of Yezo.

Kamikawa is 342 feet above the level of the sea, but it is well sheltered, and the climate, though very cold, is not quite so severe as in other parts of Yezo.

The Ainu of the upper Ishikari are nearly the same as the Saru Ainu, only somewhat taller and more ill-tempered. They show greater skill than other Ainu in wood-carving and general ornamentation. Along the banks of the river huts are scattered here and there; but the largest number is at Chubets.

At the present moment the Japanese population of Kamikawa is, with the exception of half-a-dozen policemen and as many civilians, composed entirely of convicts. These are dressed in red coats and trousers, and those who have committed murder have the top of their head shaved in the shape of a bottle (Jap., *Hetzui*). If any misbehave, they are beaten with the flat side of the long sword worn by the policeman in charge; but I must confess that otherwise the policemen are extremely kind in every way to these fellows. The well-behaved have one, two, or three small pieces of black cloth sewn to their left sleeve. They are made to work hard, but save this enforced diligence they seem to have a pretty good time. As I was talking to a policeman in charge, two dead men were brought on a cart by a man who had a towel over his mouth and a red blanket over his head. The two men had died suddenly. They had arrived only a few days previously from Southern Japan, where cholera was raging, and they had all the symptoms of having died of that deadly disease.

A very exciting way of retracing your steps down to the Sorachi River is to shoot the rapids in an Ainu "dug-out." You make one or two Ainu moderately drunk, as otherwise they do not seem anxious to attempt it, and when they are in that pot-valiant condition you get them to paddle your canoe down the stream, while you sit in the bottom holding on to the sides. You start with the velocity of a turtle, increase it to that of a horse, then to that of a swallow, and when you are well in the rapids it is like travelling on an arrow. You go rubbing against rocks, and are shot in the air when going over a small waterfall, only to fall with a splash in the water some yards further, with an increase of velocity as you go on. It really requires but little skill to navigate rapids, for it is the current itself that does all the work. All that is needed is to keep the "dug-out" straight in the water. Of course if you should happen to collide with a rock when you are going at nearly double the rate of an express train you would have little chance of saving your life; but if you are neither smashed nor drowned, and you do not come to grief in any way, you can accomplish the journey, which takes you the whole day by land, in little over one hour when there is plenty of water in the stream.

On the road from Sorachi to Poronai, and halfway between the villages of Naye and Takigawa, a new coal mine has been discovered and opened, which is said to be very rich in mineral of good quality; in fact, superior to the coal of Poronai. It is ten miles from Otaussi Nai village, where the high road has to be abandoned if the mine is to be visited.

There are many Ainu both at Takikawa-Mura (Waterfall-River village), at Otaussi, and at Poronai-buts. Poronai has in its neighbourhood some rich coal mines. As others have reported more accurately and correctly than I can on the quality and extent of these coal seams, I shall abstain from repeating or copying what has been already said. I may, however, mention that the seams cut the valley of the Ikusum River eight miles from Poronai-buts, and a continuation of them is found near the springs of the Sorachi. The coal beds of Poronai are about three and a half feet deep, and many different beds have been found deeper than these, but of inferior quality. Poronai also goes by the name of Ishikishiri, and a large penitentiary has been erected here for the accommodation of the numerous convicts exported from the Main Island to improve the scheme for the colonisation of Yezo. I was called on by the chief *yakunin* (officer), and he expressed a wish that I should inspect the prisons. A splendid horse was sent to convey me thither, and two policemen helped me on my progress through the buildings, owing to my inability to walk more than a few yards at a time. It was a large walled enclosure, with houses for the officials and cells for the *akambos*, a jocular term, meaning "babies," which is applied to convicts, because they wear red clothes like children. The buildings were beautifully clean, but what astonished me most was that no precaution whatever was adopted to prevent convicts from escaping. The outside gates were all wide open; there were neither soldiers nor policemen at the gates, and, moreover, the *concierge* was himself a convict!

"But," said I, "do not many of these fellows escape?"

"Oh, no, not many. Last month only sixteen ran away," was the *insouciant* answer of my guide.

From Poronai-buts to Sappro there is a small railway, by which the coal trains are run to the coast as far as Otaru.

WOMAN OF ISHIKARI RIVER.

AINU BARK WATER-JUGS

CHAPTER XVIII.
Nearing Civilisation.

Sappro, the present capital of Hokkaido, is a town of fairly large size, with wide streets intersecting each other at right angles. The Hokkaido-cho, a high red-brick building, the law courts, the *Kofikan*, the palace built for the Emperor, and used now as a kind of hotel, and the houses of officials, are the main buildings of the place. There are, besides, a sugar refinery, a hemp and silk factory, and a brewery, mainly supported by the Government. Neither of the first two were "flourishing industries," and one of the factories, if I remember aright, had long ceased working, and the other was soon to follow suit. The Government, I must say, have done their best to encourage and push on industries as well as agriculture in this district, but their efforts have produced but poor results. Machinery, which had been imported at great expense from England, America, Germany, and France, was left to rust and perish, and no private company seemed ready to continue the works. As a farming region the Sappro district has also proved more or less a failure from a financial point of view, though again the Government cannot but be highly praised for the money they have spent in trying to educate the people up to some kind of scientific, and therefore paying, method of agriculture. They have a large model farm of about 350 acres laid down in grain fields, as well as in meadows and pastures, stocked with cattle imported mainly from America. In the Toyoshira valley, south of the town, a cattle farm is in full operation, but it yields the Government a very poor return. However, the Government, I believe, only wish to teach the people foreign ways of agriculture, and expect no direct returns for the pains taken and the money sunk—so at least it would appear. Another colonial militia settlement is also found near Baratte, eight miles north of Sappro. Regarding these settlements, it may prove interesting to transcribe the Imperial Ordinance No. 181, dated August 28th, 1890, by which they were brought into existence and the Tondens were built:—

> ARTICLE 1.—Colonial Militia shall be composed of colonial infantry, cavalry, and colonial artillery and colonial military engineers, and shall be set apart for the defence of Hokkaido, where they shall be stationed.
>
> ARTICLE 2.—The Colonial Militia shall be organised as soldiers, in addition to their ordinary occupation of farmers; shall live in military houses which shall be provided for them, and shall take part in military drill, in cultivation, and in farming.

ARTICLE 3.—The Colonial Militia shall also be composed of volunteers from cities and prefectures, and shall change their registered residence (*Houseki*) to Hokkaido, and live there with their families.

ARTICLE 4.—The term of service of Colonial Militia shall be twenty years: the service with the colours being three years, in the first reserve four years, and in the second reserve thirteen years. Should a colonial militiaman be released from service during his term, owing to the attainment of the full age of forty years, or through death, or some other cause, a suitable male of the family shall be ordered to fulfil the remaining term of service. Such service may be remitted if there be no suitable male.

ARTICLE 5.—The Colonial Militia shall fulfil supplementary military service during ten years after the end of service in the second reserve, and shall be mobilised in time of war or other emergency.

ARTICLE 6.—The term of each stage of military service under Articles 4 and 5 shall be counted from April 1st of the year in which the soldier enters the Militia.

ARTICLE 7.—The terms may be prolonged, even though the period for each stage has fully elapsed, should war or other emergency, or the requirements of military discipline, or the inspection of soldiers (*kwampei-shiki*) demand the same, or should the soldier be then in transit from or to, or be stationed in, a foreign country.

SUPPLEMENTARY RULES:—

ARTICLE 8.—Colonial Militia enlisted before the carrying out of these regulations shall be treated according to the following distinctions:—

(*a*) Those enlisted between the eighth year of Meji and the sixteenth year of Meji shall serve in the first reserve during four years and in the second reserve during nine years.

(*b*) Those who were enlisted between the seventeenth year of Meji and the twentieth shall serve in the first reserve during four years from the twenty-fourth year of Meji, and in the second reserve after the lapse of the above period during twenty years, reckoned from the year in which they were enlisted.

(*c*) Those who were enlisted in the twenty-first year of Meji shall serve in the first reserve during four years from the twenty-fifth year of Meji, and in the second reserve after the lapse of the above period during twenty years, reckoned from the year in which they were enlisted.

(*d*) Those who were enlisted in and after the twenty-second year of Meji shall be treated in accordance with these regulations.

ARTICLE 9.—The mode of reckoning the terms of service of Colonial Militia levied before the twenty-first year of Meji shall be in accordance with Article 6 of these regulations. The term of service with the colours of those levied in the twenty-second and twenty-third years of Meji shall be counted from the day on which they were included in the Colonial Militia, and their term of service in the first and second reserves from the day next to the lapse of the full term of the former service.

ARTICLE 10.—These regulations shall come into force on and after the first day of the fourth month of the twenty-fourth year of Meji.

(Colonial Militia.) Imperial Ordinance No. 181.

We hereby give our sanction to the present amendment of the regulations relating to Colonial Militia, and order the same to be duly promulgated.

(His Imperial Majesty's sign-manual),
Great Seal.

Dated August 29th, 1890.
(Countersigned) COUNT OYAMA IWAO,
(Minister of State for War).

(*Japan Daily Mail*, September 14th, 1890.)

Sappro was a civilised place compared to others I had seen in Yezo; but it had neither the picturesqueness, nor the strangeness, nor yet the interest of more uncivilised spots.

There is no doubt that savagery—when you have got accustomed to it—is a great deal more fascinating than civilised life, and infinitely more so than a base imitation of civilisation.

It might have been thought that after the months of privation to which I had been subjected, after all the harassing experiences I had gone through, after the accident which had made the last thirty days of my journey so agonising, I should have been glad to rest in this "London" of the Ainu country, at least until I was well again. But in truth this indirectly reflected civilisation worried me. The bustle of the people, the lights in the streets, the sounds of the *Shamesen*—everything annoyed me.

His Excellency the Governor, Mr. Nagayama, kindly called on me, and when I put on some decent clothes which were lent me, he drove me to his house, where I had a lengthy conversation on the future of Yezo and the Kurile Islands. He seemed to approve of many of the points which I put before him, among which I suggested that the exports of sulphur from Kushiro, on the south-eastern coast, would be greatly increased if it were opened to foreign trade, and I was pleased to hear several months later that a motion to that effect was proposed in the Japanese Parliament. He also agreed with me that Yezo needed roads and railways badly, and that when more facile ways of communication should be established along the coast and across country, then without doubt Yezo would be rich and flourishing.

He expressed sorrow that emigration was not carried on on a larger scale from the Southern Island of Japan, and that private companies of capitalists in no way helped the Government.

His Excellency was also kind enough to drive me round the town and show me all the sights of Sappro, including the small museum containing zoological specimens from Hokkaido, and the implements of the Ainu and the Koro-pok-kuru. A huge grizzly bear which had killed two babies and a man is now stuffed, and occupies the first small room, while a bottle by the side preserves in spirit the head and foot of one baby and some parts of the man which were found in its stomach when captured and dissected.

I left Sappro for Otaru by the coal train. Otaru is situated on a semicircular well-sheltered bay, which makes it the best and only safe port on the western coast of Yezo.

The coast at the mouth of the Ishikari River curves gently round, and is exposed to the north as far as Cape Shakotan. Otaru is rapidly growing in importance, owing to the fact that it is the nearest shipping port to the Poronai coal mines. Unfortunately, three small hills, which were being levelled when I was there, had greatly interfered with the first laying out of the settlement, which accounts for the town being all crooked and irregularly planned. It has the appearance of a thriving place, and much resembles one of the small seaports of Southern Japan. In the main street a go-ahead tailor had written over his door the following inscription for the attraction of foreign clients: "Tailor. New Forms of every country shall be made here." The notice was tempting, and I went in to request his services in furnishing me with "new forms," as he called them, of English fashion; but to my great regret he had come to an end of his stock of goods, and I had to be contented with my "old forms," and go on as best I could with what I had till I should reach Hakodate, where I had left most of my baggage. At Otaru I left all my paraphernalia to be shipped to Hakodate by the first ship calling, and I proceeded by land on the north and then on the north-west coast. I felt that, suffering as I still was, I should keep alive as long as I kept moving, as long as I was distracted by new scenery and new excitements. I felt that if I were left to myself, not pitied or sympathised with, I should be able to drag on and conquer in the end. There is nothing, it seems to me, that makes people feel so ill or is so enervating as the sympathy of friends and the verdict of a doctor. Among civilised people nine out of ten do not know whether they are very ill or not until the doctor pronounces his opinion, which shows that many complaints would be scarcely felt at all if the patient did not know the name of his malady, or if he had sufficient determination as to prevent his physical pain from becoming a moral one as well. We have a proof of this in hypnotism, by which sicknesses of many kinds can be cured by impressing on the subject the belief that his body is perfectly free from disease. Of course in this case it is a stronger will acting on a weaker one, which, so reinforced, is able to overpower the physical trouble. Again, I may be allowed to state that savages and barbarians, though affected with horrid diseases of all kinds, do not seem to suffer from them as much as we do. If an Ainu man breaks his leg he does not think for a moment of lying in bed for the regulation forty days; first of all, because he has no bed to lie on; and next, because the confinement and inaction would simply kill him. He may lie down on the hard ground for two or three days, after which time he crawls about as best he can until nature makes his broken bone right again. He does not worry himself much about it. Wild animals do the same. If, then, the Ainu, and with them savages of other countries, do that, why should not I, a human being like them, do the same?

Freed from the encumbrance of my baggage, I set off on a good horse down the north coast, and moving from east to west. My baggage now consisted of a crutch which I had made for myself, a stick, a couple of Japanese *kimonos*, and a few sketch-books.

The travelling was extremely slow, and I shall not dwell at length on this part of my journey, for it has no interest in connection with the Ainu, as I met with scarcely any. On a practicable and pleasant track leading all across the hills beyond Oshoro village, a lovely view of the cliffs between that place and Yoichi, lying to the west, is to be had. In some parts the scenery is really grand. Coming down on the other side of the hill, Momonai and Kawamura, two fishermen's villages of some importance, are passed, and further west, through a picturesque and narrow entrance of rugged volcanic rocks, is Yoichi, a large village, which was entirely burnt down last year, but has since been built up again. The road to Iwanai branches off at Kawamura, across the Shakotan peninsula. This peninsula is partly volcanic, partly composed of tertiaries, on which metal veins are found, especially along the course of the Yoichi River.

About three miles from Yoichi a small flax factory was being built as an experiment by a Mr. Tokumatz Kuroda, in the employ of the Mitzui Company. Twenty-five miles further south-west of Yoichi is Iwanai. About ten miles from Kawamura, at Hando, a black tumbledown shed, like a haunted house, stands in the middle of the woods, and from here the track again goes over a mountain. On the other side is Iwanai. Five or six weeks previous to my arrival a large fire had destroyed nearly the whole of the village, and—just my luck again!—I had great difficulty in finding a place in which to obtain shelter for the night.

From Iwanai the coast-line roughly describes a semicircle, which is almost concentric with Volcano Bay on the south coast, the distance between the two seas being about twenty or twenty-five miles, so that it forms a kind of large peninsula stretching towards the south, and widening considerably at its most southern part on the Tsugaru Strait. The first two or three miles from Iwanai were a pretty flat and easy track, but then I struck the mountain trail, which was steep and heavy for my pony. It was raining in torrents, and the narrow track was literally turned into a running rivulet. By good luck the rain stopped, and when I reached the summit I had a glorious panorama of the brilliant rocks and cliffs of the Shakotan Cape to the north-east, with the Kamui and the Hurupira Mountains on one side, and the villages of Shiribets, Isoya, and Karibayama along the coast on the other. I descended into the valley and then went up again the next mountain, the Iwaonobori, a higher peak than the first. I went down its slopes on the other side in a zig-zag fashion, and then came to the snake-like river called Shiribets, on both sides of which a few fishermen's houses are found, forming the Shiribets village.

Three miles further is a larger settlement, Isoya, the half of which is called Notto Isoya, the other Shimakotan Isoya. It is a long row of fishermen's houses scattered along the coast until we get to Ushoro, eight miles further, a settlement of 120 houses.

Ushoro is connected by a road to Oshamambe, on Volcano Bay, but I went on to Shitzo, four miles north-west of Ushoro. The way was fairly good in some parts, and execrably bad in others. The heavy rain which had again come on was not exactly suited to my present state of health; moreover, it swelled all the small brooks, which fell in a series of picturesque waterfalls over the high cliffs down on to the beach. As the beach was narrow, this meant each time a cold shower-bath, which, however, did not much matter, for I was already drenched by the rain, and I had no very "swell" garments to spoil, as my readers know.

AINU HALF-CASTE CHILD OF VOLCANO BAY.

Shitzo is an old-looking place, but there is nothing attractive about it. It is in a small bay sheltered by Cape Benke, but its anchorage is only fit for junks or very small skiffs. It is much exposed to northerly and easterly winds. The coast from Shitzo to the Cape is lined with rocky bluffs and cliffs of conglomerate and volcanic formation, with bare hills inland.

There are many reefs stretching out, both along the coast and off the Cape; but in many places channels are cut in them, to all appearance produced by some remote volcanic action.

On the western side of Cape Benke is the village of Masatomari. There were formerly some Ainu villages on this part of the coast, but hardly any natives are to be found now. The few remaining have adopted to a certain extent Japanese customs and manners.

At Baraputa I heard that it was impossible to continue my journey south on horseback along the coast, for the track was almost impassable, even on foot. It was a steep and difficult trail over the mountains, among rocks and precipitous cliffs, and I was quite unable to accomplish it; so I retraced my steps to Shitzo, and from there struck across the peninsula on the road for Oshamambe, on Volcano Bay. The road is a good one, and when bridges are built where needed it will be practicable for *bashas*, the four-wheeled vehicles of Southern Yezo. The way is across mountains or among well-wooded hills. Kuromatsunai is the largest group of houses found along the road. It is about halfway between the two coasts.

Late at night, after having ridden twenty-five miles, I arrived at Oshamambe, a semi-Ainu village on Volcano Bay.

KOMATAGE VOLCANO, VOLCANO BAY.

CHAPTER XIX.
Completing the Circuit of Yezo—The End of my Journey.

Oshamambe is a group of seventy houses, just midway between Mororran and Mori. The Ainu of this bay are poor specimens of their race, as most of them have intermarried with Japanese. They are, however, those most talked about by Europeans, for they are of easy access to globe-trotters.

They are mostly half-castes, and even second and third crosses; wherefore it is no wonder that the incautious travellers who have written on the Ainu, studying only these easily-visited specimens, have discovered in them a remarkable likeness to the Japanese!

The fact that I was rapidly nearing the end of my trip half filled me with pleasure, yet pleasure mingled with regret. It was nearly six weeks now since I met with the accident to my foot, and I was decidedly better. The cold weather had greatly contributed to this improvement of my condition; and had it not been for my bone which kept sticking out of my skin, I should have considered myself in fine case. I could hop along with my self-made crutch and my stick, and when riding the pain was not nearly as acute as it had been the first fifteen or twenty days.

As the road was good, and there was nothing interesting to me on this portion of the journey, I tried to push on rapidly towards Mori. Unfortunately, at the last minute my patience was put to a trial. I hired a horse, and it was lame. No others were to be had that day for love or money. The animal had been lame for two years, they said, and though uncomfortable to ride he did not suffer any pain. This I ascertained afterwards was true, for that day the sturdy brute carried me 48½ miles without once requiring punishment. It is needless to say that what I suffered that day by the continuous jerking is beyond description. I rode fourteen hours in a fearful storm of rain and snow, and my feverish anxiety to reach Hakodate soon, so that I might receive letters, and have news of my parents and friends—from whom I had not heard for five months—helped me to pull through all the fatigue and worry of the way. The road between Oshamambe and Kunnui is fair, getting still better towards Yurap and Yamakushinai. But to shorten the journey and lessen the jerking I followed the sandy sea-beach, which, describing a smaller circle than the road, necessarily diminishes the distance. From Yamakushinai the road is very good and wide, and it has nicely-built bridges over the Otoshibe and Nigori Rivers. The small fishing villages, though not so imposing in appearance as some of those in other parts of Yezo, add to the picturesqueness of the bay, with its beautiful volcanic cone of Komagatage towering in the distance towards the south-east.

The fishing in Volcano Bay consists mostly of mackerel, sprats, halibut, and herrings.

I reached Mori late in the evening, and was received with a friendly greeting by the people of the tea-house in which I had stayed on my way up at the beginning of my journey.

The place was brilliantly lighted with numberless candles, and opposite the entrance was a kind of altar decked with flowers and cakes. A few *bonzes*, with their shaven heads and long, thin, depraved fingers, were saying their prayers and beating with a small wand on the round wooden bells. With the gods of Japan you must ring a bell or clap your hands before you begin to pray, or else the god will pay no attention to your petitions. In the next room another Japanese, with less depraved fingers, but with a more wicked face, was dressed in European clothes, and was apparently giving a sermon, and sure enough he proved to be a native Christian minister!

"Hallo!" said I to the landlord; "what does all this mean?"

"Oh," said he, smiling—for Buddhism teaches you not to show pain—"my old mother is dead. You saw her when you were here before. She died yesterday, and as she was formerly a Buddhist and had become a Christian, I have now got some Buddhist *bonzes* and a Christian minister to pray for her, for I want her to be happy in the other world."

"But do you not think," I replied, "that so much praying of different kinds might interfere with her happiness?"

"Oh, no, your honourable," he said quickly, "I have paid the *bonzes* and the clergyman in advance, and the gods cannot get angry now!"

It was curious to notice the competition between the representatives of the two different creeds.

On the one side the Christian shouted his prayers and sang his hymns in a stentorian voice, to put the *bonzes* in the shade and get the start of them in the contest; and on the other side these rattled on the wooden bells with all their might, so that their prayers should be heard first. I was more than happy when this religious race was over, and I was allowed a few hours' rest.

Instead of going straight to Hakodate by *basha* by the road I had already once traversed, I followed the coast in a south-easterly direction towards the volcano of Esan.

Near Usushiri, some two miles inland, are the hot springs of Obune, where, in a picturesque gully surrounded by mountains, are two dirty shanties for the benefit of those who wish to take the waters. At Isoya, five miles north of this place, similar springs are found, and three and a half miles south-east of Usushiri still more can be seen at Kakumi. The latter place is a picturesque little spot, with its three old sheds and the steaming bath-room framed in the multi-coloured foliage of trees with their lovely autumn tints. A clean path a few hundred yards long leads from the coast to the springs, and a track across the mountains is found between that place and Hakodate; also another leading from Obune to the latter port. By both these tracks a most lovely view of Hakodate Bay can be obtained when the summit of the mountain range is reached. From Kakumi the coast-line is wretched for travelling, set thick as it is with stones as sharp as knives, while the waves continually wash over the narrow beach, drenching the wayfarer to the skin.

I reached Otatsube, a group of a few fishermen's huts; and as there is no traffic whatever along this coast, there were no regular tea-houses. Unfortunately for me, the British Squadron in the Pacific had spent the summer at Hakodate, and the ships had often gone for gun-practice somewhere near this place, scaring the natives to death, and furthermore angering them against foreigners in general, for they said the report of the guns frightened away all the fish. When I asked for food and offered money for it, they flatly refused me, saying contemptuously,—

"You foreigners come and scare all the fish away, and now you shall die of starvation before you shall get food from us. We do not want your money. We are rich."

And so I was held responsible for the doings of Her Majesty's fleet, which until then I did not even know had been in those waters!

At Furimbé, the next small village, only a few miles further on, my experience was even more unpleasant. Not only would they not give me food, but they would not shelter me for the night in any of the houses; and many of the fishermen, taking advantage of my wretched condition, were impudent to such a point that I thought we should have come to blows.

It was getting quite dark, and I was fearfully hungry and exhausted. The only course open to me was to push on, and see if I could come across some other hut where the owners were not so churlish. As it turned out, for the first time since I had been in Hokkaido I had some good luck that night!

A few hundred yards from this Japanese village, among the trees, was a little wooden shrine. Through the grating of the door I caught sight of offerings of cakes and rice which the religious fishermen had deposited on the kind of altar, probably to appease the angry gods, and induce them to fill the sea with fish again. The door of the shrine, as is usual in country places in Japan, was not locked, but a small outside bolt was all there was to keep it closed. I had no difficulty in entering. The night was a terrible one. The rain was pouring in torrents, and having had nothing to eat all day, I felt I had not the strength to go another yard. "After all," I said to myself, "the home of the gods, Japanese or not, is good enough for me. So is this supper," I soliloquized, swallowing now a white cake, now a red one, then a green one, till nothing but the empty vessels were left. "Delicious" was my last word, when, smacking my lips over the last green cake, I proceeded to make myself comfortable for the night. It is needless to add that I left very early in the morning, when the first rays of light broke the dimness of the night, and I dare say that, for the sake of morality, I ought to add that I was sorry for committing the sacrilege; but I was not—indeed I was not!

The mountain track continued, rough and steep in many places, and the autumn tints on the foliage were lovely, though not as varied as those of Northern America. Past Todohotke another volcano, the Esan, stared me in the face. Its crater, or rather its craters, for there are several, are not on the summit of the mountain, which is well rounded, but nearly halfway down its western slopes. Accumulations of very pure sulphur are deposited in and around these craters, and a continuous rumbling can be heard inside the mountain. The craters eject sulphurous vapours, and molten lava bubbles up as if in gigantic caldrons, congealing at the mouths of the craters and cracking with the extreme heat.

The coast-line is precipitous and almost impassable round Cape Esan, therefore the track leads over the mountain. The altitude of Esan is 1740 feet above the sea-level, but owing to its rising directly from the sea it has the look of a much more lofty mountain. Komagatage, near Mori, is 4,011, or more than double the height of Esan, while Makkarinupuri volcano, or Shiribeshi Mountain, as others call it, about forty-five miles south-west of Sappro, and ten miles north of Toya Lake, reaches an altitude of 6,440 feet.

Iwaonobori, which I passed on the north coast in this latter part of my journey, is 3,374 feet. Usu, on Volcano Bay, 1868 feet. Tarumai, directly south of Sappro, only reaches a height of 2,800 feet.

When this volcanic part of the coast round Esan Cape is passed the track becomes easier and flatter. One comes again to the sandy beaches, and the coast is lively with numbers of fishermen's huts, and a couple of villages like Shirikishinai and Toi. One day's journey on horseback from here takes you to Hakodate. The Hakodate Peak can be seen in the distance to the west; and only a few more hours, only a few more miles, and I should be in civilisation, I should see a few European faces, and I should hear English spoken again.

As I approached the sandy isthmus, and the peak grew bigger before me, I wondered what had been going on in the world, and what news I should receive of my dear ones. I imagined myself already devouring with my eyes the hundreds of letters which must have been amassed at Hakodate, waiting for me during the many months I had been away. I imagined myself half buried in newspapers months old, anxiously reading the news of the world. I hurried on my pony, I crossed the sand isthmus—and there I was in the lively streets of Hakodate, gazed at by the astonished Japanese, who, I believe, were more than a little amazed—perhaps scandalised—at my turn-out.

Such as I was, and before I went to the Japanese tea-house, I called at the Consulate for my correspondence. Her Britannic Majesty's representative, who knew me well enough, was more than thunderstruck when I appeared before him in such a strange attire. He was smoking a pipe, and he almost let it drop, such was his surprise.

"Who are you?" he feebly exclaimed, looking me all over from head to foot. "Surely you are not Landor?" he said when I told him my name.

"I believe I am," I answered, "and I have come to trouble you for my letters."

"Oh, none have come; we have none," he said drily.

And now that I was not quite so well dressed as when I had called on my arrival at Hakodate from Southern Japan, he seemed anxious to see me off the premises as soon as possible, I dare say for fear lest I should expire on his doorstep.

"But there *must* be some letters," I said, as I was sadly leaving.

"No, there are none. Good-bye," he repeated.

The first glimpse of civilisation and of a civilised being was certainly not a pleasing one. In a town where there are hardly half-a-dozen British subjects, all told, I expected a better reception than one which many would not bestow on a beggar to a compatriot in a foreign country. Kindness costs nothing, and I was asking no favour.

I left the place disheartened, but feeling that the pompous official had made a blunder, unluckily at my expense.

Mr. Henson, in whose house I had left all my luggage, greeted me with open arms. He was kindness itself, and very different from the gold-collared gentleman of the Consulate. I must say that I felt most uncomfortable when, after having opened my trunks, I put on fresh clothes and boots; in fact, such was the change from my late airy costume that I caught a cold! I had now almost finished my self-imposed task. I had made the whole circuit of Yezo, and been up all its largest rivers, with the exception of that part of the western coast which lies between Barabuta and Hakodate. It would mean only a few more days of agony, and for the sake of completing my journey I left Hakodate again the next morning at 2 A.M. in a *basha* for Esashi, on the west coast. The distance is fifty-seven miles, and we employed sixteen hours in covering it. It was snowing when we crossed the hills, and it was fearfully cold. Fortunately, the road is one of the best in Hokkaido. Just in front of me sat a poor man piteously ill with *kaki*. His body was dreadfully swollen and his limbs were stiff. What the poor man must have suffered in being shaken for so many hours is beyond description. His lamentations were heartrending. He had come to Hakodate in the hope of getting cured, and now he was returning—to use his words—"to die near his home." When we reached Esashi he was truly more dead than alive. He was senseless, and had to be lifted up bodily and carried into the house.

Esashi is a large place, and is one of the oldest towns in Yezo. In front lies a small oblong island, with which various wonderful tales of treasure are connected. Its harbour is too unsafe, being exposed to all winds, and I was told that the sea is always rough except during the months of July and August. I believe that this is greatly due to the currents.

I went north to Kumaishi and Cape Ota, the most westerly point of Yezo. About ten miles west of this cape is the small island of Okushiri, peopled mostly by Japanese.

The track is tolerably fair for about twenty-four miles as far as Kumaishi. It runs either along the beach or around clay and conglomerate rocky points, occasionally over the cliffs and through ravines. North of Esashi, along the Assap River, is a good stretch of cultivable land; then the thickly-wooded mountainous region begins again towards the north.

Kumaishi is said to be the best district for herring fishing along that coast.

From Kumaishi to Kudo numerous reefs extend out at sea, and small headlands afford a safe anchorage to junks. The track is mostly on a rough coast backed by high and well-wooded hills. Striking across the mountains, which rise sheer from the sea, we come to Cape Ota, the most westerly point of Yezo. From here the coast turns towards the north-east as far as Barabuta; but as it was impossible for me to go on horseback to that place, though only a few miles distant, I turned back and returned to Esashi, then following the coast towards the south to Matsumai or Fukuyama, one of the first Japanese settlements established in Yezo, and formerly the capital of the island. The coast is rugged and picturesque from Esashi to the two villages of Kaminokumi and Shiofuki, after which a mountain path leads to Ishisaki.

I found the Japanese on this coast most polite and honest, and more like the "old Japanese" than the younger generations.

The cliffs on the south side of the Ishizaki River were resplendent in beauty under the brilliant red and yellow light of the setting sun. Oshima (or Large Island) could be seen on the horizon in the distant south. Five miles further, across a mountain track, I came to Cisango, and five more miles beyond that place landed me at Haraguchi, two small fishing villages, with houses resting on high posts and against the cliffs, somewhat similar to the villages I found previous to my reaching the Ishikari River.

After that are eight or ten miles of a monotonous hilly road, where you do nothing but ascend and descend one small hill after another, up and down a snake-like or a zig-zag path; but when Eramachi is passed the track becomes much more interesting, with its peculiar groups of rocks of all shapes sticking out of the sea, and the long line of reef over which the breakers roll foaming and thundering. From here by the side of Oshima, another small island, "Koshima," is seen on the horizon. Going south the coast gradually gets more and more picturesque, with its pretty little fishing villages hidden among the rocks and sheltered under the high cliffs. At Neptka a good road leads over the cliffs to Fukuyama.

About a mile before the town is reached, from a high point of vantage on the road, is a pretty peep of Benten Island, just off the shore, with an old temple on it, and by its side a new lighthouse. On the shore, a few yards from the road opposite the island, a large rock is literally covered with hundreds of stone images of Amida and different gods, and two *Torii*, sacred emblems of Japan, are placed in front of it.

I descended the slope gently and reached Koromatsumai, otherwise called Matsumai, or Fukuyama. It is a "dear old spot," the most picturesque of all the towns in Hokkaido. It is ancient, for one thing, while other places are modern—some villages, indeed, only a year or two old, or even less. Thus weather has toned down the light yellow colour of the new wood, which is so offensive to the eye in a landscape, and is so common in all Japanese villages of Yezo. Besides, Fukuyama has pretty temples on the surrounding hills, and prettily-laid-out gardens with tiny stone bridges, bronze lanterns, and dwarfed trees. It is more like a town of old Japan. It has a three-storied castle with turned-up roofs, as one sees on the willow-pattern plates.

The castle, formerly the residence of the Daimio, a feudal prince, is now a restaurant. The irregular streets of the town, the narrow lanes, the houses blackened by smoke and age, give a certain *cachet* which is peculiar to the place itself. The inhabitants, too, are more conservative than the younger colonists, and are quite "in keeping" with the place. Unluckily, the town has seen better days! It possesses no good harbour, and all its trade, little by little, is being carried away by its more fortunate rival, Hakodate. The population of Matsumai decreases considerably every year, as the inhabitants leave this poetical but dead-alive and decaying spot for the more exciting life to be found in newly-opened districts further east or north.

Between Fukuyama and Hakodate, a distance of over sixty miles, the road is extremely bad, and there is nothing whatever to see. Shirakami Cape is interesting as being the most southern point of Yezo, and from here the coast turns slightly towards the north-east.

Fukushima is an old village. The other headlands, and the Cape of Yagoshi, have no special features calling for attention. Near the latter cape the coast is volcanic, which renders it very rugged in shape and warmly tinted in colour. There are many villages along the coast, as Yoshioka, Shiriuchi, Kikonai, Idzumizawa, Mohechi, and Kamiiro, and the inhabitants seem well off and well-to-do people.

A great quantity of coal and firewood is carried on pony-back from these mountains to Hakodate. Rows of ten, twelve, or fifteen ponies one after the other, loaded with as much as they can carry, can be seen slowly travelling, under the care of one man, down to the principal port of Yezo, especially at the beginning of the winter season; and here and there stacks of split wood are piled ready for transportation.

Rounding the Hakodate Bay, I was again at the point whence I had first started, and happy that, notwithstanding all the ill-luck I had had, notwithstanding the strain on my physique, which is not by any means herculean, and notwithstanding all the obstacles which had come in my way, I had finally succeeded in doing what no European had ever done before, namely, in completing the whole circuit of Yezo at one time, exploring all its most important rivers and lakes, studying the habits, customs, and manners of that strange race of people, the Hairy Ainu, and visiting the Kuriles besides.

Many parts which I travelled over had never been trodden by European foot, and this made my journey all the more interesting to me. As the book stands I have related but the principal adventures which I had during my long peregrinations in Hokkaido, most of which are intended to illustrate Ainu customs and traits by my own personal experience rather than to excite sympathy for my hardships. Really, though the journey nearly cost me my life, I have never, in my extensive wanderings, enjoyed a trip more than that to Ainuland.

I have touched but slightly, and not more than was absolutely necessary, on subjects relating to the Japanese; for this is intended as a work on the Ainu.

I was happy yet sorry to be at the end of my journey! This was the 146th day since I first left Hakodate, and the distance I had travelled was about 4,200 miles, out of which 3,800 were ridden on horseback, or an average of twenty-five miles a day. The remaining 400 miles were either by steamer or canoe travelling.

From the day I broke the bone in my foot I travelled fifty-eight days, mostly on horseback, and the first time it was attended to and properly bandaged up was sixty days after it occurred, or two days after my arrival in Hakodate, by Mr. Pooley, chief engineer on board the SS. *Satsuma Maru.*

Mr. Henson was again extremely kind, and pressed me to leave the tea-house and go and stay at his place, and after five months of "hard planks" I slept again in a comfortable bed. What a treat it was! What a curious sensation to sleep in a bed again, and actually have sheets and blankets! But this was not all, for surprise followed surprise.

The pompous Consul, who for the sake of saving himself the trouble of looking into his desk, had made my last portion of the journey wretched and sorrowful, found that after all he was mistaken, and on the breakfast-table in my place I found a packet of about 100 letters and newspapers, which the Consul sent to me with a message saying that when I called last time he had forgotten who I was, and therefore had forgotten to give me my correspondence!

Now that we have travelled round and through the country in every direction; now that we have seen where the different tribes of Ainu are, I shall attempt to give my readers some insight into the Ainu themselves, and their mode of living.

WOODEN DRINKING VESSELS.

CHAPTER XX.

Ainu Habitations, Storehouses, Trophies, Furniture—Conservatism.

Ainu architecture is by no means elaborate, let alone beautiful; but though it is so simple, it is to a certain extent varied, differing according to the exigencies of climate and locality. Huts of one district vary from those of another not only in small details, but also in the whole shape; or if the shape is the same, the materials are different.

The principal characteristics of the Volcano Bay and Saru River huts is, that they have angular roofs and are thatched with tall reeds and arundinaria, while the huts up the Tokachi River are more often covered with bark, though in form they are almost identical with those others.

On the Kutcharo Lake, again, the huts are thatched with tall reeds like those of Volcano Bay, but the building itself has a totally different shape. The roof is semicircular, and each hut is in appearance like the half of a cylinder lying on its rectangular base.

On the north-east coast the huts have either roofs similar to the Kutcharo ones, or else the angle is very obtuse instead of being sharp, as with the Piratori or Volcano Bay huts.

In the Kuriles, at Shikotan, the Ainu have houses exactly similar to those at Piratori.

Setting aside the varieties of form, we shall now consider how the huts are built. A frame is first made by horizontally lashing at short intervals long poles to others at the angles of the roof. Often the roof is made first and lifted up bodily on the forked poles on which it rests. Then long reeds and arundinaria are collected in sufficient quantity to thatch the frame thickly on each side. Other poles or rafters are then placed over these reeds, and through them lashed tightly to the under frame, thus preventing the thatch from being blown or washed away. Care is taken to leave an opening for the door; and the small east window—usually the only one in Ainu huts—is cut out afterwards by means of a knife. Ainu huts have never more than one storey and never more than one room and a small porch. In districts where the climate is less severe the porch is often dispensed with. In building their habitations the hairy people make no attempt whatever at symmetry or beauty; all they aim at is to make themselves a shelter and nothing more.

There are no more professional architects than professionals of any other kind in the Ainu country. Each man is his own architect, builder, and carpenter. He may occasionally receive the help of a neighbour when he is building his hut, if all hands in the family are not sufficient to carry him through his work.

Each family has its own hut, which is used day and night by all the members. If one of the sons gets married he sometimes brings his bride to live in his father's hut, or else he goes to live in his bride's hut; but as the "hairy mother-in-law" is no better than other "mothers-in-law," the end of this arrangement is that generally the bridegroom has to build a habitation for himself and his better-half. Fortunately for him, he has to pay no ground-rent; nor has he to take a lease, nor pay the lawyer for an agreement, nor yet to buy the ground nor the materials on which and of which his not too luxurious abode is to be built. He chooses the site which is most suitable to him, and there he builds his hut as best he can; and no one is any the worse or the wiser for it. The "furnishing" is a matter of no consideration with the Ainu, as he prefers to live in an "unfurnished house." By instalments, however, as he finds his floor becoming rather damp, he provides himself with a few rough planks, which afford him comfortable sleeping accommodation; and during the winter, when fishing is not practicable, and he spends most of his day at home, he roughly carves for himself a moustache-lifter (the *Kike-ush-bashui*); a small paddle, the *Hera* (which is used both to stir the wine and as an implement in weaving); a pestle and mortar carved out of the trunk of a tree; and, if he be a very ambitious person and fond of his wife, he will probably make her a weaving loom as well as two or three "water-jugs" if we may call them so— vessels made of bark bent into shape, and lashed so strongly as to be water-tight, and used for carrying water as needed.

A few wooden bowls, a wooden hook, which is suspended over the fire when bear-meat is smoked, occasionally a *Kinna* (a mat), and a skin or two, are all the articles of furniture of Ainu manufacture which an Ainu can possess, though few of them possess so many. The Ainu hut has a fire-place in the centre, or rather, a fire is lighted in the centre of the hut. The fire is lighted with a flint and steel—a method learned from the Japanese—or by the friction of two sticks. The more civilised Ainu have now adopted matches. A hole in the angle of the roof acts as chimney, but unfortunately more in name than in practice.

Chairs, stools, sofas, beds, tables, etc., are all things unknown to the Ainu. While inspecting the hut it may be as well to see how the weaving-loom, the most complicated article of the Ainu household, is made and worked. There is a "yarn beam" (the *Kammakappe*), on which the "warp" of unwoven thread is wound and kept separated, and another "roll" by which the warp threads in the process of weaving are kept in tension between the two gratings. There then is the *Poro-usa* (the "large grating"), through the intervals of which the warp threads pass, and the *Usa*, a similar but smaller grating placed on the other side of the roll.

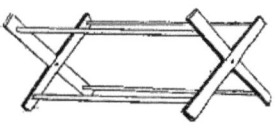

THE KAMMAKAPPE.

PORO-USA, OR "LARGE GRATING."

THE USA.

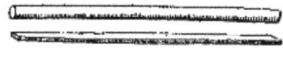

STICKS.

The cloth is wound round a stick which rests on the lap of the weaver, and is kept in tension by means of her wrists; and at the same time the *Ahunkanitte* (the "shuttle"), is passed between the two sets of warp threads carrying the transverse thread, or "woof," from one side of the cloth to the other and back again. This is then beaten up by means of a long shuttle like a netting mesh, which first draws the weft into its place, and is then used to beat it up. In some ways this form of loom is similar to that of India. The "netting mesh" is called *Atzis-Hera*. Finally, the *Pekoatnit* is a bi-forked instrument for separating the threads.

THE AHUNKANITTE.

THE PEKOATNIT.

It is needless to say that with this primitive and homemade loom it takes a very long time to weave a very short piece of cloth; but as time is not money with Ainu women, and patience is one of their virtues, it answers their purpose, and they wish for nothing better.

ATZIS-CLOTH IN PROCESS OF WEAVING.

The thread used for manufacturing the cloth is made of the inner fibre of the *Ulmus campestris* bark. At the beginning of the spring the elm bark is peeled off the trees and is put in water to soak and soften until the inner fibres can be separated, made into threads, and wound up round reeds. The material woven from these threads is very coarse and brittle, except in wet weather or when soaked in water, in which case clothes made of it cannot be worn out.

The weaving is usually plain, but sometimes a simple pattern of black parallel lines is woven in with the material. The natural colour of the elm-fibre thread is dark yellow, and the black lines are composed of the same thread stained.

The other contrivance in Ainu huts which strikes one as being simple but clever is the hook suspended over the fire. The rope is passed over a rafter. One end of it is fastened to the hook, the other, as shown in the illustration, to a piece of wood through which the hook has previously been passed.

ROASTING HOOK.

Mat-making is closely allied to weaving, and is worked entirely on the same principle, but without the aid of any kind of machinery. The bulrushes are crossed and woven coarsely, and plaited flat. One of these mats is used in Ainu huts as a door—"the *Apa Otki.*" A smaller one is hung over or by the window.

Naturally, Ainu huts are somewhat draughty. The imperfectness of the door and window-fittings, the large outlet for the smoke, besides the wind which finds its way through the thatched walls, make Ainu dwellings "ideal" to anyone wishing to "catch his death of cold." The Ainu do not much mind it.

The roof is low, and from it hang the winter provisions of dried salmon captured during the autumn. This gives an additional odour to the already strong scent of the hut—an "ancient fish-like smell," not redolent of the perfumes of Arabia. The smoke inside the hut is so dense when there happens to be a fire burning that one's eyes stream with involuntary tears, and one is nearly choked. When the days are short in winter the Ainu sometimes light their dwellings with a stick to which is fastened a piece of animal fat. It is hung up aloft, and when the lower end is lighted the fat slowly melting serves to feed the flame and keep this primitive lamp alight. Another mode of illumination is by firing a lighted piece of birch bark on a stick previously split at the upper end. The third way is by filling a large shell with fish-oil and burning in it a few strings of elm-fibre. None of these methods come much into use for everyday life, as, unlike the negroes, the Ainu are not fond of sitting up at night, except on extraordinary occasions; and when by chance they do sit up it is by the light of the fire only.

If a stranger stops for the night in an Ainu hut, he is made to sleep directly under the east window; but the family take good care to sleep all together on the north side, which is the most distant point from the door and the window. Occasional callers are received on the side nearest to the door.

The few Ainu who possess mats on which they sit during the day hang them up at night round the hut, probably to protect themselves from the liberal ventilation, which even those who are used to it find trying when a gale is blowing or the thermometer is very low.

There is no particular spot inside the hut set apart for meals, and the refuse is either thrown into a corner of the hut or flung outside the door and left there. It is difficult to say whether the inside or the outside of an Ainu hut is the dirtier. Heaps of stinking refuse are accumulated round the dwellings, and in summer-time these heaps are alive with vermin—mosquitoes, flies, *abu*, and black-flies. It is quite sufficient to move a step from the door to see a cloud of these noxious insects rise, and each one of them will have a bite at you.

Inside the house you are no better off. *Taikki* (fleas) are innumerable, and of all sizes, not to mention other well-known but usually anonymous enemies of the human skin.

The first night I slept in an Ainu hut, though I was provided with insecticide powder, I was literally covered with bites. With my fondness for statistics I proceeded to count them, and only from my ankle to my knee I counted as many as 220. The rest of my body and my head were covered in the same proportion, but I gave up the attempt to ascertain the exact number—the task was too overwhelming. My skin, however, got so inflamed by these bites as to produce fever, which lasted two or three days. After that time I never again suffered to such an extent, perhaps owing to the fact that no free spot was left to attack, or may be from that curious process called acclimatisation.

The Ainu huts are built entirely above ground, and are used alike in winter and summer.

In olden times the hut was always destroyed at the death of its owner, or when abandoned; but in the former case the custom is seldom practised now, and in the latter they are merely left to decay.

It is singular that migrating Ainu, coming across an uninhabited hut, never live in it, but build a new one for themselves.

The Kurilsky Ainu until quite recently destroyed their huts when migrating from one island to another. They also burnt the huts of deceased persons. It is needless to say that the Ainu have no churches, no hotels, no hospitals, and no public buildings of any kind. The huts in villages are a little way from one another, and each hut has directly in front a separate storehouse, built on piles or posts so as not to be accessible to wolves, dogs, or rats. These are small structures, the architecture of which has the local characteristics of the habitations, with the exception that they are invariably on piles, while the habitations are on the ground. Clothes, furs, mats, and winter provisions of sea-weed are kept in these storehouses, and access to them is by means of a peculiar ladder. It is a mere log of wood, six or seven feet in length, pointed at one end, and with five or six incisions, which serve as steps, and remind me of the steps cut by an ice-axe in a glacier or on frozen snow. Natives go up and down these ladders with ease, even when carrying heavy weights on their heads; and good care is always taken to remove the ladder when leaving the storehouse. Women principally look after these storehouses, and seem to have the whole care and control of them. I have often seen an Ainu girl— for a storehouse could hardly hold more than one—sitting on the tiny door working at her lord and master's *Atzis* robe. Hour after hour I have seen her sitting there, working patiently till the sun has set and the darkness has come. Her materials were then stowed away; the mat at the door was let down; the ladder descended and kicked away; and sadly singing in her soft falsetto voice, she retired into the dirt and dark of her habitation.

The storehouses stand about six feet above the level of the ground, and are generally on four, six, or eight piles. Upon each pile is placed a large square piece of wood turned downwards at the sides, so as not to be accessible to rats and mice. Upon these square pieces of wood rest horizontally four rafters, forming a quadrangle about eight feet square. The small storehouse has as a base this quadrangle, and is seldom high enough to allow of an adult to stand inside.

Storehouses are thatched like all other houses. On the upper Tokachi, however, they are covered with the bark of trees.

Next in connection with Ainu habitations comes the skull-trophy at the east end of the hut. This is on a parallel line to the hut wall, and only a few yards away from it, and is made of a number of bi-forked poles, upon which are placed the skulls of the bears, wolves, and foxes killed by the owner of the hut. The Ainu is proud of this trophy, and if the number of bear skulls is very large, he commands a certain amount of respect from his hairy brethren. There is nothing that Ainu admire more than courage, and there is nothing in the world that an Ainu desires more than to be thought brave. When he has gained this character a man becomes in a certain way the "lion" of the village. He embellishes his trophy with a *Nusa* and *Inaos* (willow wands with overhanging shavings—*see* Chapter on Superstitions), and he always looks on it as an evidence of his manly glory. Besides this, many Ainu possess one or two live bears kept in cages. Bear hunters often secure one or more cubs, which they bring home and allow to live in the hut like one of the family or an Irishman's pig. These cubs are nursed along with and in the same manner as the children, and Ainu say that women often put them to the breast and suckle them like their own infants. Whether this is true or not I cannot say; but though I have never seen it, and therefore cannot vouch for it, it is not unlike Ainu women to do such a thing.

When the new-comers grow big and powerful enough to be dangerous, the men make a rough cage with logs of timber,

THE APE-KILAI, OR EARTH-RAKE, AS USED BY PIRATORI AINU.

placing them one over the other in a quadrangular shape, and lashing them strongly together. The bear is driven into the cage, which is then roofed over; and after a couple of years of confinement, during which it is fattened, poor Bruin is killed for a bear festival. In the lower part of the cage there is a small wooden tray by which food is served to the captive.

On the north-east coast of Yezo I have also seen smaller cages, in which foxes, eagles, or other animals are kept; and I always noticed the care which Ainu took to feed up the imprisoned animals. That "charity begins at home" is true even among the hairy people; for if they are kind to animals it is only for the sake of making a good meal of them on the first occasion that presents itself.

PESTLE.

MORTAR.

It may be as well to state that the Ainu have never been known to make pottery. What they have of the kind is imported and sold to or exchanged with them by the Japanese. If I were an Irishman I should say that real Ainu pottery is made of wood. Nevertheless, large shells are often used by them as drinking vessels where wooden bowls are not obtainable. It is a common occurrence in Ainu households that one bowl is used by several individuals, and a more common occurrence still that none of the bowls are ever washed or cleaned after having been used.

The small Ainu porch which stands frequently at the entrance of Ainu huts answers the purpose of a stackhouse, and in it is stored the firewood used in the house. The wooden mortar and the long pestle are kept in a corner under the porch. In the more civilised parts of Yezo these pestles and mortars are general, as the natives use them for pounding millet.

The pure Ainu live principally on animal food—fish and meat—sea-weed, and some kinds of roots and herbs, which they find on the mountains. Metallurgy is utterly unknown to the Ainu. Until of late years they possessed nothing made of metal. Their arrows had bamboo or bone heads; tin or iron cooking utensils they had none; and the blades of their knives were and are of Japanese origin. Some of these blades are very old, and were acquired by the Ainu in the battles which they fought against the Japanese; others have been got by barter-metal exchanged for skins of animals.

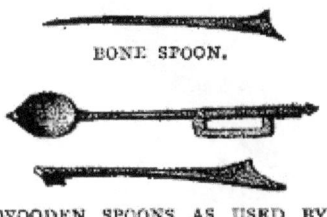

BONE SPOON.

WOODEN SPOONS AS USED BY THE MORE CIVILISED AINU.

PESTLE AND MORTAR USED FOR POUNDING SALMON.

Furthermore, save the weaving-loom, the Ainu possess no machinery of their own make. This too, as we have seen, is but a very rude and simple kind of machine. The application of wind or water power to economise human labour is in no way known to them; thus they have no windlasses, no pumps, no bellows, no windmills, no waterwheels; neither have they any signs of the rudest form of machinery moved by manual power which they have imagined and made for themselves. Furthermore, they are very loth to accept those mechanical means of economising labour which are employed by their neighbours the Japanese.

The Ainu are very conservative, little as they may have to preserve. They show a great dislike to change or reform their habits and customs, or to improve themselves in any way. Worse they could certainly not be. They have no ancestral attachment which makes them unwilling to discard their rude practices for more civilised ways; but, acting according to their instincts, and not by their intelligence, they preserve customs which seem inconvenient and unpractical to us, which habit has rendered familiar and pleasant to them.

Various natives in other parts of the world show signs of an earlier state of civilisation, but the Ainu do not. They have never had a past civilisation, they are not civilised now, and what is more, they will never be civilised. Civilisation kills them. As a hog delights in filth, so the Ainu can only live in dirt, neglect, and savagery of personal habits. They are made that way, and they cannot help it. They are excluded from progress by an impassable barrier. They have many miseries in their life, but no greater misery could befall an Ainu than to be forced to lead a civilised existence. Even after they have been educated in Japanese schools, when they return home, in a short time they forget all they have learned, and discard their acquired civilisation for the old, free, untrammelled mountain life; the wild habits of the woods and sea-shore; the nakedness of summer and the stifling squalor of the one small dingy hut in winter; the uncombed hair and matted beard; the putrid flesh of salmon, and the vile compound they revel in till they get gloriously drunk and bestial.

AINU PIPE-HOLDER AND TOBACCO POUCH, AS USED BY THE MORE CIVILISED AINU.

AINU KNIFE, WITH ORNAMENTED SHEATH.

CHAPTER XXI.
Ainu Art, Ainu Marks, Ornamentations, Weapons—Graves and Tattoos.

The expression of ideas by graphic signs is utterly unknown to the Ainu. They have no alphabet, and furthermore, they have no methods whatever of writing. Hence the utter incapacity of the hairy people to record events, time, or circumstances in their history; for even the system of picture-writing is not known to them.

Thus they have neither graven records nor any form of visible history; and tradition transmitted from mouth to mouth is all they have by way of historic continuity. The nearest approach made to graphic signs is in the owner's marks, which we occasionally find on some of their implements. The moustache-lifter is the article on which this mark is most commonly found. What these marks are meant to represent I do not know for certain; but I believe that Fig. 1 is supposed to convey the idea of a house, and Fig. 2 that of a boat; Fig. 3 a bear cage, and 4 the mere result of fancy. Even these marks are only rarely found, and have probably been suggested by Japanese writing.

The illustration shows the four specimens which I found carved on moustache-lifters.

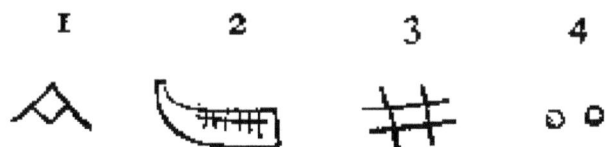

Closely allied with writing is, of course, map-drawing and ornamentations. Map drawing can be dismissed at once, like that famous chapter on snakes in Iceland, as the Ainu know nothing of it.

Rough ornamentations on bone and wooden implements are their only artistic efforts. Truthful representations of figures and animals are seldom attempted,[37] but conventionalised symbols, suggested by and based on certain forms of animal or vegetable life, are occasionally used for ornamentation.

The Ainu have no rock-sculptures, and can neither paint nor draw in any form; what they have are mere simple wood-carvings. But only a few have any aptitude for even this crude work, though of course they are not all alike. As with us we have people who are artistic and people who are Philistine, so with the Ainu, in that very humble degree which is to Western art what an acorn is to an oak.

Like all early work, Ainu art—if we may call it so—aims at a certain uniformity, especially in leaf-portraiture, so as to produce a somewhat symmetrical pattern; for at all times geometry has been the mother of design.

An Ainu does not go for his models direct to Nature, neither does he servilely copy his neighbour's work; but he gets his ideas indirectly from both these sources, and through inability to copy accurately, negligence in close study, and some amount of native imagination combined, varies the design which he has seen to such an extent as to make it in a sense original. The talent shown by different men in the art of carving varies considerably, even in men of the same tribe; while certain tribes show both aptitude and fondness for these ornamentations, whereas others have little of either.

It is the Ainu of the upper Ishikari River who chiefly excel in these carved ornamentations. The knife represented in the illustration comes from Kamikawa, and was carved with the point of a knife by the chief of the Ainu there. It took the man many months to accomplish, and it is by far the best specimen of Ainu workmanship that I saw in Yezo, though the ornamentations on it are not purely Ainu in character.

SIDE VIEW.

This man was a genius as compared to other Ainu, and his ideas of form and precision were considerably more developed than in most of his race. He has ornamented the sheath with conventionalised symbols, which were apparently suggested to him by leaves and branches of trees; and the suggestion of a flower can be noticed in the upper part of the handle. A suggestion of fish-scales has been used by him to fill up small open spaces; others he filled up with parallel lines. The sheath is made of two parts, to allow the carver to cut the space for the blade inside; but these two parts are well fitted together, and kept fast by six rings of neatly-cut bark fastened on while fresh, so that by shrinking the two sides of the sheath are brought close together, and are as if made of one single piece.

The side view of the same knife shows the clever contrivance for fastening it on to the girdle without removing the latter from around the body. This knife may be ranked among the *chefs d'œuvre* of Ainu art.

The principal characteristics of the more usual ornamentations are interesting to study.

Art of course is only the personification, so to speak, the expression of the mind, character, and knowledge of the artist; thus, in Ainu ornamentations we have patterns which could be nothing but Ainu, taken collectively, yet which show distinctly the temperament of each individual. For instance, taking

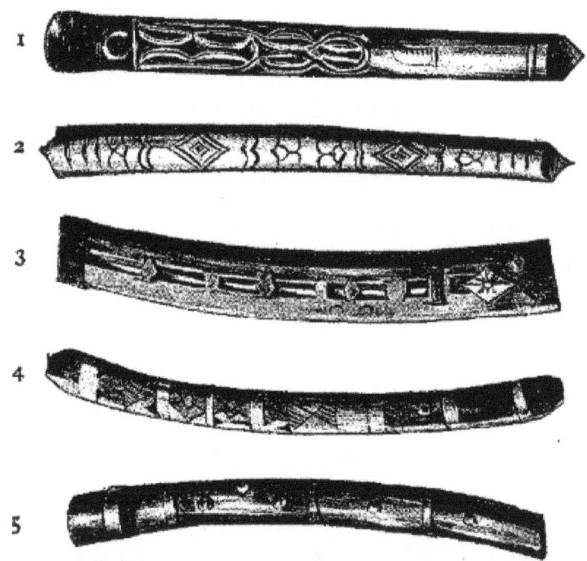

KIKE-USH-BASHUI, OR MOUSTACHE-LIFTERS.

the moustache-lifters (Figs. 1, 2, 4 in the illustration). Fig. 1, with its roundish, undecided, lines, was carved by a man weak in physique and *morale*; Fig. 2, which is much simpler and with more decided lines, was the work of a quiet but strong and proud man; and Fig. 4, with its coarse incisions, was the outcome of a brutal mind.

Ainu designs, though slightly varied by each individual, are principally formed of simple geometrical patterns; then of coils

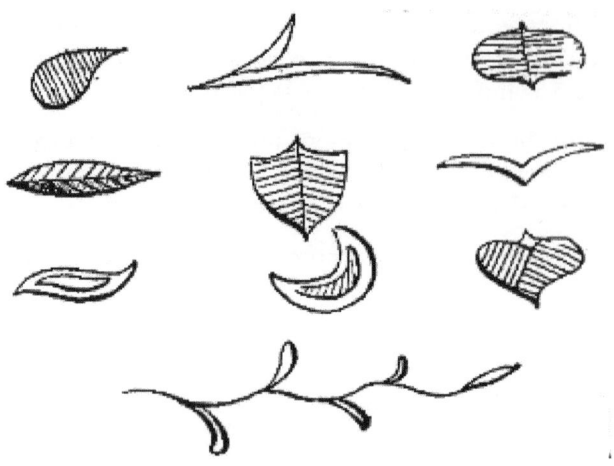

SUGGESTIONS OF LEAVES.

and scrolls; and, rarest of all, because the highest attainment of all, of conventionalised representations of animal or vegetable forms. Of the representations from animal forms the fish-scale is the only one adopted by the Ainu, but suggestions of leaves may not infrequently be found in these designs. Some of these are long and narrow; others are short and stumpy.

The above are, to my mind, the models which the Ainu have chiefly taken for their leaf patterns, following nature at a long distance indeed!

ROPE-PATTERN AND SIMPLE BANDS.

Beside these, and much more common, are the rope-pattern and the simple bands. Often the rope-pattern has bands above and below, especially in drinking vessels.

Triangles filled with lines parallel to one of the sides are

TRIANGLES.

frequently met with in moustache-lifters, and occasionally the annexed patterns are found: but as a rule the Ainu are not fond of merely straight single lines except for "filling" purposes. These patterns are mostly used on their graves. In articles of every-day use they prefer curves as a foundation of their ornamentations. The lozenge

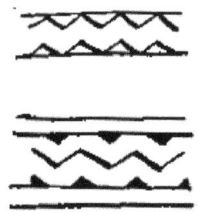  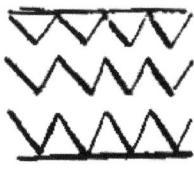

CHEVRONS.

pattern, especially one lozenge inside the other, is a favourite among their geometrical designs; also contiguous and detached circles, chevrons, double chevrons, and triple chevrons. The chevrons are mainly used by them on their graves, and they are invariably enclosed between two or four lines.

The two following patterns are elaborations of the foregoing, but are much more uncommon.

 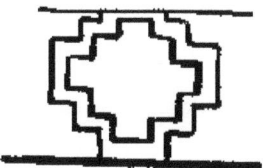

ELABORATIONS OF CHEVRONS.

The parallel incised lines and parallel lines crossing each other at right angles are met with again and again in Ainu patterns. More common still is the occurrence of a number of parallel lines meeting perpendicularly another lot of parallel lines without crossing them.

A COMMON PATTERN.

Parallel lines have a fascination for the Ainu, as we find them in most of their designs.

Concentric circles are not often met with, neither is the plain or loop coil

often found, owing to the difficulty of

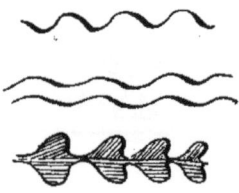

WAVE PATTERNS.

execution; but the wave pattern and double wave are typical Ainu patterns; also the reversed wave.

From these may have been derived the

REVERSED COIL.

other two, the last of which is a mere double reversed coil.

Triangular marks are occasionally

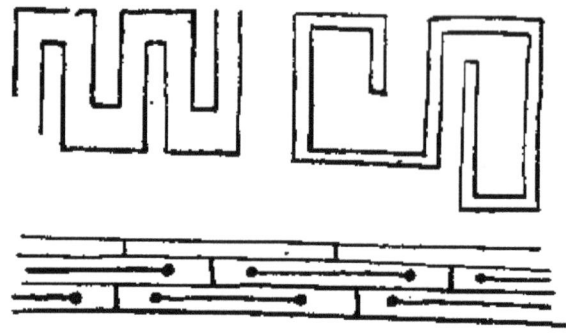

FRETS.

"put in" by the Ainu in some of their more complicated designs, and finally we find that, though rarely, they sometimes attempt a kind of fret.

Other strange forms of lines which are thoroughly characteristic of the Ainu are the following.

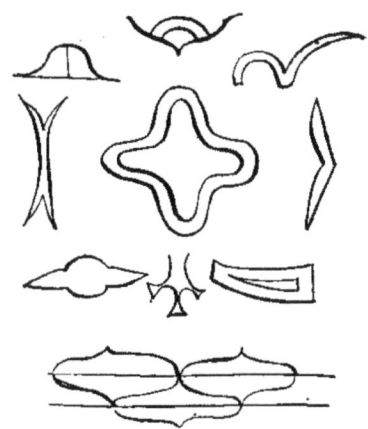

OTHER CHARACTERISTIC DESIGNS.

 I never came across any Ainu wood-carvings that were coloured, but in bone-carvings—which, I must add, are very rare—black is used to assist shade, and bring out the higher lights by contrast. The Ainu have no idea of tones, semi-tones, or gradations; the contrast is merely between the strong black and strong white. Enamelling is not known by them.

The objects which bear these incised ornamentations, beside the sheaths and handles of their knives and swords and their moustache-lifters, as has been shown, are the *Tchutti*, or war-clubs; the *Hera*, or netting-mesh used in weaving; drinking-vessels, quivers, pipes and tobacco-boxes, the thread-reeds, cloth-hangers, and graves.

The modern Ainu are not a warlike people, therefore many of the weapons which were used in former days for defence and offence are rarely found now. For instance, the old war-clubs are not used by the present generation. These clubs were long and heavy, and were carried on the wrist by a piece of rope passed through a hole at the upper end. Some were plain and straight, others were curved towards the end to

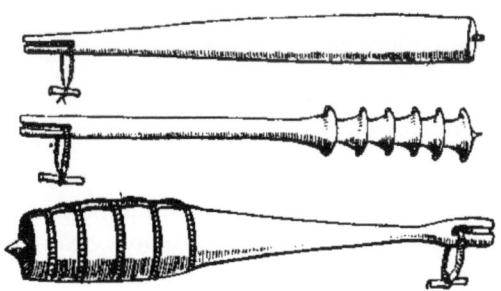

TCHUTTI, OR WAR-CLUBS.

make them heavier. Now and again some carved all over are found. Pieces of leather or rope were often knotted round the heavier part to make the blow more severe. In some of the very old clubs a stone was inlaid to add to the weight and consequent efficiency of the weapon. These clubs are from two to two and a half feet in length, and are made of hard wood.

Ainu bows are simple, and not very powerful. They are about fifty inches in length, and made of only one piece of yew. The arrows, which are poisoned, are of bamboo or bone. The poison is extracted from aconite roots mixed with other ingredients. It is somewhat greasy owing to certain fatty

TROUGH IN WHICH RESIN IS KEPT FOR FIXING ARROW-POINTS.

matters which it contains, and is smeared into the cavity in the arrow-point, which has previously been treated with pine-tree gum to fix the poison. The arrow-point is barbed, and so fashioned that when the shaft is drawn from the wound this poisoned point remains.

POISONED ARROWS.

The illustration gives two different kinds of poisoned arrows. In Figs. 2 and 3, the black part in the point shows the cavity filled with poison. Fig. 2 shows how the arrow-head is separated from the reed, and how when the arrow is drawn from the flesh the poisoned point remains inside the wound.

The arrows, when in war or hunting, are kept in a quiver, and a small *Inao* is hung to it to bring good luck to the owner.

Spears and harpoons of one barb are common, and some of the poisoned spears have heads similar to the arrows but of a larger size. Spears are out of date now, but harpoons are still employed in fishing.

Knives are the weapons on which a modern Ainu most relies. Some of these knives are of such length that they might pass for swords. The blade is single-edged, and is protected by a wooden sheath. Nearly every man possesses one, which he carries in his girdle when dressed; when naked, he carries it in his hand. The illustration shows knives of different sizes, and with different patterns worked on them. From an artistic point of view the sheaths of knives are the most carefully wrought over, and ornamented to a greater extent than any other article of Ainu manufacture.

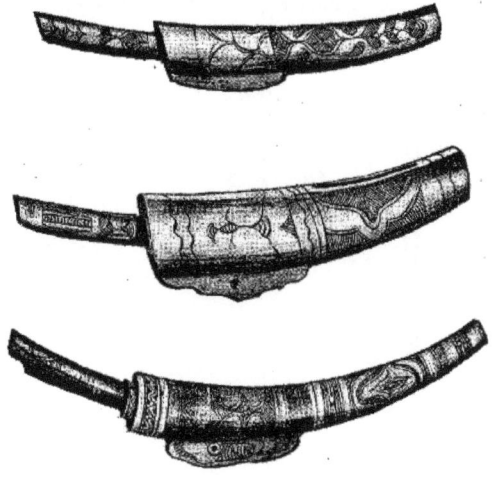

AINU KNIVES.

Then come the graves. The Ainu are very jealous of these places of eternal rest, and good care is taken to hide them either in the midst of a forest, on a distant and almost inaccessible hill, or in some remote spot, difficult to find or reach.

Each village has its own semi-secret graveyard, in which all its dead are buried. Occasionally, when the site of a graveyard has become known to others than these local Ainu, the place is deserted, and a fresh place of sepulture is chosen. The manner of burial is as follows. The body, wrapped up in a *Kinna* (mat), is fastened to a long pole and carried to the grave by two men. All the villagers follow, each carrying some article which was owned by the deceased. A grave is dug, wide and long enough to hold the body laid flat. In it are placed the bow and arrows with their quiver, the knife—from which, for the sake of economy, the blade has been previously removed— and the drinking-vessel which belonged to the deceased, if he were a man. Women are usually buried with some beads, earrings, and furs. All these articles, carried by the mourners, are broken before they are laid in the grave with the corpse; a few boards are then placed over the body, and earth is thrown over these till the ground is level again.

The grave is generally so shallow that the body is only a few inches underground—sometimes not more than four inches. The body lies flat on its back. Close to its head is erected a monument. For men it is the trunk of a tree, about six feet in length, from which the bark has been peeled off, and whereon certain ornamentations are cut. A short branch is left on one side. The top of the tree-trunk and the end of the branch are cut either in the shape of a lozenge, a hexagon, or a semicircle; and a hole is made through it. At the branch end, the cloth-earrings or the head-gear of the deceased are hung and left to decay.

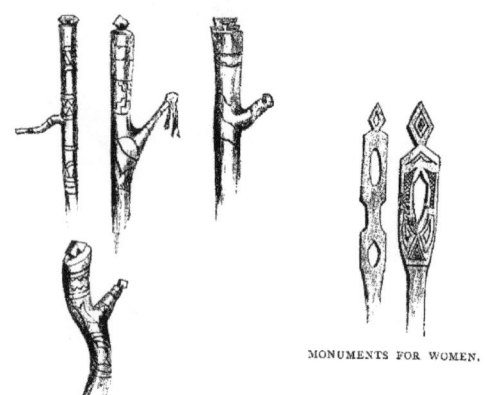

MONUMENTS FOR WOMEN.

WOODEN MONUMENTS OVER MEN'S GRAVES.

Women have simpler graves; they are flat instead of round, and are cut into the shape of a canoe-paddle. The chief of a village has a more elaborate tomb than others if he has been liked by the villagers. At Raishats, on the Ishikari River, I saw a really imposing monument put over the grave of the chief who had recently died. It was of very large size, and well carved—in the same patterns as those shown in the illustration. Its chief peculiarity was that the body, instead of being covered by earth, was covered by what appeared to be a canoe or "dug-out" turned upside down, the bottom of which had been laboriously carved. On each of the two sides, at the head and foot of the grave, was stuck into the ground a wooden blade twenty-one inches in length, resembling

WOODEN BLADE.

in shape the blade of a sword. Each of these four blades was carved alike, and had a strange design resembling the number 88. Whether a meaning is attached by the Ainu to this design I cannot say, and the curious circumstance, as my readers will remember, through which I came into possession of one of these blades, did not permit me to ask many questions on the subject. I often wondered whether it meant that life begins, goes its way round, and ends where it began? It is more likely, though, that no meaning whatever is attached to those lines, for such deep thoughts would hardly harmonise with the Ainu philosophy—such as it is. The Ainu do not stop to mourn or pray or trouble themselves about a grave when the body is once buried. Those who have touched the body wash their hands in a tub of water which has been brought for the purpose; afterwards the water is thrown over the grave and the tub is smashed. The Ainu seldom visit their graveyards except when some one has to be buried. They hate their dead to be disturbed, and nothing makes them more angry than to know that a stranger has been near their burial-ground. When a man is dead they try to forget all about him and his doings, in which they generally succeed to perfection. This naturally is not conducive to anything like continuity in the history of the country, and may partly account for their having none. Moreover, none of the tombs bear the name or the mark of the person to whom it was erected. Tombs of children are of similar shape to those of adults, only smaller in size. When carrying the dead—or, as we should say, going to a funeral—the Ainu put on their best clothes, and when the burial is over they all get helplessly drunk to make up for the loss of the departed friend.

To leave this somewhat grim subject and to return to every-day art, it may be well to mention that the designs for embroideries differ in no way from the wood-carvings. They are often more accurately finished, owing to the greater facility of materials, but the lines and all the characteristics of the patterns are the same. In the tattoos the lozenge pattern and bands are the two more commonly used. The Egyptian cross is sometimes met with (λ), and also a kind of reversed *fylfot*, or *svastika*. Moreover, the St. Andrew's cross with an additional line is not uncommon($\mathbf{X}$|). In the present volume this is all I have to say on Ainu art. I may, however, add that their ornamentations could not be more primitive, but their frequency on weapons, clothing, implements, and graves shows us that art, though not understood by the Ainu, has a certain fascination, which, in their ignorance, they cannot explain. They know art without knowing what art means. Certain lines and simple designs which are familiar to them appeal to their taste, else they would not ornament all their articles with them. But this does not show any great intellectual activity, for beyond that point the Ainu brain cannot go. As art in its natural state is merely the pictorial outcome of what the brain has grasped, we have in these crude beginnings another strong proof that the brain-power of the Ainu is indeed very limited, and their inability to represent animal form seems extraordinary in view of what other savages have done; but of course superstition may have something to say to the omission. The Ainu rank very low in the scale of civilisation; they are probably below the Australian blacks and the tree-dwellers of India, who are supposed to be among the lowest races in creation. The Terra del Fuegians and certain African tribes run them hard; but, taken all in all, the Ainu are the furthest behind in the great race of human development.

AN AINU PIPE.

CHAPTER XXII.
Ainu Heads, and their Physiognomy.

The faces of the Ainu are far from ugly, and their heads are singularly picturesque, though of course there are the finer types as there are the meaner; by which we come to gradation and comparison. The general idea that all Ainu are hideous has arisen from the accounts of the few who have travelled in the more civilised parts of Yezo, and have seen and studied only a limited number of half-breeds and actual Japanese, mistaking them for Ainu. In one of the last publications on the Ainu, photographs of Japanese and half-breeds are given as typical specimens of the Ainu race; and one or two real Ainu are given as phenomena and exceptions. That the Ainu are disgustingly filthy is undoubted; that in many ways they are monkey-like is certain; but also that on a close examination many are not devoid of good features is undeniable. As regards looks, it is a great mistake to compare savages with ourselves, and to judge of them from our own standpoint. This is no more fair than to compare a thoroughbred fox-terrier with a thoroughbred poodle-dog, to the disadvantage of the one or the other. Passing off half-breeds as pure types of course makes things ten times worse, and complicates matters for those who care for accuracy, and are interested in anthropological researches.

Ainu physiognomy is an interesting study. When seen full-face the forehead is narrow, and sharply sloped backward. The cheek-bones are prominent, and the nose is hooked, slightly flattened, and broad, with wide, strong nostrils. The mouth is generally large, with thick, firm lips, and the underlip well developed. The space from the nose to the mouth is extremely long, while the chin, which is rather round, is comparatively short and not very prominent. Thus the face has the shape of a short oval. The profile is concave and the mouth and eyebrows are prominent, though of course the nose projects more than the lips, yet without being too markedly projecting. The chin and forehead recede, as has been said, and in the supraorbital region the central boss is extremely well marked; also the brow ridges, which, however, are slightly less conspicuous than the central boss. The ears are usually large, flat, and simply-developed, with long lobes; but unfortunately, owing to the heavy weight of their enormous earrings this part of their ears is generally much deformed. Sometimes I have seen children with a hole in their lobes large enough for me to pass my finger through; with others, where the skin was not so elastic, the lobes were torn right through and the two sides hung down. In older people one does not see this so much, as their long hair entirely covers their ears. The average length of a man's ear is two and three-quarter inches; of a woman's, two and a half inches.

People have classified the Ainu as Mongolians, notwithstanding that they possess no characteristics whatsoever of the Mongolian races.

The colour of their skin is light reddish-brown, and not yellow and sallow, like that of Mongolians; they are very hairy, and the Mongolians are smooth-skinned; the features of the one race are diametrically opposed to those of the other; the mouth is strong and firm in the Ainu and weak in the Mongolian; and the Ainu eyes, the strongest characteristic of Mongolian races, do not slant upwards, nor are they long and almond-shaped, as with the Chinese or the Japanese, but with their long axes are in one horizontal plane, as in most Europeans. Indeed, the Ainu have a much greater resemblance to the northmen of Europe in their prehistoric stage than to any modern races, and least of all to the Mongolians.

But let us examine the eye more carefully. The iris is light brown, sometimes tending towards dark grey. One seldom sees black or very dark brown eyes save in half-breeds; and they are deeply set, as with Europeans. The eyelids are no thicker than those of Caucasian races, though they droop, as is common among people exposed to the full glare of the sun. The broad ridges being very heavy and prominent, cover part of the upper eyelid over the outer angle of the opening. The eyelashes are extremely long, and the eyebrows are shaggy and bushy. The eyes are full of animal-like expression and emotional warmth, a thing very rare with their neighbours the Japanese or Chinese. The long eyelashes shading the large eyes and rendering them soft, together with their pathetic and slow way of talking, make men and women singularly interesting. Like most animals, the Ainu can "speak" with their eyes.

The hair in Ainu adults is for the most part black, wavy, and easily breaking into large curls. Among children, however, one sees brown shades, which darken with years, until the hair turns quite black. Along the north-east coast of Yezo I came across several Ainu adults who had reddish hair and beard; and in the Kurile Islands, at Shikotan, several of the children had light auburn hair hanging in large loose curls and rather flaxy in texture, while the hair of adults was even darker than that of the Yezo Ainu.

The hair, which is coarse and strong, is uniformly and thickly planted over the whole scalp, and reaches well down over the forehead, where, as my readers will remember, a space is cut out or shaved off. It grows long in men as in women, but when it exceeds ten or twelve inches it is generally trimmed in the shape of a half-circle at the back of the head, and is cut off level with the shoulders at the sides. The men have a luxuriant beard, whiskers, and moustache, which grow to a great length. The hair of the beard often begins directly under the eyes, and covers all the lower part of the face. Many of the natives also have a few short coarse hairs on the nose (especially noticeable in natives of the north-east coast of Yezo). The beard, whiskers, and moustache begin to grow in the Ainu when they are fairly young. A man at about twenty can grow a good beard, and at thirty his beard is very long. Ainu women, whom nature has not provided with such a luxuriant growth of hair on the lower part of the face, make up for it by having a long moustache tattooed on the upper and lower lip, which in their idea makes them look "very manly" (*see* Tattoos). Baldness is not common among thoroughbred Ainu, even at a very old age, when, however, they generally turn grey and then white, which gives a patriarchal appearance to the hairy people.

The Ainu face seldom undergoes the marked changes common to civilised nations, as they are not subject to large emotions; but different expressions are as easily discernible by anyone who really knows and has studied the natives, as the different expressions in the eyes of animals by one who is familiar with them. When the Ainu is pleased he seldom wrinkles his face and draws back his mouth at the corners, as we do, but he shows it by a peculiar sparkle in the eyes and by an almost imperceptible wrinkle in his eyelids, which contract and diminish the opening. The corners of the mouth turn slightly upwards. The smile is an accentuation of this expression, with the additional lowering of the eyebrows, especially in the middle near the nose, causing the forehead to wrinkle.

Laughter Ainu know not. During my long stay among them I never once saw a *real* Ainu laugh heartily, for the hero of the dab of blue paint laughed less than he roared with pleasure; and I do not remember even direct crosses doing so; hence travellers have reported the Ainu to be "dull," "sad," "expressionless."

Certainly, the first thing that strikes one on coming in contact with them is, how depressed they look, and how, even in their work, their games, their festivals, sadness is greater than joy. In fact, the Ainu, with their sentimental nature, enjoy sadness.

Astonishment and surprise are expressed by a perplexed look in the wide-opened eyes, by raising the eyebrows, and by the contraction of the mouth. The hands are not raised nor directed towards the object or person causing astonishment; but if the arms be hanging down, the fingers are widely separated. With the Ainu sorrowful emotions are more marked than the more pleasing, the more joyous. Thus, when in low spirits the head is bent forwards, the eyes are staring and drooping, and the mouth is drawn downwards. In greater grief howling is added to these signs. Ainu men occasionally indulge in quiet tears without sobbing, but women weep copiously at the death of their children when these are young.

When an Ainu stands very erect, with one hand in the other in front, and, turning his head on either shoulder, throws it back and looks down at you with expressionless eyes, in the meanwhile raising his eyebrows, you may be sure that he means to show contempt. If, however, his eyes are restless and his lips quiver, if the eyebrows are rapidly brought down over the eyelids, while he opens his eyes wide showing the whole of the iris; if the nostrils are inflated and he breathes heavily; if the head is thrown forward and he is slowly arching, and, as the French say, "making a round back," you may be certain that he is in a very bad temper, and means to go for you, if he sees his way to it.

When obstinate, the pose of the arms and legs is similar to that by which he wishes to show contempt, but the expression of the face is absolutely stolid, the eyes are firm and frigid, meaning in that way to impress you with the certainty that, come what may, he will not move from his decision.

When actively angry, the Ainu sneer and snarl at one another, frowning ferociously, and showing all their front teeth, but specially uncovering their fangs or dog teeth; the arms are stretched out, but always with the fist open—if no knife or other weapon be held in the hand. Shame and disgust are two expressions which one does not often see on Ainu faces. The former I cannot describe, for I never saw an Ainu who was ashamed of anything he had done; the latter is manifested by an upward movement of the corners of the lips, and a curling of the nose, with a sudden expiration almost like a snort.

Shyness, which is the nearest approach to shame, is shown by women when meeting a stranger, and gives them a submissive look. They bend their heads and look down until the first emotion has passed, when they gaze at the new-comer with a certain restlessness and curiosity, again, as in so many of their gestures and ways, reminding one of monkeys. I never found any shyness whatever in Ainu men; neither could I detect in them any signs of fear for objects, animals, or powers with which they were familiar. Things which they do not understand of course frighten them, like eclipses of the sun or moon, or as my revolver did when I was attacked by them at Horobets; and also when I appeared as a black-winged rider on the north-east coast. In the latter case, unfortunately, I was too far off to see their faces clearly, and in the former, after the attack they showed more sensible submission to the inevitable than true cowardice. What I chiefly saw then was here and there a face with wide-open, undecided eyes heavily frowning; while some of the others shrugged their shoulders and closed their eyes, waiting for the loud report of the revolver, which unpleasant noise, heard before from Japanese guns, always gives a shock to their nerves.

When an Ainu wishes to show that something cannot be done, or that he cannot prevent someone else from doing it, he neither shrugs his shoulders like a Frenchman, nor shakes his head laterally like an Englishman; nor does he throw out his hands like a Neapolitan, but, quietly standing erect, and with his head slightly bent forward, he gently lifts it up, and slowly winking his eyes, says that he cannot do it.

When children are sulky or displeased they frown and protrude their lips, making a nasal noise similar to this—"Ohim"—without any of the vowels clearly pronounced.

Our way of nodding the head vertically in sign of affirmation and shaking it laterally in negation is not known to the thoroughbred race. Those, either Ainu or half-castes, who practise it have learned it from the Japanese. The right hand is generally used in negation, passing it from right to left and back in front of the chest; and both hands are gracefully brought up to the chest and prettily waved downwards—palms upwards—in sign of affirmation. In other words, their affirmation is a simpler form of their salute, just the same as with us the nodding of the head is similarly used both ways.

It is quite enough to look at an Ainu's eyes to see at once whether he consents or not, just as it is quite enough to look at a monkey's face to know if it will accept the apple you offer it. Slyness and jealousy are well marked in the Ainu face, and the former is seen in the glittering, restless eyes, the latter in the sulky glance and protruding mouth. Slyness is a very common characteristic among Ainu men; jealousy is recognised and frequent in women.

I could give a large number of other characteristic expressions, of less ethnological importance, but in the present work I shall limit myself to the principal ones which I have attempted to describe, leaving out altogether "expressions" of half-castes, so as to avoid confusion.

I must beg my reader's forgiveness for the "dryness" of the imperfect description I have given of the Ainu physiognomy, as many will agree with me that it is a great deal easier to notice unfamiliar expressions on faces than to describe them accurately in so many words.

AINU MAN WALKING WITH SNOW-SHOES.

CHAPTER XXIII.
Movements and Attitudes.

The Ainu people may be called physically strong, but yet they are not to be compared to the Caucasian races. They are fairly good walkers, capable mountaineers, and deft marksmen, but they do not excel in any of these exercises, either by speed and endurance in the former two, or by special accuracy and long-range in the latter.

In the Ainu country most of the hard work is done by the women, who thus surpass the men in both endurance and muscular strength. Ainu men are indolent, save under excitement. They will cover a long distance—say forty miles—in one day, bear-hunting, and not suffer from great fatigue, while they will not be able to walk half that distance under less exciting conditions. The average distance which an Ainu can walk in one day on a fairly level track does not exceed twenty-five miles at the rate of two and a half miles an hour. The distance he can run would not go beyond ten English miles, and this is partly from want of training, as he never runs if he can help it. If, however, the walk of twenty-five miles, or the run of ten miles, had to be kept up for several days in succession at the same pace, few Ainu could manage to hold out for more than three days at most; while a walking average of fifteen miles and a running average of six miles each day could be kept up for a week. In walking and running women are as good as men in one day's distances; but, contrary to what they are in manual labour, they lack endurance in locomotion, and break down after the second or third day. Men regard running as unbecoming after childhood. "If we must go quick, why not go on horseback?" says the practical Ainu, who is as perfect a horseman as the Indian.

When riding, he is able to cover a distance of fifty-five miles easily in one day on a good pony, and about seventy miles if he changes his quadruped four times. Both men and women ride in the same fashion, astride, and nearly always on bareback, or with simply a bear-skin thrown over the horse. Pack-saddles are only used when carrying wood, fish, sea-weed, or other heavy articles; and though the Japanese of Yezo designate these by the name of *Ainu kurah* (Ainu saddles), they are only in reality rough imitations of their own pack-saddles. Though women do ride on occasions, it is the men who are the true equestrians. From their infancy they spend a great deal of their time on horseback, while women ride only when obliged. Being, therefore, accustomed from their earliest days to ride pretty nearly from morning to night, men can stand many days of hard riding, and are not so easily exhausted as by walking or running. The Ainu are good at horse-racing, as we have seen at the Piratori festival, but foot-racing, even when the distance was short, gave but poor results.

Weights and burdens are carried entirely by women, and they carry them either on the head, if the load be not too heavy, or on the back by means of a *Thiaske Tarra*, or simply *Tarra*, a long ribbon-like band tied round the bundle, leaving a loop which goes over the forehead, thus dividing the weight between the shoulders and the forehead. When carrying a weight with the *Tarra* the woman stoops, and the greater the weight the lower the head has to be. The strain on the forehead and muscles of the neck is greatly modified by bending the body more or less; the weight increasing on the shoulders in proportion as the pull decreases from the forehead. The advantage of this contrivance is that it leaves both hands free. Very heavy loads can be carried by average women with this simple contrivance, and its common use may account for the strong and well-developed necks noticeable among them, but not among the men. Children are carried on the back of other children by means of a modified *Tarra* that has a stick about twenty inches long, the two ends of

THE THIASKE-TARRA, FOR CARRYING CHILDREN. which are fastened to the two ends of the band. The child carried sits comfortably on this stick while the centre part of the *Tarra* rests on the head of the child-carrier. This centre part is generally lined with a piece of skin or cloth, and ornamented with a few simple Ainu designs. A weight which cannot be lifted with both hands is easily borne for a long distance by the aid of the *Tarra*; and I should think that with it a strong woman could carry on her back a load, say, of from eighty to ninety pounds. It is difficult to institute comparative tests of strength, as constant practice, without counting "knack," often enables a person to perform feats which baffle a much stronger man. Taken altogether, the Ainu strength is relative to their height; but they are somewhat below the average Caucasian races both in endurance, and yet more in speed and muscular power.

When actively employed, the Ainu can abstain from food for fourteen or sixteen hours; when quiescent for about twenty. They can go without drink (when it is not alcoholic) for ten or twelve hours without feeling inconvenience. A pebble is often sucked, or a straw is chewed when fluid is not obtainable, thus causing a flow of saliva, which to a certain extent quenches their thirst. However, the reason given by the Ainu is not this. According to them, certain stones and some kinds of grass contain a great amount of water.

More interesting to me than their physical characteristics were their movements and attitudes, which I was able to study and note correctly without their observation. For instance when Ainu try to move some heavy object they pull it towards them. Thus, when they drag their "dug-outs" and canoes on shore, and again when they launch them, they never push from them, but always pull towards them. If an Ainu has to break a stick planted in the ground he does it by pulling it; whereas a Japanese will push it. Again, in pulling a rope the Ainu pull; the Japanese push by placing the rope over one shoulder and walking in the direction wanted. In a crowd where a Japanese would push his way through by extending his arms and thus separating people, the Ainu seizes a man on each side, pulling one to the right and the other to the left till space for him to pass is made.

As muscles are only strengthened by exercise, it is not astonishing that we never find well-developed arms among the hairy people, who so seldom make vigorous use of them. Children are as fond of climbing trees as the average English boy; and sometimes this is done in our way, by putting the legs and arms round the trunk and gradually "swarming" up; but with trees of a small diameter the ways of monkeys are adopted. The arms are stretched, and one hand is placed on each side of the tree. Both feet are then pushed against the trunk, keeping the leg slightly bent, but stiff. One hand goes rapidly over the other, one foot above the other, and so on; and the more rapid the movement the easier the climb, if care be taken to plant the feet firmly so as not to slip. Ainu boys are dexterous at this; but I have never seen full-grown men attempt it, though I am sure they could if they chose. Elderly people are very sedate in Ainuland, and violent movements are generally avoided.

Where the Ainu are indeed great is at making grimaces. The Ainu resemble monkeys in many ways, but in this special accomplishment they beat monkeys hollow. It would take volumes to describe all the different grimaces which I saw them make, especially at myself while I was sketching them; but one or two of their "favourites" may prove worth describing.

One Ainu at Shari, on the north-east coast, excelled in moving his scalp, and by raising his eyebrows at the same time creased the skin of his forehead to such an extent as to make his eyebrows almost meet his hair. The nostrils were expanded and the upper lip was raised so as to show the teeth firmly closed. The same man was also good at moving his ears. Others preferred to put out their tongue, emitting at the same time a harsh sound from the throat.

Although many Ainu could not voluntarily move their scalp they often did so unaware. When eating, especially if a piece of food required some effort to swallow, the neck was outstretched, the mouth closed tight, the eyebrows raised high, and the scalp brought far forward over the forehead. In masticating, the ears would sometimes move involuntarily, as with dogs or monkeys.

The Ainu are also good at rapid "winking," first with one eye, then the other, each eye playing at an inexpressibly funny kind of bo-peep. *En revanche*, they make no great use of their hands, and it is not uncommon for them to use their feet to assist their hands. Indeed, their toes are supplementary fingers, and they often hold things between the big toe and the next, as when making nets or *Inaos* (wooden wands with overhanging shavings). When making nets, the string is firmly held by the big toe bent over; when shaping *Inaos* the lower point of the wand is passed between the two toes, which keep it fast while the long shavings are cut.

When women wind the thread made of the *Ulmus campestris* fibre, they often let it run between the two larger toes while they wind it on a spool or a reed. Then, again, the toes are often used to pick up small objects out of the reach of the hands, and also to scratch the lower extremities. The two middle fingers of the hand and the three smaller toes of the foot are seldom used by the Ainu, and are somewhat inert. The little finger is slightly more active. Whenever Ainu point at anything they habitually do so with the open hand, for they have a certain difficulty in using any finger separately. This difficulty is not so great with the first finger; but where a European would use only his thumb and first finger, an Ainu uses all four fingers and his thumb as well, as in carrying food to his mouth, picking up small objects, lifting a cup, pulling his own hair, scratching his ears, &c. That the Ainu have more muscular power in the head than either in the hands or feet when violent exertion is required is certain, as I had frequent proof when requiring natives to make my baggage fast with ropes to my pack-saddle. Where a European would have done this by passing the ropes round the baggage and pulling them fast to the saddle, the Ainu set his foot (generally the right) against the baggage and pulled the ropes with his teeth. By this method he used one-third more force than he would had he done his work with his hands. Though the Ainu are very supple about the body, they are nevertheless stiffer than we are about the knees and hands, which last peculiarity prevents them from learning any kind of sleight-of-hand. They are supple because of the singular flexibility of their spine and the "looseness" of their arms about their shoulders. When resting or tired, the shoulders droop so far forward as to prove that the muscular tension which we constantly exert to have "square shoulders" is foreign to the hairy people. The Ainu are deficient in biceps, and such an arm as a blacksmith's or athlete's, which is not uncommon among ourselves, is in Ainuland a thing unknown. Their muscles have not the firmness of those of civilised men. Want of use entails loss of power in the muscular system, and that, unfortunately, produces further results in paralysis, *kaki*, and rheumatism. In the legs the *tendo Achillis*, which often assumes such enormous proportions with us, is only moderately developed with them, though it is generally larger than the biceps, owing to the habit of walking and riding. Notwithstanding this, the centre of muscular power, as we have seen, is undoubtedly in the head, as with inferior animals; and the Ainu are fully aware of this, for if not why should they carry all weights on the head or by the help of the head? Why should they use their teeth instead of their hands when an extra powerful pull is required? And why should they *push* with their heads when pulling with their teeth is not practicable?

Having examined the different movements of the Ainu, let us now take some account of their attitudes. What struck me most was the unconscious ease with which they stood, sat, and slept, no matter in what circumstances.

It may be well to repeat here that the Ainu are not burdened, as we are, with articles of furniture and a code of manners which so greatly modify our attitudes and make us conscious of all we do. Moreover, we wear crippling boots and nonsensical garments, which, besides not being ornamental, more or less alter and deform different parts of our body, considerably restrict certain attitudes, and greatly stiffen some of our limbs; as, for example, the exaggerated smallness of waist in women.

It is remarkable what a close resemblance the hairy people bear to the prehistoric man as constructed by *savants* out of skulls and skeletons—a resemblance found, I believe, in no other race of savages.

Take an Ainu standing at ease; he carries his head straight, but without stretching his neck, so that if a horizontal line were passed through the *meatus auditorius* it would cut the face directly under the eyes. If another line were drawn perpendicular to the horizontal, we should find that the front of the face is not on the same plane with the forehead, but projects considerably beyond in its lower part. In thoroughbred Ainu the head is well posed on the cervical vertebræ, and seldom shows an inclination from back to front, from right to left, or *vice versâ*; but in half-castes an inclination forward, and also slightly from the left to the right, is a marked characteristic.

The body when standing still is a trifle inclined forward, but when walking the inclination is greatly increased.

The body is well balanced, and this inclination is partly due to the head being abnormally large for the body; also to the habit of keeping the knees slightly bent either when standing still or when in motion.

The women, through carrying heavy weights on the head, are straighter than men when standing as well as when walking without a burden. Their spinal column describes a gentle curve inwards, while with men it has a slight tendency outwards. When an Ainu is standing at rest his arms hang by his side, the palms of the hands are turned inwards with a small inclination towards the front. But a pose which is even more characteristic than this is when both hands are placed in front, the fingers of the right hand overlapping those of the left. When sitting this is their invariable attitude, but in walking the arms hang by the side, and no swing is given to them to help the motion. In running, the arms are bent, and sometimes the hands are kept half opened about the level of the shoulders.

The Ainu legs, notwithstanding their greater muscular power than that of the arms, are neither stout nor well-developed—but they are wiry. The hips are narrow, and the legs are slightly curved.

The gait is energetic but not fast, each step being flat, with the foot firmly planted on the ground. When in motion the feet are perfectly straight, and move parallel to each other, and at each step the heel and toes touch the ground at the same time—an undeniable proof that the body is well balanced when they walk.

The Ainu walk mostly unshod, and the average length of the step in men is twenty-six inches (from heel of left to tip of right foot), and in women about twenty inches. The average number of steps to the minute is ninety-two in men and ninety-eight in women. Where the Ainu is seen at his best is when he is riding bareback. He sits so firmly that animal and rider seem to be only one body. The knees are slightly bent, and the legs and feet hang so that the toes are a great deal lower than the heels, and are also turned in. No voluntary muscular contraction is affected on the muscles of the legs; for if the knees are bent this is because of the shape of the horse's body, and if the rider "sticks" on his steed it is merely by the counterbalance of the dead weight of his two legs. The body of the rider is quite erect when riding gently, but on increasing speed the body is thrown backwards, the legs remaining in the same position. The single rein is held in the right hand resting on the horse's mane, and the left arm habitually hangs or rests on the rider's leg. When feeding in his hut, the Ainu sits cross-legged, but in places where he can lean against something, or out in the open, he squats, bearing his weight on both feet, but with the legs bent to such an extent that his head is on a level with his knees. Often his arms are rested on the knees themselves, and food is passed with the hands to the mouth, to be then torn by the teeth. No forks, spoons, or chopsticks are used by the thoroughbred Ainu; but Japanese influence has induced some of the more civilised specimens of Volcano Bay and Piratori to give up partly the use of mother Nature's forks and take to the *Hashi* (chopsticks), also to adopt some ugly tin spoons as the sign of their adherence to civilisation. Lastly, when asleep the Ainu generally lie flat on the back. Sleeping on the right side and resting the head on the bent elbow is also a common posture; and when sleeping for a short period of time during the day I have often seen men still sitting, bring up their legs, cross their arms on their knees, and then rest the head on the arms; thus placidly having a "nap" without waking up with a stiff neck, stiff legs, and "pins and needles" in their arms, which would be the sure result if the average European tried that mode of repose.

Most Ainu have no bedding of any kind, and most of them sleep on hard rough planks or on the ground itself. Some of the people, however, sleep on bear-skins in winter, as it keeps them warm, and the colder the night the closer all the members of the family pack together to warm each other with their natural heat. A strange peculiarity, when Ainu are asleep, lying flat on their back, is, that instead of keeping both legs fully stretched out, one, or sometimes both, are raised and bent, with the sole of the foot planted on the ground. This peculiarity is chiefly noticeable in men, and I have observed it many times, especially in old people. The reason of it is this. The Ainu having no pillow, the head has to be turned so far back to rest on the ground itself that action at the other end of the body is necessary to counterbalance the strain on the spine. I came to this conclusion by being often placed in the same circumstances as the hairy people themselves, when I found that lying flat on my back on the hard unpillowed ground, if the legs were straightened only a small portion of the spine between the shoulders was supported, but by raising the legs the whole spinal column rested on the level surface.

As we have now seen the Ainu asleep in a "comfortable attitude," we shall leave them for the present, and I shall take my readers to examine their clothes, their ornaments, and their tattoos.

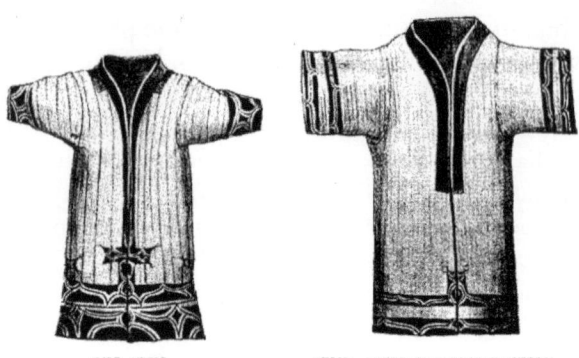

THE ATZIS.   ATZIS, AFTER JAPANESE PATTERN.

THE ATZIS.

CHAPTER XXIV.
Ainu Clothes, Ornaments, and Tattooing.

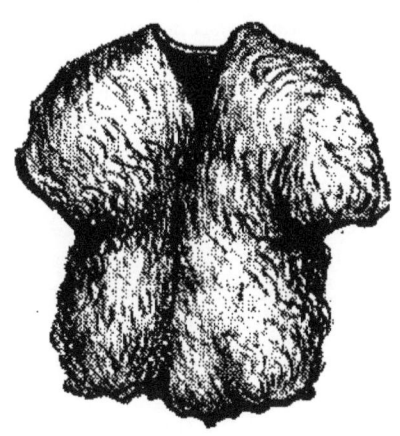

WINTER BEAR-SKIN COAT.

The Ainu men generally go naked in summer time, but in some parts of Yezo civilisation has forced them to adopt cheap Japanese clothes. It must not be supposed from this that the real Ainu never wear any clothes at all, for indeed on grand occasions they dress gaudily enough, but always in a rude, elementary kind of way. For winter use they sew together the skins of either bear or deer, fox or wolf, making a kind of sleeveless jacket, which protects the chest, the shoulders, and the back. Another kind of fur garment of deer-skin is longer and has sleeves, is large at the shoulders, and very narrow at the wrist, as a still further protection against the cold. This deer-skin coat is mostly worn by women as an under-garment. Besides these fur garments for winter weather, they wear the *atzis*, a long reddish-yellow wrapper, made of the woven fibre of the *Ulmus campestris*. It has sleeves similar to the deer-skin coat, only these sleeves are a great deal wider.

BACK OF ATZIS.

On the southern coast some of the civilised tribes have either adopted Japanese *kimonos* altogether, or make their *atzis* after the same pattern, to ingratiate themselves with their masters, on the principle of imitation being the sincerest flattery, and perhaps also because they come cheaper in the end. The *atzis* reaches below the knees, and is folded round the body. It is kept in position by a girdle or belt of the same material, or of bear or sea-lion skin. This *atzis* is ornamented with embroidery both back and front, round the sleeves, round the neck, and all round the border, or, as we should say, hem. The embroideries are done in Japanese coloured cottons and threads. The colours are invariably red, blue, and white, on a background of this yellow *Ulmus campestris* cloth. They have the same characteristic patterns, and are identical with the ornaments on knife-sheaths, drinking-bowls, moustache-lifters, &c., as the readers will find in the chapter on the "Arts of the Ainu." Men and women wear *atzis* of the same shape, only those of the women are longer than those of the men, and reach nearly to the feet. Moreover, the patterns which are embroidered on the men's dresses are not considered suitable for the women's, and *vice versâ*. Women—who, by the way, do all these embroideries—have to content themselves with the simplest patterns devisable—a mere thin line of blue stitches; but they give to the men a more elaborate ornament. They first sew on heavy bands of material, which then they embroider in highly complicated patterns, thus giving a much heavier and handsomer appearance to the male *atzis*. In winter the sleeveless fur jacket is sewn over the *atzis*, and, as has been said, women wear the deer-skin gown as an under-garment. Ainu embroideries vary considerably, not only in different tribes and different villages, but also in each family, according to the talent and patience possessed by the embroidress. It takes an affectionate wife a year or longer to ornament the elm-bark dress of her beloved husband, and in the case of a chief's robe the work never comes to an end, as additions are constantly made. Children have an extremely simple embroidery, when any, round the sleeves and hem of the *atzis*, but never any, simple or elaborate, either on the back or front.

I have often seen women working patiently hour after hour while sitting on the tiny door of their storehouses; and the result of their labour would be half an inch of coarse stitching, which for them was a great work of art. Most Ainu now possess needles of Japanese manufacture, but in former days they had only bone needles, and instead of fine well-dyed Japanese thread were obliged to be content with the fibre of the elm tree dyed black. The ornamentations on the *atzis* of Ainu who have no Japanese needles are necessarily a great deal coarser and simpler than those which are done with steel needles and cotton threads. The essential characteristics are the same in both. In sewing together skins for winter garments fish-bone needles are often used up to this day.

These embroidered clothes, when new, are only worn on grand occasions, as at a bear festival, or when paying a visit to a neighbouring village. A few rags constitute the usual every-day costume, and no difference is made between the in-door and the out-of-door clothing. In fact, most Ainu sleep in their clothes, such as they are.

THE "HOSHI."

One article of dress which is worn by all alike, young and old, male or female, is the *hoshi*, or leggings. Like their gowns, these are sometimes made of the inner fibre of the elm-tree bark and sometimes of rushes and reeds plaited as in the ordinary rush matting. When of elm-tree bark, they are often embroidered in the upper part, as can be seen in the illustration. They are fastened just under the knee by means of the two upper strings, then wrapped tightly round the leg and bound round the ankle with the lower and longer ribbon. The Ainu go barefooted in the summer, but during the winter months, when the cold is too severe for this, they cover their feet with mocassins and long boots made of salmon-skin, and often of deer-skin. When the Ainu goes for a long journey or a hunt, during which he has to traverse rough ground, he generally protects his skin boots—the soles of which would soon be destroyed by the sharp stones and ice—by slipping over them a pair of thick rope sandals, which protect the sides, the back, the toes, and sole of the foot. If to this

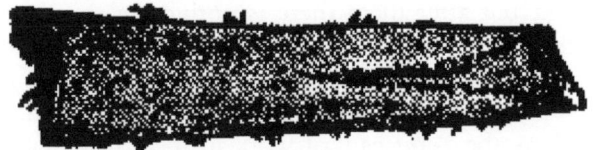

BOOTS TO BE SOAKED IN WATER SO AS TO TAKE SHAPE OF FOOT, AND TO BE KEPT UP WITH A STRING.

DEER-SKIN SHOE.

inventory be added a head-gear consisting of a band wound round the head, and an occasional apron, the whole of the Ainu wardrobe is catalogued. This band, which is worn principally by women, is untied and removed when saluting or meeting a man, whether on the road or in the woods. A

THE TARRA OR HEAD-BAND.

Japanese towel often takes the place of the native manufacture. I am inclined to think that this custom of covering the head has been acquired from the Japanese, as none of the Ainu of the Upper Tokachi—the only pure ones remaining—wore anything in the shape of band or kerchief, while it is extremely common with the Ainu of Volcano Bay and Piratori to wear these unbecoming towels. At Piratori the Ainu women give a more artistic character to this ugly headgear by embroidering it in front and wearing it like a tiara. An apron is occasionally worn by Ainu, but this too, in my opinion, has been borrowed from the Japanese. Ainu clothes often get undone, owing to their shape, and therefore Ainu men sometimes wear these aprons, but rather because they are made to wear them than from native modesty or inclination to be commonly decent. I have seen Ainu on the north-east coast of Yezo and on Lake Kutcharo wear coarse hats of matted rushes. When laid flat, these hats have a diameter of about thirty inches; but when worn, they are folded in two, and kept in this position by a string tied under the chin and passed through the hat. They are used principally in winter as a protection against the snow. The Ainu care more to adorn than to clothe themselves. A few glass beads, a metal earring, a silver coin, or anything that shines, can make a man or a woman as happy as a king. Intoxicants come first of all things, but after them there is nothing in this world that Ainu cherish more than personal ornaments, and this is, of course, even truer of women than of men. What strikes a stranger when looking at an Ainu for the first time is, as I have already said, the size of their metal earrings and heavy glass necklaces. As the Ainu cannot work in metals or make glass, these ornaments have been purchased from Japanese, Chinese, and Corean adventurers, and many costly skins of bears, foxes, wolves, or seals are gaily bartered for a few beads, worth next to nothing. The Ainu is fond of metals, but he does not know the difference between one and the other. All that glitters is gold for him; and if it is not gold then it must be silver. Therefore some Ainu are known to have invested all their fortune of valuable furs for a pair of brass earrings, and, what is more, they have never grudged the bargain! Previous to the importation of these worthless articles their ornaments were made of wood, bone, and shells, of which "survivals" are still to be seen with the Ainu of the Upper Tokachi.

The large circular earrings are much prized: men and women alike wear them. Many men, however, do not wear these metal earrings, but prefer instead a long strip of red or black cloth, or skin.

The lobes of the ears are frequently torn down by wearing these heavy earrings from early childhood, and they know not how to mend them by sewing them. Another hole is sometimes bored in the upper and sound part.

Ainu women of civilised districts occasionally wear metal finger-rings, but these are of course of foreign make, and imported.

Ainu *menokos* (girls) seem to have no partiality for bracelets or amulets, but necklaces are the dream of their life. The delight of an Ainu woman in a new necklace is in proportion to the size and number of the beads. A woman who possesses one of extra large beads is envied by all her less fortunate neighbours; and she who has several strings is at once admired and hated by all the womankind of the village. For, indeed, Ainu women are "human" enough to know how to hate each other! The beads which most take their fancy are the blue, black, white, or metal ones. The larger beads in the necklace are in front; and the rough wooden pendants with bits of bone, metal, or broken beads inlaid in it, which hang to the necklace, rest on the breast. Large Japanese sword-hilts are often used as pendants by the Volcano Bay natives.

The Ainu of the Upper Tokachi region had none of these beads, but a rough wooden pendant was suspended round their neck by a leather string.

Girdles are worn by men and women for two purposes—first, to keep their clothes together; next, to support the large knives which the Ainu always carry with them.

The Ishikari Ainu who lived formerly in Sakhalin wear leather belts, and the women wear besides a peculiar cloth headgear. Both these articles are ornamented with drops of melted lead and Chinese cash sewn on to the cloth.

These are all the articles of clothing and ornament which are in common use among the Ainu. None of them are worn as symbols of rank, or to denote virginity. No Ainu can explain why he or she wears one thing more than another, except for the reason that he or she likes it. There are no Ainu laws as regards clothing, and with the exception of the "chief," who on special occasions dresses more gaudily, and wears a crown made either of willow-tree shavings or dried sea-weed, with a small carved-wood bear head in front, they all dress pretty much alike. A chief could not be distinguished from a commoner by his everyday clothing.

Speaking of personal ornamentation, I may as well describe the way in which the hair is dressed, and also the tattoo-marks.

Little care is taken of the long hair, which reaches down to the shoulders. It is never washed, nor brushed, nor combed. At the back it is cut in a semicircle round the neck. Over the forehead the men shave a small part of the long hair, which, falling over their eyes, is uncomfortable to them; but women do not. Until lately this shaving was done with sharp shells, and wives shaved their husbands. The process was said to be rather painful, and the thoughtful women have now adopted knives for that purpose, to the great delight of the stronger sex. The part shaved is in the shape of a lozenge two and a half inches by two inches respectively from angle to angle. This open space causes the hair to part in two different directions and hang down in large wavy curls. The fingers are occasionally passed through it, and then with the palms of the hands it is plastered down on both sides.

A characteristic Ainu method of making the morning "toilette" is to bend the head low and let the long hair fall over the forehead. The two hands are then placed under it on the temples, and suddenly and violently the head is shaken and thrown back, the hair being pressed down by the hands at the same time. If the first attempt at neatness is not approved of, the process is repeated two or more times. I must confess that personally I could seldom see any marked difference between a head of hair "dressed" and one "not dressed"; but it must be remembered that the Ainu have no looking-glasses, and what they think is right is of course right for them.

Formerly, when an old woman lost her husband she had her head entirely shaved, and when the hair had grown long again she repeated the process as a proof of fidelity and affection to her deceased spouse. It is very rarely done now. She used to wear a sort of cap, with an aperture at the top, round the crown of the head during the time that her hair was short; and it was incumbent on the widow to wear a look of sorrow and pain till her hair grew long again.

The Ainu men have long beards and moustaches, which are never trimmed, with the exception of the Kurilsky Ainu, who trim theirs. The beard begins to grow when they are very young, but it is shaved till they reach manhood. It is then left to grow naturally, and never touched again as long as they live. Ainu women, whom nature has not favoured with such a manly ornament, supplement their deficiency by having a long moustache tattooed on their lips. Their hands and arms are also tattooed.

The tattooing among the Ainu is limited to the fair sex, and it is confined to the head and arms. Why and when the fashion was adopted is not known, and the semi-Ainu legends on the subject are very vague. One legend says that when the Ainu conquered Yezo, which was then inhabited by a race of dwarfs—"the Koro-pok-kuru"—some Koro-pok-kuru women came to the Ainu camp to beg food from them, and they did so by passing their arms through the reed walls of the Ainu huts. One day an Ainu clutched one of these arms and pulled it in, when a tattooed pattern on the tiny arm was greatly admired by the hairy conquerors, who adopted the practice from that day.

A simpler reason is that the women, not being so hairy as the men, are humiliated by their inferiority in that respect, and try to make up for it by tattooing themselves. In support of this theory may be quoted the fact that women are only tattooed in parts which are left uncovered when clad in their long *atzis* gowns.

The Ainu process of tattooing is a painful one. The tattoo marks are usually done with the point of a knife; not with tattooing needles, as by the Japanese. Many incisions are cut nearly parallel to each other. These are then filled with cuttlefish-black. Sometimes smoke-black mixed with the blood from the incisions is used instead. On the lips the operation is so painful that it has to be done by instalments. It is begun with a small semicircle on the upper lip when the girl is only two or three years of age, and a few incisions are added every year till she is married, the moustache then reaching nearly to the ears, where at its completion it ends in a point. Both lips are surrounded by it; but not all women are thus marked. Some have no more than a semicircular tattoo on the upper lip; others have an additional semicircle under the lower lip; and many get tired of the painful process when the tattoo is hardly large enough to surround their lips. The father of the girl is generally the operator, but occasionally it is the mother who "decorates" the lips and arms of her female offspring. Besides this tattooed moustache, a horizontal line joins the eyebrows, and another line, parallel to it, runs across the forehead. The tattoo could not be of a coarser kind. A rough geometrical drawing adorns the arms and hands of women, the pattern of one arm being often different from that of the other. Frequently only one arm is tattooed. I never saw tattoos that went further than the elbow, neither did I see any other part of the body tattooed. The four specimens given in the illustration show the patterns most usual in different tribes, though each individual has some slight variations.

Fig. 1 was copied by me from the arm of a woman at Frishikobets (Tokachi River); Figs. 2 and 3 are the two arms of Kawata Tera, a girl of Tobuts (northeast coast of Yezo); and Fig. 4 is the left arm of a girl at Piratori.

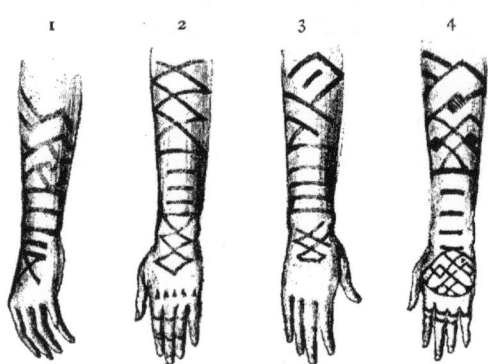

TATTOO-MARKS ON WOMEN'S ARMS.

It will be noticed that in the regions where the Ainu have come in contact with Japanese, rings are tattooed round the fingers, while the Tokachi Ainu women have none. In the two arms of Kawata Tera (Figs. 2 and 3) the dissimilarity of the two patterns is very marked at first sight, but on a close examination it is easy to perceive that the operator meant to carry out the same pattern on the right arm as on the left; only through his incapacity to reproduce correctly his former lines, or for other reasons, he got muddled up in the design, and left his work unfinished. If all the lines in the upper half of Fig. 3 were continued, the design would be very similar to Fig. 2.

Tattooing is considered an ornament, besides, as I have already mentioned, adding the coveted air of "virility" to women. There is no religious feeling connected with it, and the practice is rapidly dying out, as the Japanese men make fun of the Ainu women, who after all only tattoo their mouths and arms, while they themselves often tattoo the whole of the body. The Ainu have no rules as to when the girls are to be operated on. They are done both before and after marriage, contrary to what has been said, that the women do not tattoo themselves after they have become wives. The moustache is generally finished before a girl gets married, as she herself is anxious to be thus decorated; but there are no rules as to virginity or marriage, for the arms and hands are as often tattooed after marriage as before. Indeed, in the Ainu country, "tattooing" one's wife seems to be one of the pleasures of the honeymoon. The design of these tattoos is meant to be, but is seldom, symmetrical. The Ainu apparently execute these designs on a preconceived plan, but the results rarely come up to expectation, as no drawing of the design is prepared beforehand. The bluish-black colour of the tattoo is very permanent and strong, and many an Ainu woman is disfigured for life, who, according to our ideas, would otherwise be good-looking.

SNOW-SHOES.

AINU SALUTATION.

CHAPTER XXV.
Ainu Music, Poetry, and Dancing.

The music of each nation has certain characteristics of its own; and though according to European ideas the music of what are called barbarous peoples may sound in some sense excruciating, it always has a certain occult charm, more especially to one who is able to forget his former training, and teach himself to see, hear, and think in the same way as the natives he is studying.

Undoubtedly we Westerns have brought music to a pitch of refinement that no savage nation has even attempted to reach; but in my opinion we do savages injustice when we call their music "unmitigated discord." Barbarians like the Ainu do not indicate their rhythmical effects and modulations by means of a musical notation; and harmony is of course very defective with them, from our point of view. On the other hand, the feeling and passion with which they chant their songs make them go straight to the heart, if as a melody they are not always pleasing to the cultivated Western ear.

An Ainu seldom sings for the mere pleasure of art as art, and it is only when full of joy or "crazed with care" that he gives expression to his feelings in music. Then he pours out his whole soul in that which to him is melody beyond the power of words to compass.

After a hunt, a fishing expedition, a journey, or a misfortune, the Ainu enters his hut and seats himself cross-legged on the ground. He then holds out both hands with the palms together, and rubs them backwards and forwards three or four times; after this he raises them, palms upwards, to a level with his head, gracefully lowers them to his knees, and then, raising them again, strokes his hair and beard. Again he lowers his hands twice, thrice, or even more times, according to the amount of respect to which the person saluted is entitled, the latter following in every smallest detail the motions of his saluting friend. When this complicated salutation has been performed separately before each male member of the household, the new arrival relates the tale of his good-or ill-luck; and if the events be of an unusual character the story is chanted in a sort of sing-song which makes each note of joy or lamentation vibrate in the heart of the listener. It is only in such circumstances of stress of feeling that I ever heard the Ainu sing, though sometimes women and young folks when alone, fishing, riding, or travelling, sing out bits of their past lives as they remember this scene or that event.

Ainu music is almost entirely vocal, and their singing has more the character of the *recitative* than of the *aria* proper. Their songs are always for *solo*; and during my stay among the hairy people I never heard a concerted piece, nor even an air or a single voice with a chorus for a number of voices; neither did I hear any songs performed by men and women together, but invariably by men to other men, and by women to other women. It seems to me that the reason why they have no choruses is their strict etiquette, which forbids them to interrupt a speaker till he has finished his narrative; and as their songs are only narratives which the musical sing-song makes more impressive, it seems more than probable that the reason I have given is the right one. If a singer during his narrative stops, and is silent for a minute or two, another takes up the "lost chord" in exactly the same intonation of voice, asking a question or singing words of comfort, anger, or scorn, as the case may be; but no Ainu ever joins in the song before the person singing has stopped.

The hairy people are fond, not only of their own, but of all music, and their ear is acute enough to hit a tone or note when sung to them, and even to remember with more or less accuracy a short air after they have heard it two or three times. Many who have come in contact with the Japanese have learned from them songs of a totally different character from their own. Of my personal experience I can speak of a boy who, while I was sketching, heard me sing a few bars of the *Trovatore*. An hour or two later I heard him repeat this passage, certainly with an Ainu *libretto*, and somewhat Ainuized; but for all that he had managed to catch the melody, which showed that the lad must have had some musical instinct as well as a good musical memory.

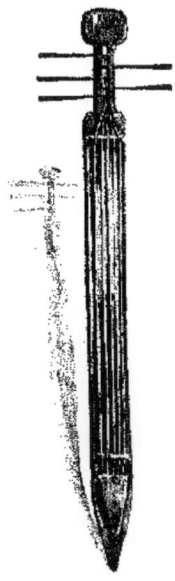

A "MUKKO," OR MUSICAL INSTRUMENT.

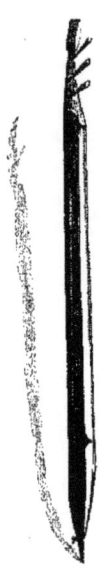

SIDE VIEW OF THE "MUKKO."

The Ainu are remarkably quick at reproducing sounds which are direct imitations of noises, cries of animals, &c., and it is instinctive in them, as when children they are not taught or trained to do so. The education of Ainu children is indeed a thing far to seek in every way, and what they know is self-taught. Nature is their only school. The Ainu voice is pleasant, flexible, and very soft in quality. The men are mostly baritone and bass, the women alto; but when singing, a falsetto is preferred to the natural voice, especially by the women, and this always without an instrumental accompaniment. Musical instruments are more than rare among the Ainu; indeed, I saw only one, which is now in my own possession. It is a black-stained wooden instrument, fifty-one inches in length and three wide. The upper part is flat, the under is half a cylinder scooped out by a knife, while five keys are fixed in the short neck, in which a cavity is cut, leaving a space for the strings to be tied to each key. The top is circular, and flattened on each side. One very small hole is bored exactly in the middle of the instrument and another is at the lower end, where the point of a triangular piece of leather, seven inches long, is passed through and fastened by a knot tied in the leather on the opposite side. The five strings, which are of *Ulmus campestris* fibre, are fastened to this leather piece and then to each key. A peculiarity of this instrument is, that it has two prism-shaped bridges, and they are placed at each end of the harmonic case. The Ainu call it *mukko*, which word, however, means only a musical instrument; and as it is applied by them to all Japanese instruments of music, it shows that they do not distinguish very sharply one instrument from another. Though in my long journeying I found one of these *mukkos*, I was never able to discover any Ainu who could play on it, and the Ainu of Ishikari from whom I bought it told me that the man, the only one, who could play on it, was dead. This was unfortunate, as none of the others could tell me how he tuned it; and one old man, in attempting to solve the problem, broke three strings. Seeing that I was then quite unable to learn any of the tunes of the deceased Ainu Paganini I purchased the instrument, and found by cross-examining the natives that it was played by twanging the strings with the fingers, and not with a plectrum, as is the case with the Japanese *shamesen*. In the illustration I have faithfully drawn a front and a side view of this instrument, so as to give the reader an exact idea of its shape. The Ainu of Volcano Bay sometimes make bamboo jew's-harps for their children; but even those are very uncommon, so we might as well define Ainu music as entirely vocal. Ainu music is sentimental, and not displeasing, but it is monotonous, and continually repeats itself. It is difficult to establish a rule as to what order of intervals their music is founded on, as their progressions, modulations, and rhythmical effects are often so peculiar as to make it impossible to indicate them accurately by means of our musical notation; but the nearest approach to it is the diatonic minor scale. The Ainu are fond of chromatic intervals, and when their recital comes to an exciting point they make use of this method in a *crescendo* to give strength to the narrative, especially at the end of the tune, which invariably winds up in the tonic. The intervals which are of most frequent occurrence in the Ainu tunes are as follows:—

The tunes seldom contain modulations from one key into another, except in the case of genius-gifted improvisators, who sometimes indulge in such a luxury, especially when intoxicated; but the usual modulation is generally begun *pianissimo* and in irregular time, and is sometimes like a slow lamentation gradually and irregularly increasing in force, some notes marked violently and the next very faintly, thus giving a weird effect of light and shade. When a sentence comes to an end, there is a chromatic interval *fortissimo*, and the keynote generally concludes the tune. The melody repeats itself again in the next sentence, sometimes altering the *pianissimo* into *fortissimo*, and *vice versâ*, according to the force which the narrator wishes to give to certain words. The Ainu, as far as I could judge, have no fixed rhythmical method, and each man constructs his own. Their melodies are generally short and simple, and the same phrases and passages—in fact, usually the whole melody—occur again and again in their songs. No Ainu melody that I heard was constructed according to any rule of musical form.

All were invariably of one part only, in which the name of the tune was often applied to a certain form of rude poetical composition. For instance, some of the folk-lore legends—which, unfortunately, are not purely Ainu—are chanted in a musical intonation, and are a kind of extempore composition, though the roots of the songs and the verse have probably been brought down from former generations. This is proved by the preservation in them of some obsolete words and forms of speech which are never used in current conversation, and which none of the younger folks can understand or explain. I believe, however, that none of these legends are very old. The Ainu, having no written language, it is but natural that their tradition and legends should have been greatly changed and corrupted, especially by intercourse with the more imaginative Japanese. It is to be noted, however, that the Ainu, though to a certain extent as imitative as monkeys, have also a large amount of personality and originality, due to their shy and unsocial habits. This originality is not surprising when we remember that they are taught nothing, and that each man provides for himself and his family, but has no markedly friendly feelings towards his neighbours; in other words, it is a state of degradation very similar to that of wild animals. Perfect indifference is shown by the people of one village towards those of another. They are neither friends nor foes. All have a right to live, but as for helping one another, that is out of the question.

Having no written documents, each man, in his easy-going manner, recites and sings as best pleases himself such verses or legends as he has heard from his father or from some other person, and the result is that, according to the reciter's greater or smaller poetical and musical tastes, the grandfather's composition, already altered by his father, is again altered by the son, which makes it a composition of his own. This transformation of a given theme is common even among civilised nations when people are set to repeat the same story verbally transmitted from one to the other—the version of the third person has but little in common with that of the first. If this we do with a spoken narrative, how much more with tunes learned by ear only, and characterised in the delivery by individual temperament and transient mood.

The Ainu do not teach these legends to their children, and if learned at all they are merely "picked up" by ear and, in a manner, at random; therefore, most Ainu profess ignorance as to their existence, and a man, when I asked him if he knew any, scornfully answered in these identical words, translated:—"The Ainu are taught nothing, and they know nothing."

The few legends, &c., that I heard were told me by Benry at Piratori, and by another old man, the chief of a village up the Saru River. The title of one was "Tushi-une-pan"—"Twice Below;" the story of Yoshitsune, a Japanese hero, and Samoro-kuru (a Japanese man-friend of Yoshitsune), who came to Yezo and had a great struggle with a huge fish, which was harpooned by them and disappeared twice under the water, capsizing the boat which contained the two fishermen. Yoshitsune's temper was roused, and he cut the *nipesh*[38] rope to which the harpoon was fastened. The fish went to die at the mouth of the Saru River, when plains of hemp sprouted out of its body.

Another legend, called "Kimta-na," is a rather different and more simple version of Tushi-une-pan's story which I have just related.

Yet another variant of the same legend is found in the "Inu-sapk"—or "A Summer Story" (literally translated: *Inu*, hear, relate; *sapk*, summer), which was so very confused that I could not make head or tail of its minuter details; but, like the "Kimta-na," it was about a famine in the Ainu land.

Then there was a fourth, which went by the name of "Abe-ten-rui"— "Burning to embrace," or love-sick. It was again about Yoshitsune, who had fallen in love with a pretty Ainu maid, and could not eat either good or bad fish until she appeared to him in a dream. As Yoshitsune was a strong-minded man he got over his love, and taught the Ainu not to be deceived by woman's wiles.

These and other similar legends, some of which do not bear repeating, being too improper, can be collected at Piratori or on Volcano Bay from the half-civilised Ainu; but I am inclined to think that they are mostly concoctions of Japanese ideas construed or misconstrued in the Ainu language.

Ainu do not indulge in poetic compositions which have a definite metre, nor do they use special words for rhyme or rhythm; but all the words in their songs are intelligible, and seldom meaningless syllables are used, as in many of the chants of other savage nations. This of course is because, as has been said, their songs are merely a form of conversation adopted on certain occasions.

Some of their music seems to have been suggested to them by such animal sounds as the plaintive howling of bears, wolves, and dogs.

Music is believed by the Ainu to have the power of curing illness, or rather, of scaring away from the body those evil spirits which are supposed to have taken possession of it; but, when used as exorcism, the music is no longer grave, slow, and sentimental, but verily diabolical, consisting mainly of wild howling with an accompaniment of stamping feet and the rattling of sword and knife, and followed by a disgusting expectoration of chewed convolvulus roots, which are said to be powerful in expelling the evil spirit and restoring the sick person to health.

Furthermore, music is invariably used by the Ainu—especially by the women—to facilitate manual labour, as when pounding millet, rowing, pulling canoes on shore, or drawing water from a well, when packing seaweed, or when preparing salmon for the winter; and also in their games, which I have already described in the chapter on the festival at Piratori.

During the process of pounding millet—which is only practised in the southern part of Yezo—two or three girls stand round a mortar in which the millet has been placed, and each girl, holding with both hands a pestle, beats and sings, one after the other, the words "*Huye, huye*," as the pestle is let down, increasing in loudness when the grain requires harder pounding, and slowly decreasing in volume towards the end. This pounding begins about sunset, and the place chosen for the operation is generally the small porch of the huts. It has indeed a weird effect to hear these many voices from the distant huts gradually dying away as darkness comes on, till finally only two or three break the stillness of the coming night. Then even those wear away, and everything becomes as silent as the grave.

When riding on horseback, especially if alone, young men are fond of singing, and when going through forests, chopping and collecting firewood, Ainu invariably sing.

I have often heard two or three Ainu, when packing sea-weed within a few yards of one another, each singing to himself, and each so much absorbed in his own composition as not to even hear his neighbours. An Ainu does not and cannot sing unless he feels in the mood for it; but if he sings he is carried away by his own music. Of course this is a good quality in Ainu music, as in all arts where "feeling" is to be appreciated as much as execution. The latter is to be got by constant practice and teaching; but the first has to be born in one.

My readers must forgive me if I am judging Ainu music, not from the European, but from the native standpoint, for I think it is only fair to give things as they are, without too much reference to our own ideas.

With savage nations, music is the expression of the feelings and passions of the musician. Thus, it is necessary to well know the man himself before we can understand his productions and appreciate them; and such knowledge is only attained by constantly living with natives, not as a mere stranger, but as one of them.

Very few travellers have seen the real Ainu, or studied them accurately, while many, partly owing to their inability to differentiate one race from another, have given us highly imaginative descriptions, and even photographs, of Japanese half-castes and actual Japanese, describing them as Ainu. If such worthy ethnologists as have visited the "civilised part only" of the Ainu country, have been unable to distinguish types of the hairy Ainu race from those of the hairless Japanese, or from mixtures of the two, undoubtedly racial characteristics have been but imperfectly recorded.

It is more particularly in music and poetry, as I have already explained, that temperamental characteristics are shown, and one ought to be careful to clearly define what is native music and poetry—in which I include legends, traditions, and folk-lore—and what has been transmitted by neighbouring and conquering races. Loud music is not appreciated by the Ainu, and makes them grin with more scorn than enjoyment. I could only try experiments in this direction by singing to them, as I had no European musical instruments with me; but I found that singing *con brio* at the top of my voice was not so pleasing to them as when I sang *piano con passione*. For instance, the song "Toreador," in the opera *Carmen*, created fits of merriment from a crowd at Frishikobets, while the same crowd, a few minutes later, listened attentively and silently to Gounod's "Ave Maria," sung in a kind of "miaoling" voice.

I may here mention incidentally, to show the different musical tastes of Ainu and Japanese, that some months previous to this I was at a concert at Tokio in which the same "Ave Maria" was performed by some distinguished European musicians. The large Japanese audience, who had been attentive and well-composed till then, went into fits of laughter when Gounod's masterpiece was played, and all through it the noise of people laughing was so great as to drown entirely the orchestra and singers. Some of the women in the audience nearly went into hysterics at the long *legato* notes at the beginning of the piece. Louder melodies and of a livelier character did not affect them so. I wish to draw attention to this fact, that amongst all primitive peoples the native music is sad and slow—the livelier melodies coming later; and also, that with both wild and domestic animals the most noteworthy effects are produced by slow and simple music. We all know how dogs will remain quiet and calm when a soft and gentle air is played, but get furious to the point of savageness under the "plan-plan-rataplan" of a merry noisy tune. As for the last item connected with Ainu music, viz., dancing, it is rarely practised, even by the Ainu women, to whom alone it pertains. At the best it is of a very rude form. In the Piratori festival (Chapter IV.) we have seen that their dancing is accompanied by rhythmical sounds imitating the noises produced by implements in everyday use, as the squeaking of a paddle by the friction on the canoe, the cry which accompanies the pounding of millet, blowing alight the fire, and similar sounds. Time is kept by clapping the hands and by vociferations which tell the partners what position or action to assume, each action being accompanied by a different sound, but all performed while the hopping is kept up. I have not felt justified in classifying these rhythmical sounds, which accompany the dancing, as choruses, for there is not enough in them to constitute either a tune or a melody. They are suggested more by the action of the arms and upper part of the body than by the steps; in fact, if it were not for the continuous hopping it would be more accurate to describe Ainu dancing as "posturing." The dancers form a circle, with sometimes one or two children in the centre. As there are no professional musicians, there are no professional dancers; but though each man may be his own composer of music, the women never alter their dances, which are handed down unchanged from one generation to another. It is only at festivals that the dance is performed, and never inside the huts, but in the open air. It is not for the amusement of spectators, for besides one or two of the older women, spectators there are none; but it is for the enjoyment of the dancers themselves. The men do not seem to take the slightest interest in the dancing, and apparently regard it as unmanly. They remain in the hut drinking while the girls enjoy themselves in this way outside, and should one of them by chance come out, he would stop and look on no more than men in civilised countries would stop and watch little children at play. On the other hand, on such occasions Ainu matrons squat in a semicircle not far from the dancers, and keep up a lament-like or sometimes quarrelsome conversation among themselves, and occasionally encourage the girls in their hopping, and suggesting *encores* of this figure or that, which, between one quarrel and another, has taken their fancy.

A WOODEN PIPE.

CHAPTER XXVI.
Heredity—Crosses—Psychological Observations.

The mental qualities of the Ainu are not many, and what they have are by no means great; nor are they improved by education, for what they know comes more from inheritance than personal acquirement, though naturally every rule has its exceptions. I repeatedly noticed that talent, such as it was, ran in certain families, the members of which were all more or less intelligent. Certain families were more musical than others; other families were more artistic—if, indeed, such a word could be applied to the very low development of the artistic faculty when at its best among the hairy people. Various members of one household were potently insane; others were as potently idiotic. I shall not class under this heading of heredity transmitted disease, like leprosy, consumption, &c., but I shall limit myself to heredity in physical traits and mental qualities. Unfortunately, with the Ainu intercourse between the sexes is so imperfectly regulated as to often lead one to erroneous conclusions. The reader may easily imagine the difficulty of establishing precise rules of transmission in a race like the Ainu, where castes are not marked, with the exception of the chieftainship in each village, the only necessary qualifications for which are a sound, sharp intellect, a strong physique, and personal courage. The office is hereditary if these qualifications are also inherited; but should the sons or brothers of the chief prove unworthy of his place, the Ainu would assemble in a "village council" and elect another strong, clear-headed, and brave man in place of the *roi fainéant* thus summarily deposed. These chiefs have no absolute authority, though the men often consult them in their quarrels and difficulties, which they are asked to settle. Thus, because of these qualities necessary for the office, these chiefs are a slightly superior type to the other natives; for with savages, as with civilised people, sharp-witted, strong, and brave men are naturally of a finer type than those who are their inferiors in these qualities: but the difference among the best Ainu and the worst is so small that I do not feel justified in classing chiefs as of a different caste. Besides, exceptional beauty, strength, or larger stature is not necessarily transmitted in the families of chiefs, nor do the Ainu themselves consider them better-looking than others.

As Ainu laws of marriage have no relation to the physical and moral improvement of the race, the only way of classifying the natives for purposes of heredity is by tribes, each village being considered as a tribe. Ainu villages are generally very small, and the inhabitants of each village intermarry among themselves, therefore each member of the community is in some way related to every other member; hence heredity in certain physical traits, mental qualities, and diseases shows itself in one community and not in another. The difficulty of tracing the exact connection of each individual with his or her relations beyond the acknowledged father and mother also baffles research in more minute details. Abnormal formations are sometimes transmitted to many members of one tribe, as, for instance, the hare-lip and webbed fingers, of which deformities two or three specimens could be found in a small village numbering fifteen or twenty houses. Malformation of the umbilicus is common—sometimes in almost every member of one small community—while it is very rare in others. Children are mostly affected by this, as in some villages the cord is not treated at all at birth; and this leads to an abnormality till the child grows older, when the few who survive seem to get all right. In other villages the cord is fastened in a very primitive, not to say imperfect, manner, with a common string of *Ulmus campestris* fibre.

Albinism is very uncommon among the Ainu. I do not know of any case when it has been transmitted, as albinos are greatly disregarded by the Ainu, and, I was told, seldom marry.

Red hair, or hair with red shades in it, is common among the Ainu of the north-east coast of Yezo, and also among the Kurilsky Ainu of Shikotan, where nearly all the children have light hair. It darkens considerably as they grow older, as many of the men said they had light hair when young, which turned dark with age. Members of certain communities have inherited the love of bear-hunting; others the love of fishing; some tribes have a musical aptitude, and a certain artistic talent for rough ornamentations on wood; others have developed their inherited power of sustaining hunger and thirst. The only characteristic which all the different tribes have inherited, without exception, is love for intoxicating drinks; and this love is not only inherited by thoroughbred Ainu, but also by half-castes.

Mixed marriages between Japanese and Ainu are frequent, but the progeny are unfortunate beings, of whom a large percentage die when very young: those who live are generally malformed, ill-natured, and often idiotic. Their sight and hearing are not so acute as with the pure Ainu, and crosses are said to be sterile, with very few exceptions. If children of second crosses are born they seldom live to be more than five years old.

Half-breeds are invariably from a Japanese man with an Ainu woman, but occasionally an Ainu man marries or cohabits with a half-caste woman. I have never seen a pure-blood Ainu man marry a pure-blood Japanese woman. The majority of half-breeds are males: I should think two-thirds males and one-third females. The half-caste women are physically finer than the men, but they are said to be very generally, if not uniformly, sterile.

The products of the first cross greatly resemble in general look the Ainu parent, without being quite as hairy, though still very hairy; but a strange peculiarity is, that they get bald while quite young. One can easily detect them by their eyes, which are frequently like those of the Japanese, by the wide flat forehead, and by the pose of the head, which inclines forward. They generally walk with their toes turned in, instead of keeping their feet perfectly straight, like the pure Ainu. The moral and intellectual position of these half-breeds is a pitiful one. They are rejected by both the Ainu and Japanese, and are held inferior to both alike.

A high moral standard, whether got from philosophic breadth or Christian virtues, does not suit a despised barbarian race like the Ainu. Nothing could or does kill them quicker than civilisation. Experiments have been tried to civilise certain Ainu: they were made to wash, bathe, and live in comfortable, clean quarters: they were instructed and got good food; but after a few months they had to be sent back to their native place and ways, for civilisation only killed them.

The half-castes have none of the good qualities of either race. They are neither as brave as the Ainu nor courteous and light-hearted like the Japanese. The following remarks, which I take direct from my diary, were written by me between Shimokebo and Tomakomai, on the south-west coast of Yezo, where many half-breeds are found along the sea-shore, and I shall pass them on untouched to my readers.

"The Ainu along this coast were decidedly ugly. Many half-breeds are also found along this coast. These half-breeds invariably grow bald in early life, whereas the Ainu do not. The hair on their back, arms, and legs is not so long or so thick as with the pure Ainu. Their teeth are neither so strong nor so sound. As is usually the case when a mixture of two or more races takes place, the lower and upper jaws not being of the right proportion, it follows as a matter of course that unusual pressure and friction injure and wear out the enamel of the teeth, thus causing premature decay. The Americans and Australians are good examples of this premature decay caused by the disproportion of the upper and lower jaws. Also, teeth which do not fit well together sometimes grow so long as to be a nuisance to the person who owns them. I found that these half-breeds have all the bad qualities of both the Ainu and the Japanese, and have not retained any of the good ones. They are ill-tempered, lazy, and vindictive. It is well to mention that, on the Japanese side, they have come mostly from the criminals exported by the Japanese Government, which fact partly explains why they are so evil-minded and untrustworthy. Instead of falling into the more civilised ways of the Japanese, these half-breeds prefer the wild life of their Ainu ancestors; and if anything they are wilder than the Ainu themselves. Insanity is very common among half-breeds. The head is in most instances of an abnormal size; the frontal bone is generally more sloping than with the thoroughbred Ainu; and though the skull be wide from one temple to the other, it is not spacious enough from the frontal bone to the back of the head. They have heads so shaped that the animal propensities are in excess of the moral and mental faculties.

In thoroughbred Ainu I found the bumps of amativeness, philoprogenitiveness, and tune very well developed. In the half-breeds these bumps hardly show at all, and in some cases the back of the head—where the two first bumps are found—is almost flat.

"Ainu half-breeds never live to be very old. They are often affected with rheumatism—*kaki,* a disease peculiar to the Far East—leprosy, and consumption, and they suffer from these diseases much more than do the pure Ainu. I found leprosy quite common among half-breeds—while I have seen but few Ainu affected with it. In most instances, though, leprosy had only attained its first stages—contraction of fingers and subsequent dropping off of the three phalanges, ears, and nose; but this may be explained by the fact that the sufferers in general succumb before the disease attains its more serious character, when the whole body is visibly affected by it."

Precise laws as to the degree of quickness of perception, power of reasoning, and learning of the Ainu race cannot be given, for, as I have mentioned before, almost each individual would require a special rule for himself. My readers may have noticed that, while some Ainu were but little above monkeys, others were sharp, and gave answers very much to the point. This may apparently be regarded as a contradiction on my part by people who have neither lived with savages, nor studied the temperament of beasts. But it is not a contradiction. There are in this world clever monkeys and stupid monkeys: some can never be made to learn any tricks; others will learn them in no time. Intelligence is instinctive, and not acquired, though of course it can be greatly developed with education; thus, the Ainu are instinctively intelligent, but I wish my readers clearly to understand that their intelligence does not go much further than that of an intelligent monkey, though of course the Ainu have the advantage over beasts of being able to talk, and therefore, to a limited extent, discuss and combine. The Ainu memory is a perfect blank in certain respects, as with arithmetic, science, mechanics, reading, writing, drawing, and delineating maps; while in other directions it seems to be fairly keen, as in hunting, fishing, tracking, and acquiring languages up to a certain point. This last faculty is noticeable in nearly all the lowest races, as the Australian aborigines, the Tasmanian natives (now extinct), the Tierra del Fuegians, &c. The Ainu ideas of time are vague, and if you add to that the extreme difficulty which they experience in counting even up to ten, and their inability to count beyond that number, it is easy to understand why we can never learn the exact age of Ainu individuals.

Like the monkeys, the Ainu cannot concentrate their attention, and they are easily wearied. Beads and shiny objects have a fascination for them; but other objects, even perfectly new to them, arouse but little curiosity, which soon passes, and they show no intelligence and less imagination as to the probable use of these strange objects. They show no inquisitiveness, and no wish to be taught the use of anything new and unfamiliar.

It will be remembered that at Yamakubiro, on the Tokachi River, beyond the natural astonishment caused by the first appearance of my ponies, the strange baggage, and myself, the Ainu did not pay much attention to this novel sight, and did not show any wish to have it explained, while more civilised people, like the Japanese, would not have been satisfied until I had shown and explained every article in my possession, and allowed each person to try its use, &c., after which they would talk for hours of what they had seen. The Ainu are not "built" so, and therefore they have never made any progress. In the more civilised parts of Yezo we have a proof of it. Their backwardness in acquiring the habits and customs of their conquerors the Japanese, arises from incapacity more than from conservatism. Yet for all that the Ainu are so incapable of improving themselves, they are very persevering in what they do attempt, as in their rough wooden carvings, the hollowing of their "dug-outs," the construction of their wooden tools and weapons, the weaving of their rough garments, and the ornamentation thereof; but in all these they appear to act more automatically than with keen and constructive intelligence.

The Ainu are not to be taken *au pied de la lettre*, for the illusions produced by ignorance and untutored imagination prevent anything like literal accuracy; but they are not what we may call conscious and immoral liars. A good example of this is my adventure at Horobets, when, although they knew that they would be severely punished by the Japanese policeman, the Ainu confessed their attack on me, and did not attempt either denial or evasion. They are often plucky, and even distinctly courageous; as, when out bear-hunting, a man armed only with a large and not over sharp knife unhesitatingly attacks this formidable beast, who sits up on his hind quarters, sure to crush the life out of his assailant should he miss his stroke. The Ainu, protecting his head with his left arm, and having taken the precaution to cover his back with skins, goes merrily for the embrace; and while Bruin squeezes, the hairy man splits its body open with the large knife.

The Ainu are cool-blooded. They are not subject to strong emotions, and therefore they are not much affected by dreams and nightmares. They are not affectionate except for a momentary impulse; but, like most animals, they are faithful when they love. Mothers are fond of their children till they have reached puberty; but after that the affection seems to fade away. Paternal love is much less strong.

The pure Ainu are comparatively honest people, which may be due to the incapacity for being dishonest. In a country where there is no exact definition of property, where anybody can get what he requires without resorting to theft, there is no reason why everybody should not be honest. Then, according to Ainu ideas, stealing is not always stealing. For instance, if an Ainu, without asking, takes away some of the salmon caught by one of his hairy brethren, he will be blamed for it, he will get into a row, and probably be beaten; but if the theft is perpetrated on a Japanese or a stranger he will be praised, though the Ainu well knows that he is not acting right. Their desire is stronger than their conscience, such as it is; and having no laws of their own to rule them worth speaking of, they often do according to their desire, without deserving the accusation of conscious dishonesty. It is exactly the same case as when a dog jumps on the dining-table when everybody is absent and carries off the leg of mutton which he knows he ought not to touch; but the temptation was too strong, and he could not resist it. The Ainu are fond of independence, though in many instances I found them gentle, and apparently submissive to a stronger will than their own. The field of their brain-power is of course very narrow, and the same rough, rude, primitive thoughts and ideas are constantly repeated in their conversation as well as in their designs.

NAKED AINU MAN FROM THE NORTH-EAST COAST OF YEZO, PACKING SEAWEED FOR WINTER USE.

CHAPTER XXVII.
Physiological Observations—Pulse-beat and Respiration— Exposure—Odour of the Ainu—The Five Senses.

The following physiological remarks are mostly from observations made on Ainu of the Upper Tokachi district, the natives of which have had no communication with Europeans and little with Japanese previous to my own visit to them. Observations made on the semi-civilised Ainu of Volcano Bay and Piratori, on those of the north-east and west coasts, and the Ishikari River, as well as on half-castes of different districts, have been taken into consideration.

Owing to the lack of a clinical thermometer and other instruments, I, unfortunately, was not able to ascertain the normal temperature of the body; nor could I get any very accurate observations as to the frequency of the pulse-beat, owing to the miserable condition of my watch and the difficult task of getting natives to sit perfectly still while their pulse was felt. A superstitious fear, too, that some evil would befall them accelerated the pulsations, and they invariably moved away rubbing the spot I had touched on their wrist. Though I could not count the exact number of pulsations to a minute, the movement of the pulse was as a rule slow and rather weak. Respirations were fourteen to seventeen to a minute in men, and about sixteen to twenty in women, and the respiratory movements were similar in both sexes, viz., costal breathing was predominant. In half-castes I have sometimes noticed abdominal breathing.

The Ainu not only bear cold well, but prefer it to heat, though, indeed, their country is never very hot. The sun's rays have no fascination for them, as with so many other races; and I have seldom seen Ainu basking in the sun for purely physical pleasure, although they go about with uncovered heads, and do not seem to suffer any ill effects from the practice. The Ainu of Piratori wear Japanese hats of wicker-work; and others, especially women, tie round their head a Japanese towel—a fashion, as we have seen, also adopted from the Japanese. With this head-dress the crown of the head is left uncovered.

The Ainu are not massively formed, but they are sturdy, and, as we have seen, can bear almost any amount of privation as regards food and drink. Sleep is necessary to them, and they require a great deal to be in anything like good condition. The sleeping hours are generally from an hour or so after sunset to sunrise; but during the day they are often drowsy, and turn in to have a siesta after food and exercise. In men the voice is soft and deep; shriller but still gentle in women. The Ainu seldom perspire, partly because the pores of their skin are blocked with dirt; partly because their long hair absorbs a great quantity of natural moisture; and mostly because they do not drink much except when they can get hold of intoxicants.

The skin is greasy—the natural result of many years of an unwashed existence; and this gives to the hairy people a peculiar and strong odour, much resembling that of monkeys. Many are familiar with the peculiar odour of an uncleaned monkey's cage, and the same, intensified a thousand times, characterises an Ainu village. Hundreds of yards off you can distinctly smell out a village, or if the wind is blowing towards you, that peculiar odour is perceptible for a full half-mile. Although the sense of smell is acute in the Ainu—for they sometimes employ it in tracking animals—they are not aware of their own strong odour; but they are quick in distinguishing that of other races. I have several times heard Ainu of the coast remark that I possessed a different odour from that of the Japanese; but they could neither define it nor assimilate it to that of any animal they knew, though several of them one day held a lengthy pow-wow about it; and in the interest of anthropology I submitted to the unpleasant process of being smelt all over by them. The Chinese unanimously assert that Europeans smell like sheep, and they say this is the reason we constantly wash and bathe, being aware of our infirmity, and doing our best to diminish it by soap and water. We ourselves attribute to Jews one distinct odour, and yet another to the Russians; not to speak of those belonging to the negroes, the Chinese, and, in fact, all other nations. Thus, the odour has some importance in the classification of peoples, as it largely depends on the kind of food as well as the personal habits of a race. Meat-eaters smell differently from fish-eaters, and these again from vegetarians. As regards the Ainu, their filthy habits of course increase their offensiveness, while bodily exercise renders them intolerable. The Japanese recognise the Ainu odour as a distinguishing mark of the race, and Japanese fishermen have often said to me, "*Aino shto taihen kusai*"; "*Saru,*" or else "*Kumma onaji koto*"—"Ainu men smell bad, just like a monkey or a bear."

As an Ainu grows older this peculiarity increases. The weaker sex is generally more "strongly scented" than are the men, owing to the fact that women wear skins and rough cloth rags nearly all the year round, while in summer the men go about either entirely naked, or very lightly clad.

On the north-east coast of Yezo and in Shikotan (Kurile Islands) I saw some Ainu who, contrary to the rule, had red hair, and their animal odour was terribly offensive. The Ainu do not use any unguents like palm-oil, cocoanut-oil, or the like, by which the unpleasantness of certain African tribes and Eastern peoples is to be accounted for. What they have is natural and national, and due to their food, habits, and race alone.

The Ainu have no partiality or dislike for any particular scents, and their sense of smell shows itself mainly in their power of tracking game or animals, as was said before. The same might be said of the sense of "touch," which they seldom apply practically, notwithstanding their sensitiveness in certain parts of the body, especially under the arm-pits and on each side of the spinal column and the back of the head—just those parts which in most animals are the most sensitive; but they have no developed sense of touch in their finger-tips, as with civilised nations.

Most Ainu find it difficult to declare which is the heavier of two not very unequal weights. Differences in the temperature of two bodies, and in the smoothness or texture of two surfaces, are also extremely difficult for them to define, while it is easy for them to judge of weights and texture by eyesight. The palms of the hands, which are so sensitive with us, owing to the papillæ being more thickly studded there than in other parts of the body, are less intelligently sensitive with the Ainu. When they touch cold or hot objects they feel pain, but not difference of temperature, as when with us a wound is touched it makes little difference whether it is by something hot or cold, it is simply pain, and not discrimination. Their lips, as well as the tip of the tongue, are slightly more sensitive; the lower lip more so than the upper. I was never able to determine the relative sensibility of the sensitive parts of the Ainu body, as my experiments either caused anger and impatience, or hilarity and mockery. If the first, the observations had to be stopped before they were well begun; if the second, beyond the general results which I have quoted, the answers were mere guesswork on their part, and therefore not worth recording. Most of my observations are based on experiments made while the men were unaware that they were observed at all. Often, when asleep, I have touched them on the soles of the feet and the palms of the hands without causing them to awake, while when touched on the lower lip or in the lumbar region they invariably woke up startled. One day I tried this experiment on an Ainu who was sleeping on his back, with his mouth wide open. I touched his tongue with a well-sharpened lead-pencil, and the effect was subitaneous; more so than on either the lips or the lumbar region. The skin directly over the spine was dull, but the ears showed a certain amount of sensibility. The sense of "taste," which is a mere modification of the sense of touch, is also dull, although naturally, when stimulated by very acid or bitter substances, it produced distinct impressions. Even with ourselves, though more perfected than the sense of smell—which, however, often comes to its assistance—few can boast of having the sense of taste very acute. In our lower classes an extraordinary amount of salt, mustard, pepper, or sugar is needed before they can call their food "tasty," whereas a person of more refined education will detect the lack or excess of even the smallest portion. Over-stimulation of the lingual nerves and extremes of heat or cold deaden the sensibility of the tongue, palate, and fauces, and destroy the power of distinguishing flavours; bad digestion also frequently affects the organs of taste. From this we may argue, then, that the sense of taste, though born in one, has to be cultivated before it is brought to any degree of refinement. The Ainu not only do not possess this acquired refinement, but, through monotony of food, learn only one kind of flavour, and cannot distinguish differences. Thus, as many labourers in our country would not find any difference between a beef-steak slightly underdone and one over-cooked, so an Ainu finds no difference whatever between a piece of salmon properly dried and one perfectly rotten. In this respect the Ainu are far below beasts.

In tribes of natives like the Ainu, who have lived an adventurous life, mostly in the open air, it is but natural that the two senses of "sight" and "hearing" should be more developed than those of "touch," "smell" and "taste;" as life itself depends mostly on their accuracy and acuteness. The Ainu possess good sight. Inflammation of the eyes is very common among their children, owing to their filthy condition; but it seldom affects their permanent sight; very few Ainu suffer either from myopy or cataract, or other eye affections such as are frequent among civilised and more studious nations. In very warm climates, where the sun is powerful and the light strong, the eyes are generally shielded by specially long and thick eyelashes and eyebrows, which last prevent the sweat from running down the forehead into the orbit; but, strange to say, the Ainu, who are a northern race, and have always lived in cold climates, have eyelashes even longer and thicker than any race of people in tropical climates. The iris is of a somewhat greyish tint, sometimes traversed with brown shades. The white of the eye is less pearly than with Caucasian races, and the eyes, shaded as they are by long eyelashes and heavy eyelids, seem to possess all the qualities necessary for abnormally long vision. And this we find to be the case, for the Ainu can distinguish objects a long way off, but they are dense as to minutiæ. In other words, the eye of an Ainu is ready to receive an impression, but very slow in transmitting to the brain the impression received.

As we have seen, they cannot reproduce the "human form divine," or any faithful representation of anything animate or inanimate which they have seen. They see *en gros*; thus, should an Ainu's attention be drawn to some very distant object rapidly moving on the shore, he will at once say that it is a horse, because he knows that the chances are it is a horse, but he will be unable to describe its colour, and whether cantering or galloping, saddled or unsaddled, by a single glance at the horse, unless his attention is called to each particular detail, when he will answer each question correctly enough. The Ainu vision is then strong, but the brain is not quick in response. Testing their sight by "test dots," as used in the British Army, was not a success, greatly owing to their inability to count and the inaccuracy of their answers.

The most fully-developed sense in the hairy people is, in my opinion, that of hearing. Distant sounds are clearly recognised and specified, and they are also aware that by placing one ear near the ground, far-off sounds of horse's hoofs and the like can be clearly distinguished. The ticking of a Waterbury watch could be heard by Ainu at a distance of twenty and twenty-two feet, while I could only hear it nineteen feet away. I was often struck by the quickness with which they detected the tick-tack even when the watch was in my pocket, and they were six or eight feet away. The unusual sound fixed their attention and made them curious as to the cause, and they showed a childish kind of surprise and delight when the watch was produced and passed round among them, each one being allowed to enjoy his share of the ticking.

Resuming these few remarks on the characteristic points of Ainu senses, my readers will probably have noticed certain facts which strongly support Darwin's theory of evolution, and the hairy arboreal ancestor with pointed ears from which the races of men are descended.

TROPHY OF BEARS' SKULLS.

CHAPTER XXVIII.
The Ainu Superstitions—Morals—Laws and Punishments.

I cannot begin this chapter better than by saying that Ainu religious ideas are essentially chaotic. They recognise no supreme God, and no intelligent Creator; and they cannot be called polytheists, for indeed they are not *worshippers* of any power—taking the word in its full meaning. The Ainu worship nothing.

If they have any belief at all it is an imperfect kind of Totemism, and the central point of that belief is their own descent from the "bear." This does not include the smallest reverence for their ancestor. They capture their "Totem" and keep it in captivity; they speak to it and feed it; but no prayers are offered to it. When the bear is fat, it is taken out of the cage to be ill-treated and baited by all the men present. It is tied to a stake and a pole is thrust into its mouth; and when the poor beast has been sufficiently tortured, pricked with pointed sticks, shot at with blunted arrows, bruised with stones, maddened with rage and ill-usage, it is killed outright, and, "ancestor" as it may be, it makes the chief dish and *raison d'être* of a festival, where all the members of the tribe partake of its flesh. The owner of the hut in which the feast takes place then sticks the skull on to a forked pole, and sets it outside with the others at the east end of his hut. The skin is made into garments, or is spread on the ground to sleep on.

In addition to this rudimentary kind of Totemism—if I may call it so—the Ainu show a certain amount of fear and respect for anything which supports their life or can destroy it. This, however, is under the form of an "instinct" rather than a "religious feeling." Dumb animals of any kind are similarly affected by powers which they cannot explain; but as we would not think for a moment that when a dog is barking at the moon the dog is worshipping the orb of night, or when it basks in the sun that it is offering prayers and reverence to the orb of day, no more should we think that the Ainu, who are not much above dumb animals, worship all they respect and fear.

If other writers, most of whom have never visited the Ainu country, had not written on this subject, I would have limited myself to saying that the Ainu, properly speaking, have no religion, but as certain untenable theories and false ideas have been published, I feel bound to state what I know on the subject, that, so far as I can, I may correct these erroneous impressions. I regard myself as qualified to speak with some authority, as I am the *only* foreigner who has seen and studied *all* the different tribes of Ainu in Yezo and the Kuriles; while other writers, the few who have actually been there, have based their statements on a few half-castes or Ainu in the more civilised part of southern Yezo, collecting from them ideas left behind by previous travellers, and offering them to the public as purely Ainu. That these hasty travellers and cursory writers have been deceived, or have deceived themselves, is not astonishing; for it must be borne in mind that the Ainu language is as poor in words as the Ainu brain is deficient in thoughts. Thus it is no easy matter to explain to an Ainu what is meant by "religion," by "divinities," and by "worship." The nearest approach can be made only by comparisons and analogies, which often lead far from the point aimed at. Like all savages and barbarians, the Ainu are more apt to answer as they think will please the questioner than to give a definition of their own beliefs. The manner in which a question is put gives the keynote to the reply, which is in no sense an independent statement of their own thoughts.

For instance, if you were to say to an Ainu, "You are old, are you not?" he would answer "Yes"; but if you asked the same man, "You are not old, are you?" he would equally answer "Yes." Knowingly speaking the truth is not one of their characteristics; indeed, they do not know the difference between falsehood and truth. This is a common failing with all savages as well as with all Orientals; but with the Ainu it is even more accentuated; and when, in addition to this, the difficulty of making them understand exactly what one means is taken into consideration, it is not astonishing that a traveller arrives at a wrong conclusion if the utmost pains be not taken in pursuing one's investigations.

Of course the Ainu who have come in contact with Japanese know of a God, and some of them, at the instigation of Japanese *bonzes*, have become nominal Buddhists. Benry, at Piratori, showed me a small Buddhist shrine, of Japanese manufacture, which had been put up on a neighbouring hill. All the time I stayed at Piratori I never observed any Ainu worship at it. One day I saw two boys throwing stones at it, but that could hardly be called an act of reverence, even among my hairy friends.

On my inquiring as to the origin and use of the shrine, I was told by some that it was erected to the God of the Japanese. Benry, who was always "well informed," both in things that he knew and those that he did not know, said that it was built in honour of Yoshitsune, the Japanese personage who, as we have seen, is the hero in semi-Ainu legends, and whose image or spirit, according to travellers' tales, is worshipped by the Ainu.

It always appeared strange to me that the Piratori Ainu had this Japanese hero in their legends, but still more strange that they should make him their deity. Yet what was most singular of all was, that with the exception of Benry and a few others at Piratori, no other Ainu I met in any other part of Yezo seemed to know about Yoshitsune—or Okikurumi, as he is sometimes called by them; and, moreover, they knew nothing of his doings, or of the reason of his being worshipped. The Ainu of the Tokachi knew nothing whatever of this personage.

The Ainu idea of soul is always associated with "breath" or "life;" and as for the resurrection of the body and the future life of the soul, they have never even dreamt of it. Metempsychosis is equally unknown to them.

As my readers have seen, in the description of a burial the implements and weapons which belonged to a deceased person are buried with him. The articles, however, previous to being thrown into the grave, are smashed to pieces; for the idea is, not that the dead body should profit by these things in the other world, but that no other person should make use of what had been his property in this. The reasoning power of the Ainu does not carry him beyond what is purely material; his mind has never been trained to go beyond that limit, and he finds that he can live well within it. Like all animals, he is guided by his instinct, which tells him what is good and what is bad for him; but as to any attempt to find out *why* such things are good or bad for him, he is utterly at a loss, and has to give up the quest. Though not devoid of a rudimentary kind of shrewdness, the Ainu is dense and ignorant to the last degree, and just as he is reluctant to adopt new modes of living, so he is unable to accept new ideas or larger thoughts. The mere conception of a Superior Being, who is the Maker of all things and above all things, is far beyond the comprehension of any Ainu. Eating and drinking are what he principally lives for. He does not thirst for knowledge, nor strive after the Divine; and he has no creed of any kind and no formula of sacrifice or worship, which two conditions are essential to even the most elementary religion.

What the Ainu do really possess in the way of supernaturalism is the ordinary savage's credulous superstition, which manifests itself in certain charms or fear of certain omens. However, after that degree they take the world as it comes. They have no idea of who made it, and they are not anxious to learn. The sun, the moon, bears, salmon, water, fire, mountains, trees, are all things for which an Ainu has a dumb kind of regard, not amounting to reverence, as he knows that he could not live without them. This has led some persons to define these objects as the principal divinities of the Ainu, and to call the people themselves polytheists. The word *Kamoi*, or *Kamui*, has been rendered as "god," gods "divinity." Now, what does the word *Kamoi*, or *Kamui*, really mean? Translated literally it means "old" or "ancient"; but amongst a hundred other meanings it also denotes "large," "beautiful," "strange," "it," "the man," "he who," &c. In fact, it is used to qualify anything, whether good or bad; and in some ways corresponds to our adjectives "wonderful," "awful," "grand"; but assuredly the Ainu do not by this word mean to designate the objects thus described as so many gods. Anything for which they entertain respect or fear is described as *Kamoi*, or *Kamui*, which thus is applied to the sun, the moon, the stars, mountains, rivers, old trees, bears, salmon, large stones, &c., not with the intention of making them divinities, but simply to specify their power, greatness, or antiquity. The word is applied to every kind of thing, animate or inanimate, good or bad, respected or derided, dreaded or revered, admired or abhorred. It is sometimes a prefix, sometimes an affix, and is the most universal attribute the Ainu world or language contains. We are, therefore, forced to the conclusion, that either the Ainu are polytheists or pantheists to such an extent as occasionally to make everything and everybody a god; or else, that translators have given their own, and a greatly exaggerated, meaning to the word *Kamui*, and that these so-called gods are not gods at all. To me there is no alternative opinion on the matter. The Ainu have no gods in our sense.

Basing conclusions on wrong premises, writers on the Ainu religion have been naturally led astray altogether. For instance, the composite word *Kotan-kara-kamui*,[39] which a learned missionary has translated "Creator," only means "the man who made the village"—a description which hardly corresponds to the grandeur attributed to the words by its imaginative translator.

Then again, *Kamui kotan*, which according to some means "the home of God," in its real signification is "an ancient village; a beautiful place." When *Kamui* is applied to persons, it is generally a suffix; when to things, it is a prefix.

But let us come to the *inao*, which by some have been called the "Ainu gods," by others "Divine symbols." These *inao* are willow-wands, with shavings depending from the upper end, sometimes from the middle, and occasionally from near the lower end as well.

The larger wands are about four feet in length, and have either one or two bunches of shavings at the upper end only. They go by the name of *inao netuba*, or "big *inao*." Other smaller *inao*, like the *Chisei-kara-inao*,[40] are kept in the house, and stuck in the eastern corner of the hearth, and in the wall directly opposite the entrance door. Some of the *inao* are shaved upwards from the bottom, others downwards from the top; and one, a big *inao*, is often thrust through the small window facing the east. Sometimes they are placed about singly, especially inside the huts; but outside, close to the eastern wall, I have often seen eight or ten standing together in a row. When so taken collectively they are called *nuza*. On Volcano Bay, up the Saru River, and on the Lake Kutcharo, where it is the custom of the Ainu to make trophies of the skulls of bears and deer which have been killed in the hunt, one or two *inao* are placed at the foot of the trophy. Sometimes, but very rarely, a whole *nuza* is to be seen in front of a trophy; but in most cases the *nuza* I saw were near huts that had no trophy at all, and, as I say, only very seldom were they in front of the trophy itself, unless a bear feast was going on. I am therefore under the impression that these *nuza* are only put up when some festival takes place, and that they are not kept there permanently. I remember that at Piratori there were no *inao* and no *nuza* outside Benry's house, but on the day that the festival took place one was put up, and several *inao* were placed inside the hut, in the hearth and on the north wall. Likewise, a *nuza* was put up on the same day at the east end of the hut in which the feast was given, and the inside was also adorned with *inao* of various sizes and descriptions. Each *inao* is pointed at the lower end, so as to be easily stuck in the ground. The *inao* of all sizes and shapes impressed me as being mostly for ornament. Then some are held as charms against misfortune and disease; but they never impressed me as being offerings to the gods. *Inao* are placed near springs, so that the good water may not turn into pestilential, and occasionally *inao* of a peculiar shape are hung in the doorway of newly-built huts. They are made of a number of small willow sticks tied together, from which hang five or six bunches of shavings; they are hung horizontally, and not in a vertical position, like the other *inao*. They are very uncommon, and only used on certain specified occasions. For example, when a child is born an *inao*, in the shape of a doll, is made of a bunch of reeds folded double and tied with a string about an inch from the bend, which thus forms the head; it is then tied lower down to indicate the waist. By dividing the reeds into two equal portions they produce a pair of legs, and a stick is then passed through the reeds between the head and the waist to form the arms. When this doll is made it is placed near the infant, so that should any disease or misfortune, in the shape of a kind of evil spirit, be tempted to enter the child's body, it may be averted, and enter the doll instead. Should a person fall ill new *inao* are stuck in the hearth, as the Ainu share our own idea that evil spirits dwell mostly in fire; others are placed near the sick person. They are not meant as offerings to the gods for his or her quick recovery, but merely to bring good luck to the individual whose body they think has been taken possession of by "animals inside," or, in other words, evil spirits.

Even at the present day in England and on the Continent horseshoes for luck are hung over entrance doors, and if a horseshoe be fastened on to a stable-door, the beasts within are supposed to be held free from accidents and illness.

In Spain and Italy little red rags tied to a small wand, not dissimilar in shape to a small Ainu *inao*, are stuck in flower-pots near windows, over beds, doors, and up chimneys, to keep witches at bay, red being a powerful exorcist in the way of colours, and as good as the "running stream which witches dare not cross." Some hysterical women have declared that they have seen witches hiding in the smoke of the boiling *Pentola* (the earthenware pot in which the soup is boiled)—but that on seeing the red rags they vanished, and never visited the house again. Italian and Spanish women and children almost invariably carry charms round their necks, that are to keep them safe from harm; and, furthermore, when a child falls ill, one or more red rags are fastened to its bed before a doctor is sent for. Then, again, people suffering from epileptic fits have often been supposed to be "possessed," and beaten to death or burnt alive, so that the evil spirit which was in them should thus be destroyed. It must be borne in mind that not many centuries ago similar beliefs were prevalent even in free and enlightened England.

If we compare these beliefs with those of the Ainu, we find that they differ very little either in form or substance. In place of the witches which our own ancestors, modern Italians, and Spaniards, and some benighted peasantry still to be found in the West of England, believed, and do still believe in, the Ainu have imaginary animals or evil spirits. The wands and red rags of our Latin neighbours are represented by their *inao*; and our lucky horseshoe is with them the horizontal *inao*. Charms are worn by the Ainu men, women, and children; and when going to war or to hunt the men carry a block of wood to which their knife or sword is attached, and on the right-hand side of which hangs a small *inao*.

These blocks of wood are flattened, and are elliptical at both ends. Their length varies from four to fifteen inches, and sometimes ornaments— generally circles—are carved on them. A string is fastened on one side so as to sling them to the shoulder; but they are usually carried under the arm. They are supposed to protect the carrier from accidents, and also to bring him good fortune.

We see, then, that similar ideas are entertained by utterly different peoples thousands of miles distant from one another; and that certain superstitious beliefs left on this side of the globe find their parallel among the hairy people on the other. Of course with them it is natural that their beliefs should count for more than with Europeans, as civilisation has not in any way enlarged or improved their minds; but it seems to me unfair that the same identical beliefs should go under the name of *superstitions* when applied to Europeans, and called the "Ainu religion" when practised by the hairy inhabitants of Northern Japan. Though to this I know it may be replied that, as all things spring from germs, so these ignorant superstitions of the Ainu may be in a manner called their religion, as the germ of a more developed system—the cotyledonous state of what might grow into a more advanced spirituality. Like the ancient Greeks and Romans, the Ainu wave their moustache-lifters, during their libations, towards the sun, the fire, and the person who has paid for the wine, before they address themselves to the large wooden bowls wherein lies their happiness; but this also is not a religious ceremony, and no religious feeling whatever is connected with it. It is a mere *toast*—part of their etiquette—which exactly corresponds to the German "*Prosit*," or to our

English "Your good health." The Ainu of course have no special high-days, no Sundays, no religious services, no prayers, no priests, no sacrificial priests, no churches, and no bells; but they can "swear"; and as the Neapolitans invoke their saints, so they occasionally call the sun, the moon, the fire, and everything else, all sorts of bad names if things do not go as they ought. This "swearing" has been defined as *Ainu praying* by one authority on the Ainu religion; moreover, the same authority calls the Ainu a "distinctly religious people," and an "exceedingly religious race!" To anyone who visits a country and regards all that he finds from one point of view only, it is not difficult to interpret words and things in accordance with the preconceived idea; but however high the principles sought to be established, I do not consider a man justified in attributing to definite facts an importance and significance to which they have no claim. I have no doubt that a native who had associated with or been in the employment of a Christian would make statements in accordance with his master's belief as it had been taught him; but it is incorrect to offer these "borrowed statements" as the religious beliefs of a whole nation.

I shall not discuss this question at greater length; but for the sake of readers who are interested in the subject it may be well to make two or three more statements before closing this chapter. The Ainu do not know of a heaven and hell; but in one of the latest publications on the aborigines of Japan we are told that they do; and, moreover, that they are fully aware of the resurrection of the body in the other world!

Even assuming, for the moment, that the Ainu are theists, or polytheists, after what we have heard of their gods, this is a somewhat surprising statement. It will be remembered that anything good or bad, dreaded or repulsive, respected or not respected, is qualified by the Ainu as *Kamui*, and we shall attribute for a while the imaginary meaning of "God" to the word. Now, if everything and everybody, good or bad, is equally a god, I myself fail to see the necessity of a hell, as the chances are that all the gods would inhabit heaven. This alone serves to show how absurd the theory is; but I wish to give the exact translation of the words *Kando* and *Teine-pokna-moshiri*, which are said to be the two Ainu expressions for "heaven" and "hell."

Kando means "sky," not "heaven." *Teine-pokna-moshiri*[41] stands for the "wet earth under(ground)." As the Ainu are in the habit of burying their dead, I find it more rational to apply to the words in question the meaning of a "burial-place," a "cold place of rest" rather than that of Hades or Gehenna.

"They" (the Ainu), says a learned missionary, "seem to conceive of men and women as living in large communities in the other world in the same way and under the same conditions as they do in this, excepting that they can know no death." In other words, resurrection of the body and eternal life.

Strange to say, the writer of the same lines asserted in the "Transactions of the Asiatic Society of Japan,"[42] that "The Ainu *know nothing* of a resurrection of the body."

It must not be argued that because they have no religion the Ainu are bad people. They are far from it. They are decidedly not moral, for nothing is immoral among them. The Ainu must be considered more as animals than as human beings. When we speak of a dog, we do not ask whether it is a moral dog, but only if it is a good dog. The same can be said of the Ainu. We cannot compare them to ourselves, nor judge them by our own standard of morality. Taken by themselves they are gentle, kind, brave, and above everything they are simple. Their language, manners, customs, arts, habits, as we have seen, are the very simplest and rudest possible. Thus, it is absurd to suppose that such simple brains could entertain high religious ideas. If they had brains enough to compass high religious beliefs they would long ago have used those brains in bettering their miserable condition and filthy mode of living. They would have striven to make the beginnings of a history and a literature, or at least to have devised or adopted some mode of writing with which they could preserve these high ideas, and pass them on from generation to generation. Even their language is so poor in words as to hardly express their everyday wants. The Ainu are low in the scale of humanity. They have always been low; they have not sunk, for they have never risen. They have never done any harm in this world, and they will never do any good.

The Ainu are without laws, which, paradoxical as it sounds, to a great extent makes them good. People are never so good as when no harm can be done. There are indeed few crimes among them; no voluntary infanticides; very very rarely murders; no suicides; little theft, and as little treachery among people of the same tribe. Though usually retiring and reserved, they are hospitable on special occasions, and generous with what little they possess. The young show an instinctive reverence for the aged, without considering it a virtue or a duty. Cowardice is despised by the Ainu, but courage, endurance of pain, and hardship, drunkenness, and similar qualities, are looked on as the chief virtues in men. Punishments are seldom inflicted by Ainu on any of their tribesmen, and the crime must indeed be great to raise the whole community against the criminal. If by rare chance some great evil has been done, the chief of the village and all the men assemble, and decide on the punishment to be inflicted. Flogging is the general punishment for the lesser crimes, which, according to Ainu ideas, are theft and assault. The murder of a tribesman is sometimes punished by cutting the tendons of the hands and feet of the murderer, thus disabling him from hunting or fishing. If, however, the man murdered was of another tribe, or a Japanese, this Draconian kind of justice is not administered. Quarrels among tribesmen are settled by private retribution, and no one interferes either one way or the other. These quarrels, however, very seldom occur, as the Ainu are naturally a peaceful people. Imprisonment does not exist, for the simple reason that the Ainu have no prisons. They do not know what a prison is; neither is capital punishment practised by them. According to their own ideas they are not cruel to children, for we seldom see them wilfully ill-treating them; but according to civilised notions Ainu women make shockingly bad mothers. They love, but they do not look after, nor practically take care of, their little ones after these are about a year and a half old; and as to washing them, combing their hair, educating them, or trying to cure them of the thousand and one wretched skin diseases, which come chiefly by their own neglect, an Ainu mother puts her hand to these things no more than the men put theirs to the building of a temple or the creation of a literature. This neglect is not with them, as it would be with us, an intolerable crime, but is the natural result of their animal instinct as contradistinguished from rational development. For if a baby is not old enough at one and a half years of age to take care of himself, he is of no good as an Ainu. It is needless to add that, in these circumstances, most of them are of no good, and that the percentage of infantile deaths is appalling to a civilised mind.

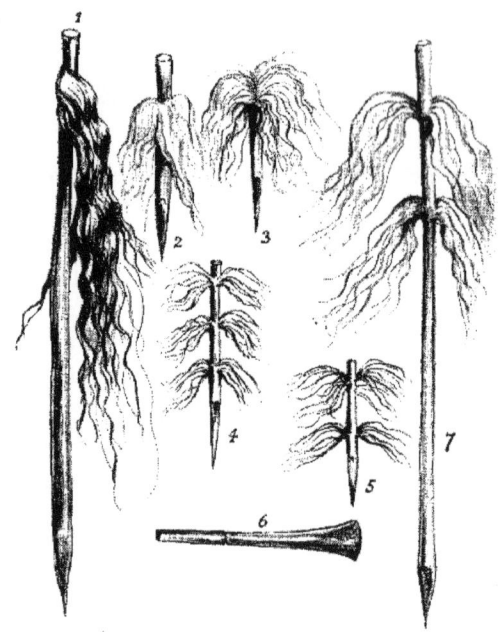

1, 7, INAO-NETUBA. 2, 3, 4, 5, CHISEI-KARA-INAO. 6, A PESTLE OR POUNDER.

CHAPTER XXIX.
Marital Relations, and Causes that Limit Population.

The laws of marriage in the Ainu country are not very stringent; in fact, there are no laws. If a young man takes a fancy to a pretty hairy maid, and the maid reciprocates his affections, all they have to do is to go and live together, and there is no Mrs. Grundy to be scandalised at the want of closer forms and ceremonies. There is no function to celebrate the occasion; there are no wedding presents, no bridesmaids, no officiating clergyman, and no old slipper flung after the happy pair as soon as the knot is tied. The bridegroom either goes to live in his bride's hut, or, if he does not care for his mother-in-law, he will bring his lady-love to his own father's hut. Usually, however, the two, especially if their respective families are large, prefer to build a hut of their own. The honeymoon is spent in house-building, and while the bride carries the loads of timber and long reeds, the bridegroom accomplishes the more difficult task of putting them together as well as he can for future shelter. All goes well with the happy couple until the roof has to be lifted up bodily and perched on the forked poles, during which process "family rows" generally begin. But they do not last long, and when the house is finished, though not decorated, home peace reigns within, and the bridegroom, as we have already seen, proceeds to ornament his chief treasure—his wife—with tattoos on her arms. This idyllic state of things is not specially permanent, for soon after this first marriage the Ainu feels that he would like another wife, and, without thinking twice about it, he marries again. Though savage and barbarian, the Ainu is shrewd enough not to take his second wife to live with his first, for he knows what the result would be, human nature being the same in Yezo as it is in London, and jealousy as strong among the tattooed women of the hairy people as among the fair-skinned daughters of the West. All women are bad enough when out of temper, but the Ainu women are pre-eminent in this respect. Our shock-haired bigamist calls his first wife *poro-machi*—"great wife," and he calls the other *pon-machi*—"small wife;" and as long as the two females do not live under the same roof they are all happy with the arrangement. If, indeed, he chooses to have more than these two wives he thinks small blame to himself. There is no bar of any kind in his code to his having a third "half;" but this seldom happens now, for the women are not in such over abundance in the Ainu country as to allow each man to indulge in a "triple alliance." The Ainu are therefore polygamists when they can find the third woman, and almost always bigamists when this is possible. The wife does not take her husband's name, for no Ainu has a family surname; and each man or woman is called after some peculiarity which he or she possesses, or after some event or accident which has befallen them. For instance, *Una-charo*, a man's name, means "Sprinkled-ashes," and *Yei-Ainu*, "Dangerous Ainu," &c.; and *Korunke*, a woman's name, means "Ice-eater;" *Reoback*, "Who burst three times," and so on, each person having a different name, which is nothing more than a nick-name. When the girl gets married she does not drop this nick-name, neither, as has been said, does she take her husband's name, though sometimes she is called So-and-So's wife. Supposing that Miss Burst-three-times were to marry Mr. Sprinkled-ashes, she would be Mr. Sprinkled-ashes' wife, and would still be called by her maiden name, Burst-three-times.

It is impossible to quote exact statistics of the Ainu population, and whether the women outnumber the men, but from my own observation I should think that females are in excess of the males in some districts, and about even in others.

The man, naturally, is the lord and master of the household, and the wife is like a kind of inferior being or a slave, whose duty it is to obey her male companion. She has to yield in everything, whether she is right or wrong; she is occasionally beaten; she never takes active part in any of her husband's Bacchanalian revels; but though she leads a sad kind of life, a life of hard work and no pleasure, she does not seem to be any the worse for it. There are wives, of course, who, as in other countries, give a "pretty rough time" to their husbands; but in the Ainu country these are certainly the exception. As there is no ceremony of marriage, there is naturally no "divorce;" but if an Ainu gets sick of his wife, all he has to do is to leave her and go elsewhere, or else to banish her from his hut. This, however, very seldom happens, for that rare creature the henpecked Ainu husband is willing to put up with a lot; and though brave enough to encounter single-handed a bear, the hairy man is by no means valiant enough to face his wife's temper; while, for all that she is practically a slave, and personally an inferior, is sometimes in Ainuland, as everywhere else, the strongest factor in the domestic sum.

As long as the wife does her duty well as a "beast of burden," little more is required from her. Her morals, as far as I could make out, are not well looked after. Adultery is not considered a crime. I do not mean by this that adultery is practised on principle, for it is not so: there is no reason whatever why it should be, for each man has his own wife or wives; but if adultery were practised by any members of a community, what we consider a dreadful crime would be regarded as a mere "joke" among the hairy people. The husband, like any other animal, dumb or not, would naturally resent the intrusion, but the community would in no way interfere, or punish the offender. A girl is considered fit to be married when she is about sixteen years of age; a man about twenty, or as soon as the body is fully developed.

People as a rule marry in the same village. It is but seldom that a girl marries a man or a man a girl of a different village. Villages, as we have seen, are generally composed of only a few houses, and the result of this strict endogamy is, that marriages take place among very near relations. In very small villages of only one or two houses, the father has been known to marry his own daughter, the uncle his own niece, &c. But enough of this. The result of this dreadful state of affairs is, that the race is rapidly dying out, destroyed by consumption, lunacy, and poverty of blood. All the members of one village are necessarily related to one another; and, as I have demonstrated in a previous chapter, this is the main cause why certain diseases are common to one community and utterly unknown to others, and certain hereditary talents or tendencies are frequent in one village and imperceptible in the next.

The Ainu seem to have no Platonic love; their love is purely sexual. It is not to be wondered at, in a country where marital relations are so peculiar, that very little love is felt for children beyond a certain age. The mother suckles her own child usually for seven or eight months. She can bear children till she is about thirty-five, though some who seem to be much older are still fruitful. It was difficult to ascertain this fact for no Ainu knows his own age. As far as I could learn fertility is neither hindered nor checked in any way— either by adopting a peculiar diet or by other practices. On the other hand, many a woman is sterile, and many are also affected with the most horrible of all diseases. I am inclined to think, however, that this special malady was imported to Yezo with Japanese civilisation, for it is in the more civilised parts of the Ainu country that it is most frequent.

There is probably no country in the world where there is so much loss of infant life due to want, accidents, and diseases, as with the Ainu. Abortion is common, owing to the severe exertion of the mother during pregnancy; and many a child dies not many days after birth for the same reason, and consequent disappearance of milk in the mother's breasts. The greater mortality of children, however, is between the age of six and ten. Only a small percentage of these poor creatures live to take part in the game of life; while many succumb to ill-treatment and the most horrible skin eruptions. Thus we have a good explanation of the frightful rapidity with which the Ainu race is fast disappearing. Naturally, those few who survive grow strong and healthy; but their great fondness for alcoholic drinks, which they can now so easily procure from the Japanese, destroys even them.

One is generally struck in Ainuland by the number of old men and children, and by the almost entire lack of young fellows between the age of fifteen and thirty. This is due mainly to the great increase of mortality in children during the last two generations. The sadness which seems to oppress the Ainu, and which we see depicted on the face of each individual, is nothing but the outcome of this degeneration of the race. As a race the Ainu will soon be extinct. I dare say that in fifty years from now—probably not so long—not one of the hairy savages, who were once the masters of Sakhalin, Yezo, the Kuriles, Kamschatka, and the whole of the southern Japanese Empire, will be left. Not one of these strange people—soft, good, and gentle, but savage, brave, and disreputable—will live to see their country civilised; and in the life which they have led of filth and vice they will die in front of that greater scourge, civilisation, leaving behind no traces of themselves, of their past, of their history, nor of their present—nothing but a faint recollection, a tradition, that in Yezo and the Kuriles died the last remains of those curious people, the Hairy Ainu.

APPENDIX.

I.—MEASUREMENTS OF THE AINU BODY, AND DESCRIPTIVE CHARACTERS.

The following measurements were taken on five men and five women of the pure Ainu of Frishikobets (Upper Tokachi River). They were carefully chosen among the best types.

The names of the men were:—

1. Unacharo: *Una*, ashes; *charo*, sprinkled = "Sprinkled-ashes."

2. Aba pukuro: *Aba*, a relation; *pu*, storehouse; *kuro*, a man = "Related to the man of the storehouse."

3. Pe chantwe; *Pe*, undrinkable water; *chan*, to run away; *we*, to tell = "Who ran to tell of the undrinkable water."

4. Kosankeyan: *Ko san*, to go down; *ke*, eating; *yan*, cold.

5. Yei Ainu: *Yei*, dangerous; *Ainu*, Ainu.

The following were the names of the women:—

1. Usattean: *Usat*, cinders; *tean*, long.

2. Korunke: *Korun*, ice; *ke*, to eat = "Ice-eater."

3. Sho kem: *Sho*, so; *kem*, blood = "Covered with blood."

4. Uina mon: *Uina or Una*, ashes; *mon*, tranquil.

5. Reoback: *Re*, three; *oback*, to burst = "Who burst three times."

HEIGHT

	MEN. inches.				WOMEN. inches.	
1.	61	}		1.	58¾	}
2.	65	}		2.	59⅞	}
3.	60½	} Med. 62-19/40.		3.	59½	} Med. 58⅜
4.	64⅞	}		4.	54⅝	}
5.	61	}		5.	59⅛	}

LENGTH FROM TIP TO TIP OF FINGERS WITH ARMS OUTSTRETCHED.

MEN. inches.				WOMEN. inches.		
1.	64⅝	}		1.	59⅛	}
2.	65	}		2.	62½	}
3.	63½	} Med. 65⅜.		3.	62½	} Med. 61-13/40.
4.	69½	}		4.	60	}
5.	64¼	}		5.	62½	}

It is interesting to notice the great difference between the height and this latter measurement, showing the great length of the arms in the Ainu race.

THE HUMERUS.

MEN. inches.				WOMEN. inches.		
1.	9	}		1.	8½	}
2.	9⅝	}		2.	8¾	}
3.	8½	} Med. 9-9/40.		3.	10⅜	} Med. 9-19/40.
4.	9	}		4.	9¾	}
5.	10	}		5.	10	}

THE ULNA.

MEN. inches.				WOMEN. inches.		
1.	9¼	}		1.	9¼	}
2.	10¾	}		2.	9⅛	}
3.	9⅛	} Med. 9-37/40.		3.	8⅞	} Med. 9¼.
4.	11	}		4.	9⅜	}
5.	9½	}		5.	9⅝	}

THE HAND.

MEN. inches.				WOMEN. inches.		
1.	7⅜	}		1.	6⅞	}

2.	7½	}		2.	7	}
3.	7¼	} Med. 7⅖.		3.	6⅞	} Med. 6-9/10.
4.	7⅞	}		4.	6¾	}
5.	7	}		5.	7	}

THE SPINE (dorsal and lumbar vertebræ to the sacrum).

	MEN. inches.				WOMEN. inches.	
1.	25½	}		1.	27	}
2.	28⅝	}		2.	26¾	}
3.	27½	} Med. 27⅘.		3.	28¼	} Med. 27⅝.
4.	29⅝	}		4.	27	}
5.	27¾	}		5.	29⅛	}

THE LEG (Femur, Tibia and Foot.)

	MEN. inches.				WOMEN. inches.	
1.	34⅜	}		1.	32⅞	}
2.	36¼	}		2.	35½	}
3.	32½	} Med. 35-1/20.		3.	34	} Med. 33-13/20.
4.	37⅞	}		4.	30½	}
5.	34¼	}		5.	35⅜	}

FEMUR.

	MEN. inches.				WOMEN. inches.	
1.	17½	}		1.	18⅜	}
2.	18⅜	}		2.	19⅞	}
3.	17⅛	} Med. 18⅝.		3.	18½	} Med. 17-33/40.
4.	20	}		4.	14	}
5.	20⅛	}		5.	18⅜	}

TIBIA.

	MEN. inches.				WOMEN. inches.	
1.	14	}		1.	14¼	}
2.	14⅞	}		2.	13	}
3.	12⅝	} Med. 13½.		3.	13½	} Med. 13⅘.
4.	14⅞	}		4.	14	}
5.	11⅛	}		5.	14¼	}

(The Tibia is very flattened with the Ainu.)

TARSUS (from ground to Ankle).

	MEN. inches.				WOMEN. inches.	
1.	2¾	}		1.	2	}
2.	3	}		2.	2⅝	}
3.	3	} Med. 3.		3.	2	} Med. 2⅜.
4.	3¼	}		4.	2½	}
5.	3	}		5.	2¾	}

CHEST (from Arm-pit to Arm-pit).

	MEN. inches.				WOMEN. inches.	
1.	13½	}		1.	12⅝	}
2.	13⅝	}		2.	14¼	}
3.	13½	} Med. 13-19/40.		3.	14¼	} Med. 13-7/20.
4.	13	}		4.	12¼	}
5.	13¾	}		5.	13⅜	}

AROUND CHEST.

	MEN. inches.				WOMEN. inches.	
1.	36½	}		1.	33⅜	}
2.	35⅜	}		2.	34½	}
3.	37½	} Med. 37-3/40.		3.	35½	} Med. 34⅕.
4.	37⅝	}		4.	32⅞	}
5.	38⅛	}		5.	34¾	}

AROUND WAIST.

	MEN. inches.				WOMEN. inches.	
1.	33	}		1.	28⅜	}
2.	37	}		2.	31½	}
3.	34	} Med. 34-7/10.		3.	34⅞	} Med. 31-7/20.
4.	36	}		4.	31	}
5.	33½	}		5.	(37⅝ but was conceived.)	}

MAXIMUM BREADTH OF SHOULDERS.

	MEN. inches.				WOMEN. inches.	
1.	19¼	}		1.	15½	}
2.	16	}		2.	13⅝	}
3.	18	} Med. 17½.		3.	13⅞	} Med. 14⅖.
4.	18	}		4.	13⅞	}
5.	16¼	}		5.	15⅛	}

THE FOOT.

	MEN. inches.				WOMEN. inches.	
1.	9¼	}		1.	8⅝	}

2.	9⅝	}		2.	9⅛	}
3.	9½	} Med. 9-23/40.		3.	9⅛	} Med. 8⅘.
4.	10¼	}		4.	8¼	}
5.	9¼	}		5.	8⅞	}

THE HEAD (around the Head, just above the Ears).

	MEN. inches.				WOMEN. inches.	
1.	23½	}		1.	23⅜	}
2.	23½	}		2.	22⅝	}
3.	24⅜	} Med. 23¾.		3.	23⅝	} Med. 22-29/40.
4.	22⅜	}		4.	22	}
5.	23⅛	}		5.	23	}

LENGTH OF FACE.(From Hair to Chin.)

	MEN. inches.				WOMEN. inches.	
1.	7½	}		1.	7¼	}
2.	9	}		2.	6¾	}
3.	7½	} Med. 7-31/40.		3.	6¾	} Med. 6⅞.
4.	6⅞	}		4.	7	}
5.	8	}		5.	6⅝	}

WIDTH OF FACE FROM EAR TO EAR (over Forehead and Cheek Bones).

	MEN. inches.				WOMEN. inches.	
1.	11⅞	}		1.	11⅛	}
2.	12½	}		2.	11	}
3.	12	} Med. 11-19/20.		3.	11¾	} Med. 11-21/40.

| 4. | 12 | } | | 4. | 11⅞ | } |
| 5. | 12⅛ | } | | 5. | 11⅛ | } |

HEIGHT OF FOREHEAD.

	MEN. inches.				WOMEN. inches.	
1.	2¼	}		1.	2¼	}
2.	2⅞	}		2.	1¾	}
3.	2⅜	} Med. 2-2/5.		3.	2⅛	} Med. 2.
4.	2	}		4.	2	}
5.	2¾	}		5.	1⅞	}

WIDTH OF FOREHEAD.

	MEN. inches.				WOMEN. inches.	
1.	5	}		1.	6	}
2.	5¼	}		2.	5½	}
3.	5½	} Med. 5⅕.		3.	5	} Med. 5⅜.
4.	5¾	}		4.	4⅞	}
5.	6	}		5.	5½	}

LENGTH OF EARS.

	MEN. inches.				WOMEN. inches.	
1.	3	}		1.	2⅜	}
2.	3¼	}		2.	2⅜	}
3.	2¾	} Med. 2-23/40.		3.	2¾	} Med. 2-23/40.
4.	2½	}		4.	2⅞	}
5.	2⅝	}		5.	2½	}

LENGTH OF FINGERS.

	MEN. inches.				WOMEN. inches.	
1.	3⅛	}		1.	3	}
2.	3⅜	}		2.	3	}
3.	3	} Med. 3-9/40.		3.	3	} Med. 2-39/40.
4.	3⅝	}		4.	2⅞	}
5.	3	}		5.	3	}

(*a*) Colour of skin (in parts not exposed to air)—light reddish slightly tending towards brown, but almost as light as with Europeans.

(*b*) Colour of hair—black, dark-brown, reddish-black, red.

(*c*) Colour of eyes—light-brown tending towards dark-grey.

(*d*) Character of hair—wavy.

(*e*) Amount of hair—abundant on face and all over the body in males more so than in females.

MEASUREMENTS OF SHIKOTAN AINU.

The skin and eyes are the same colour as with the Yezo Ainu. The hair is black, dark-red, or dark-brown. Black is the prevalent colour. Children often have fair hair, which grows darker as they grow older. The hair is abundant over body and face, and it is wavy.

The face possesses the identical characteristics of the Yezo Ainu.

Medium height: 61 inches to 62¾ inches.
Round waist: 32⅞ inches.
Chest: Empty, 35⅞ inches; inflated, 37½ inches.
Humerus: 11⅞ inches.
Ulna: 8-11/16 inches.
Hand: 6¾ inches.
Foot: 9½ inches.
Spinal vertebræ: 24 inches.
Scapula (from shoulder to shoulder): 17 inches.
Between shoulder-blades: 5⅞ inches.
Femur: short.
Tibia: very long.

(Natives objected to have their legs measured.)
The Tibia is much rounder than with the Yezo Ainu.
Length of face: 7½ inches.
Width of face from ear to ear: 11⅛ inches.
Round head above ears: 21⅝ inches.
Ears: small.
Forehead: 2⅜ inches high; 5¼ inches wide.

With arms outstretched and from tip to tip of fingers the Shikotan Ainu measure generally the length of one hand (about 6¾ inches) more than their own height. Consumption, *kaki*, and syphilis are common complaints among them.

II.—GLOSSARY OF AINU WORDS, MANY OF WHICH ARE FOUND IN GEOGRAPHICAL NAMES IN YEZO AND THE KURILE ISLANDS.[43]

- A.
- A = (a suffix).
- Apa = an open space, a doorway.
- Aikap = impossible, impassable.
- Ambe = that is.
- An = to be.
- Aota = near.
- Apta = rain.
- Apun = gently.
- At = a tree.
- Atsu = barren, naked.
- B.
- Bets, or pets, pet = river.
- Be, or pe = pestilential water.
- But, or put = mouth of a river.
- C.
- Cha = old.
- Cha cha = very old.
- Chip = fish.
- Chippe = a canoe, a boat.
- Chup = the sun.
- E.
- Erimu = a rat.
- Etoko = formerly, in front of.
- Etu = a cape.

- F.
- Fu = bare.
- Fun = green.
- Fure = red (also pronounced Hure).
- Frishiko = old.
- H.
- Haru = grass.
- Hattara = a deep pool in a watercourse.
- Hure = a bad smell.
- Hure = red.
- I.
- I = a suffix for "a place."
- Ibe = to feed.
- Ichan = a canal made by salmon in river-beds to lay their, spawn.
- Ikam = against.
- Iwa = stone, a rock.
- Itapk = word, story.
- Iwashi (Japanese) = sardine.
- Iwao = sulphur.
- K.
- Kama = cliffs, rocks, to go over.
- Kamui = great, wonderful, ancient.
- Kap = bark of a tree.
- Kara = to take, to make.
- Kashi = towards.
- Kerimba = a berry.
- Kene = an alder tree.
- Kem = blood.

- Kenashi = a meadow.
- Keshup = head.
- Kesh = towards the west.
- Ki = rushes.
- Kim = mountain.
- Kinna = mat.
- Kinna = reeds.
- Kinna = grass.
- Kiri = to know.
- Kitai = mountain.
- Koi = the waves of the sea.
- Kochi = level.
- Kombo = sea-weed.
- Koro = to possess, to have.
- Kotan = a village, a place.
- Kotcha = in front of.
- Ku = a bow.
- Kuano = straight.
- Kume = black, very dark.
- Kuru, or guru = a person.
- M.
- Ma = to swim, deep.
- Mak = behind.
- Makta = away.
- Mata = winter.
- Meak = female.
- Mean = cold.
- Mo = tranquil.

- Mon = small, tranquil.
- Mom = to flow like a river.
- Moire = slow.
- Moi = a bay, a sheltered bend in a river where the water is quiet.
- Moshiri, or mushir = island, country, place, land.
- Moshiri Kes = the east.
- Moshitte-chu-pok = north.
- Moshiri pok = west.
- Moshitte-chu-pka = south.
- Mun = grass.
- N.
- Na = again.
- Na = bigger, or smaller (also sign of comparative).
- Nai, or Nae = a rivulet, a small stream.
- Nai yau = a tributary stream.
- Nak = where.
- Nam = cold, as water, as ice.
- Naoak = yet more shallow.
- Ne = together, where, and, also, which, &c.
- Neatka = also, again.
- Nen = who.
- Neto = where.
- Ni = wood, or tree.
- Nikam = leaves of a tree.
- Nibeshi = name of a tree (probably *Tilia*).
- Nikap = bark of a tree.
- Nipek = a fire, a flame.
- Nisei = valley.

- Nisusu = scenery, panorama, view.
- Nitat = swampy ground, a swamp, a lagoon.
- Nitai = a forest.
- Nitt = a thorn.
- Nitek = branches of trees.
- Nituman = trunk of a tree.
- Nobori = mountain.
- No = (meaningless ending of words).
- Noshike = middle.
- Noshihike = half.
- Nupka = a forest.
- Nup = a treeless plain.
- Nup = a deep silent pool in a river.
- Nuburi = mountain.
- Nupuru = turbid (as water).
- Nupuri = a mountain (volcano).
- Nutap = the projecting part of a river bend.
- O.
- O = a meaningless prefix, sometimes used as an adjective.
- Oara = one.
- Oboso = to pass through (as water).
- Oak = shallow—not deep.
- Oha = empty.
- Ohoho = deep.
- Okai = at a place.
- Okai = a male.
- Okari = around.
- Oakau = to hide.

- Oakan = a male.
- Omanne = to go.
- Oma = to be inside.
- Onne = large, old, great.
- Opattek = a volcanic eruption.
- Opeka = straight.
- Oro = to be in.
- Oropak = as far as.
- Oshima = to go in.
- Oshimak = behind.
- Ota = sand.
- Otaru = sandy.
- Opke = a spear.
- Ot = in, inside, into.
- Oya = another.
- Oushike = a place.
- Oyapk = away, abroad.
- Oyapk moshiri = away, country (foreign country).
- P.
- Pa = smoke.
- Pa = east-end of villages.
- Pai = bushes.
- Pakne = as far as.
- Panke = lower.
- Paru = the mouth.
- Pase = heavy.
- Patek = only.
- Pe = pestilential water, bad water, not good to drink.

- Pei = something.

- Pene = inland.

- Pet, pets, bets = river.

- Pet bena = source of a river.

- Pet samo = bank of a river.

- Petsamata = by the side of a river.

- Pet put = the mouth of a river.

- Pet-urara = a stream.

- Pet yao = an affluent.

- Pet-ka-shu = to wade a river.

- Penke = upper.

- Pinni = ash-tree.

- Pinne = male.

- Piuta = sand (coarse).

- Pipa = a spring of fresh water.

- Pira = a bank, a cliff.

- Piri = a wound.

- Pirika = pretty, good, well, all-right.

- Pishita = sea-beach.

- Pita = to untie, to undo.

- Pitara = a dry place in a river-bed.

- Po = a small thing.

- Pon = small.

- Poi-shuma = pebbles, stones.

- Poka = only.

- Popke = hot, steaming (also Topke).

- Poro = large.

- Pui = a hole.

- Puri = natural, very, usual.
- Put, Putu (corrupted into Buto by the Japanese) = the mouth of a river.
- R.
- Rai = death.
- Rakka = seal.
- Rahuru = a fog.
- Ram = low.
- Ran = to descend (a mountain).
- Rangu = a kind of tree.
- Rarumani = a kind of tree (*Taxus cuspidata*).
- Re = three.
- Repun = to go, in the sea, surrounded by water.
- Repun moshiri = an island.
- Rera = wind.
- Retara = white.
- Ri = high.
- Rikkin = to ascend.
- Riri = a wave.
- Riri-shiye-tuye = ebb tide.
- Riri-ya = flow tide.
- Roru = at the head.
- Ru = a road, a track, a pathway
- Rui = to burn.
- Rukoppe = where roads cross.
- Rui = great, big.
- Rubeshipe = a ravine.
- Rupne = large.
- S.

- Sapk = summer.

- Sak = without.

- Sama = by the side of.

- San = to descend.

- Sara, Saru = a grassy plain.

- Sat = dry.

- Sattek = shallow water.

- Sesek = hot.

- Seta = dog.

- Shep = broad.

- Shi = high.

- Shibe = autumn salmon.

- Shiki = a kind of tall grass.

- Shiko = a view, a sight.

- Shimon = on the right-hand side.

- Shimoye = to shake, to move.

- Shenai = a large river.

- Shirari = a cliff, mass of loose texture.

- Shirau = a horse-fly.

- Shiretu = a cape.

- Shiri = land.

- Shiruturu = a small island in a river.

- Sho = so.

- Shoi = a hole.

- Shum = foam.

- Shuma = a stone.

- So = a waterfall.

- Shupun = a kind of fish.

- Shusu = a willow tree.
- T.
- Ta = to, towards, to take, to cut.
- Taanni = on this side.
- Taksep = a rock.
- Tapne = short.
- Tanne = long.
- Tap kop = an isolated hill.
- Tat = Birch-tree (*Betula*).
- To, or ko = a lake, a swamp.
- Toambe = that.
- Toi = earth.
- Tokap = day, light.
- Tomari = a harbour, a sheltered place.
- Top = scrub bamboo.
- Tope = *Acer*—a kind of tree.
- Tukara, also Tokari = sea-otter.
- Tunni = *Quercus dentata*.
- Tureshi = to ascend.
- Turep = a plant, the roots of which are eaten by the Ainu.
- U.
- U = a suffix to indicate a place.
- Uhui, also Ouye = a fire.
- Uhui nobori = a volcano.
- Un = a particle denoting that something is to be found at a place.
- Upas = snow.
- Ush = a bay.
- Ush = a gulf.

- Ush = a locative particle.
- Uta = a master.
- Utka = the rapids of a river.
- W.
- Wa = from.
- Wakka = water.
- Wen = bad.
- Y.
- Ya = land.
- Yai = danger.
- Yaikap = awkward.
- Yam = cold, a chestnut.
- Yuk = a deer.
- Yutta = greatest.

FOOTNOTES

[1] *Nobori*, mountain, volcano; *bets*, river, stream.

[2] *Shirao*, horse-fly; *i*, a suffix meaning *a place*.

[3] *To*, lake, swamp; *mak*, behind; *oma*, inside; *i*, a suffix meaning *a place*, or "a place behind which a hidden swamp is found."

[4] *Yu*, springs; *huts*, mouth of river.

[5] *Horo*, large; *hut*, *huts*, *put*, the mouth of a river.

[6] Small Japanese dinner tables.

[7] At-pets—Elm-tree river (*at*, elm-tree; *pets*, river).

[8] Nii-pak-pets—also called Nakap-pets. *Nii*, a wood; *pak*, under; *na*, more; *kap*, bark of tree.

[9] Shibe-gari-pets—Salmon-trout river.

[10] *Ikan*, a canal made by salmon on river-beds to lay their spawn; *tai* thick.

[11] *Poro*, large; *nam*, cold; *bets*, river.

[12] Moyoro. *Moy*, a bay; *oro*, to be in.

[13] Onnito. *Onni* or *Onne*, great, large; *to*, lake, swamp.

[14] Bitatannuki. *Bita*, to undo; *tannu*, long; *ki*, rushes, reeds.

[15] *Pero* or *Pira*, cliff; *Hune*, *Hun*, a particle indicating the existence of something at a place.

[16] *Toy*, earth; *o*, (?) *i*, a place; *pets*, river.

[17] *To*, lake, swamp; *buts*, mouth of a river. *O*, a meaningless prefix; *puts*, mouth of a river.

[18] Rev. John Batchelor, 'The Ainu of Japan,' chap. xx.

[19] *U*, place; *par*, mouth; *pe*, undrinkable water; *nai*, stream; *Upar-penai*, a place at the mouth of a stream of undrinkable water.

[20] *Me*, in front; *mu*, sheltered spot in a river; *ro*, track; *puto*, mouth of river; *Memuro-puto*, track in front of a sheltered spot at the mouth of a river.

[21] *Otto*, into; *i*, a place; *nai*, stream; *Ottoinnai*, a place in a stream.

[22] *Nitumap*, open trunk of a tree.

[23] *Ni*, wood; *piri*, wound; *bets*, river.

[24] *Puro*, great; *ke*, I; *nashpa*, deafening noise.

[25] *Ke*, I; *nashpa*, deafening noise.

[26] *Beppo* or *pet put*, at the mouth of a river.

[27] *Nesan*, a corruption of *annesan*.

[28] *Ko*, lake; *shto*, man. *Ko* is probably a corruption of the Ainu word *to*, a lake or a swamp, and it is used by the Japanese of Yezo for "lake," instead of the word "*numa*."

[29] The correct name and pronunciation is *Shimushir*.

[30] The opposite coast of Nippon can be seen plainly from Hakodate.

[31] The Japanese always begin their meals with sweets.

[32] *Shimushir*, High Island.

[33] *Urup*, name given to a kind of salmon.

[34] *Krafto*, Ainu word for Sakhalin.

[35] *Poro*, large; *nai*, stream.

[36] Sometimes also pronounced *Krafto*.

[37] The only attempt at animal representation is the small bear-head in chiefs' crowns.

[38] *Nipesh*: a kind of hemp.

[39] *Kotan*, village, place, site; *kara*, to make, build; *kamui*, the man, ancient, strength.

[40] *Chisei*, house, dwelling, hut; *kara*, make; also, have.

[41] *Teine*, wet; *pokna*, under; *moshiri*, earth, place, island.

[42] Vol. X., Part II., §6.

[43] The vowels to be pronounced as in Italian.

www.ingramcontent.com/pod-product-compliance
Ingram Content Group UK Ltd.
Pitfield, Milton Keynes, MK11 3LW, UK
UKHW031826270325
456796UK00002B/281